WYRD TIMES

Self-portrait by Nigel Pennick, 1992.

WYRD TIMES
Memoirs of a Pagan Renaissance Man

Nigel Pennick

Wyrd Times: Memoirs of a Pagan Renaissance Man
by Nigel Pennick

Edited by Michael Moynihan and Joshua Buckley
Interior design by Joshua Buckley
Cover design by Aaron Davis
Cover photograph: Nigel Pennick as the Lord of Misrule at Trumpington Orchard Wassail, courtesy of Eric Haynes (photographer unknown). Celtic interlace art by Nigel Pennick.

ISBN: 978-0-9997245-9-0

© 2023 Nigel Pennick

Thanks to Eric Haynes, Linda Kelsey-Jones, Rosemarie Kirschmann, Ann Pennick, Waltraud Wagner, and Jon Ward for their photographs; and to Annabel Moynihan, Ian Read, Ehud Sperling, and Lothar Tuppan for other assistance.

Despite all efforts, the author and publisher were unable to identify the photographers for several images in this book, which have been left uncredited. Any uncredited photographer is welcome to contact the publisher for proper acknowledgment in future printings.

All rights reserved. No part of this publication may be reproduced or transmitted in any form or by any means, electronic or mechanical, including photocopying, recording, or any information storage or retrieval system, without prior permission in writing from the publisher and copyright owner.

Arcana Europa Media
P. O. Box 6115
North Augusta, SC 29861

www.arcanaeuropamedia.com

Submit yourself with good grace to Clotho, and let her spin your thread out of whichever material she will.

—Marcus Aurelius[1]

1. Marcus Aurelius, *Meditations*, trans. Maxwell Staniforth (London: Penguin, 1964), no. 35.

CONTENTS

Prologos
We Wunt Be Druv
3

I. Early Years
9

II. Student Days and the Start of My Career in Science
55

III. Notes from the Underground
93

IV. Sacred Land and Measure
141

V. The Elder Faith
209

VI. Crossing the Borderlines
255

*VII. Spiritual Arts and Crafts,
Music and Mumming*
283

VIII. Matters of Life and Death
327

Epilogos
Vast and Strange Realms: A Continuing Quest for Knowledge
353

Editors' Note:

Nigel Pennick wrote *Wyrd Times* during the pandemic seclusion of 2021 and 2022. In it he recollects—almost entirely from memory—various salient details of his life and activities over the past seventy-five years. The first few sections are largely chronological, leading up to his entry into adulthood in the mid-1960s. Once he became involved in underground culture, however, his work rapidly branched out into an array of different cultural spheres. From this point on, the best approach was to organize the material into broadly thematic sections. As a result, there are necessarily points of chronological overlap between these sections. Nevertheless, it is hoped that this arrangement will enable the reader to see the organic development of his larger interests, and how his creative impulses found expression over time.

PROLOGOS
WE WUNT BE DRUV

Power, like a desolating pestilence,
Pollutes whate'er it touches; and obedience,
Bane of all genius, virtue, freedom, truth,
Makes slaves of men, and, of the human frame,
A mechanized automaton.

—Percy Bysshe Shelley, *Queen Mab*

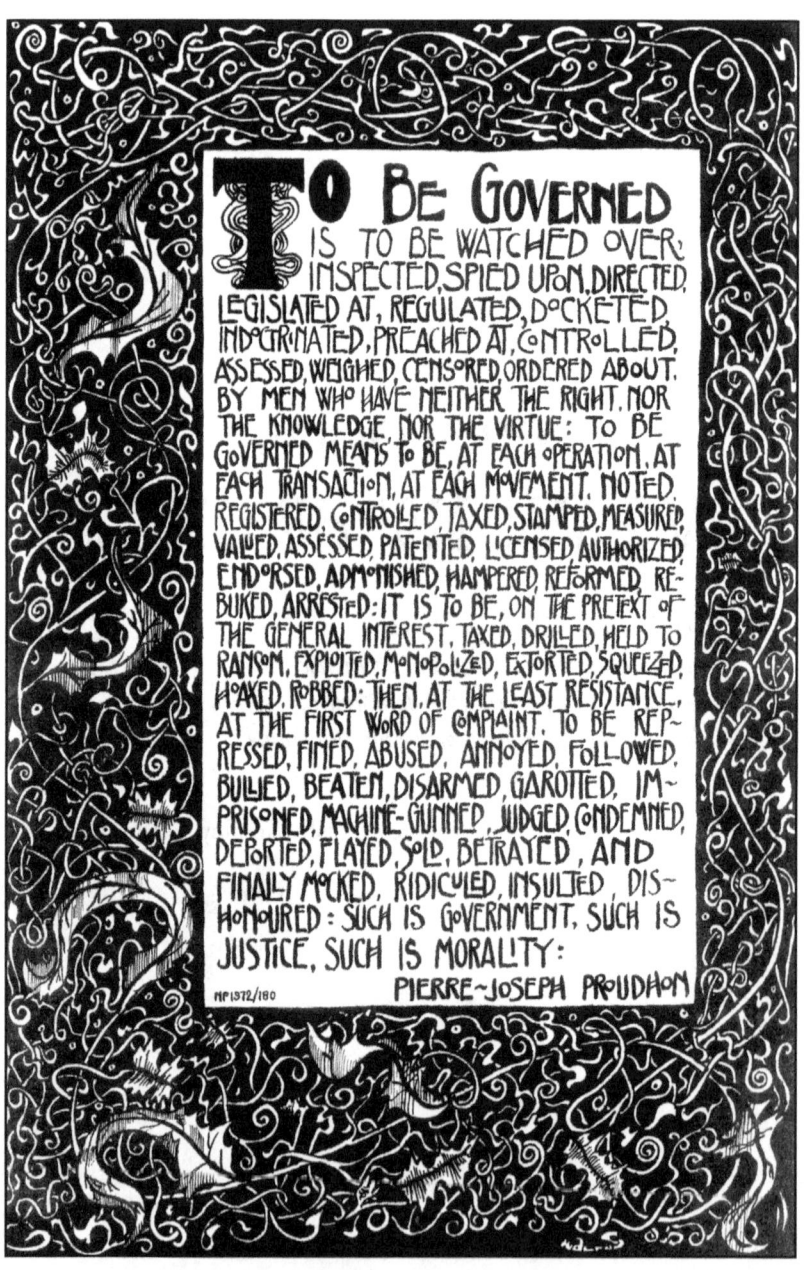

Hand-drawn and lettered poster by Nigel Pennick, 1972.

Part of my ancestral tradition is from "Old West Surrey." In this part of England, the yeomen, farmworkers, and craftspeople were fiercely independent, proudly holding their own against those who would force them to do things against their will. "*We wunt be druv*" was their motto— "We won't be driven" in standard English. Tragically, the culture of Old West Surrey was driven almost out of existence during the twentieth century as the result of those twin scourges of tradition, commercialism and war, the two-headed spawn of militant materialism. But the spirit of "We wunt be druv" refuses to die and still lives on, as you can plainly see.

The traditional view of existence, outside the adversarial strictures and doctrines of religious systems, is subtle, in contrast with the instrumental materialism of modernity. The world is in constant change; there are no boundaries, things alter, and they fade into one another imperceptibly. Those who view the world instrumentally operate by means of a fixed taxonomy, the assertion that there are unchanging discrete "things" that can be isolated and manipulated. This way of thinking has limited uses, but nevertheless is the dominant one in contemporary society. However, the phenomena we experience are not eternal realities; they are brief fragmental snapshots, small parts of a continuing process in space and time. In one is all.

From birth, we are surrounded by unrest and disquiet that manifests in the human sphere as envy, jealousy, anger, hatred, and violence. This is nothing new. The world has always been cruel and unfair, and present-day woes are only different from those of the past in outward appearance. He or she who won't be druv

Marchers in Lewes, Sussex, carry their flaming motto as part of the annual Bonfire Night celebration on November 5. The march commemorates the thwarting of the 1605 "Gunpowder Plot" in which a group of Catholics, including the infamous Guy Fawkes, planned to blow up the House of Lords.

has awareness that no one is immune from the vicissitudes of the world, and anything that can happen to one person can happen to another. Events that one experiences, however bad, cannot be unexpected if one recognises this truism. No one is excepted from the misfortunes of the world; as Seneca noted: "Nothing can happen to a wise man contrary to his expectations." Reality is having no illusions and expecting the unexpected. Anything can happen in the next half hour—and it probably will. Those who allow themselves to be druv complain that their distress is an anomalous condition that ought not to exist if "someone" did something about it. Then the world would be perfect.

This is a delusion.

While we must "dree our wyrd," we may not use the situation in which we find ourselves as an excuse for shortcomings. We have free will to alter those things that fail to satisfy us, but if they cannot be changed, then this recognition need not bring despair and inaction. One should accept them and find another way. We refuse to be druv by external conditions. If we cannot find the circumstances we need ready-made, then we must create them. John Nicholson once said: "I want to make a world that doesn't exist." Awareness without illusions frees the mind. As Seneca counsels us: "Let all labour have some purpose, some aim. Not industriousness, but false conceptions of things disturbs those who are restless and foolish." And attributed to Henry Ford is the truism: "Whether you think you can, or think you can't—you're right."

Of course, everything we attempt is fraught by problems and hindrances, but often these can be overcome through diligence. Retaining awareness at all times and not being distracted from one's task by uninformed opinion or trivial arguments is vital. Those who won't be druv do not suffer fools gladly. The *Chaldaean Oracles of Zoroaster* advise us: "We should flee, according to the oracle, the multitude of men going in a herd." In contemporary terms, this means not taking part in media-driven frenzies and empty public rituals, neither participating in imaginary competition with others. These activities are a waste of time and sap one's energy in futile conflict. Comparing oneself with others is a pointless exercise. Epictetus noted that "Whatever anyone may say about you, do not take notice of it, for this is no affair of yours."

Not being druv is also recognising that one is not part of some group that one has never volunteered to join. When I was born, I was, without my consent, registered as a subject of King George VI, monarch of the United Kingdom and Emperor of the British Empire. I was the *subject* of a king, and when the king died, of a queen. People are in subjection even when life is comfortable and they are unaware of their condition. Not being druv recognises this anomalous status where one is apparently free, yet actually the property of a state—which in some circumstances can abolish that freedom at will. Only if we voluntarily align ourselves consciously with any group are we a part of it, and even then, we do not give up our critical faculties and follow leaders blindly. "Orders must be obeyed at all times without question" is anathema. We wunt be druv.

Question everything. One cannot be a conformist when one expresses one's true nature. Everything we do must be voluntary. Being true to oneself entails rejecting what is merely fashionable, whether that fashion is of the mainstream commercial or the subcultural variety. This means not becoming a stereotype, whatever form that may take, whether conformist or transgressive. Inevitably, one will have titles and descriptors thrust upon one describing status in society, one's work or one's calling, but these are a means of communication, not realities that define our true being. Recognition of these limitations, and refusing to conform to destructive norms, is the essence of not being druv.

It is an autonomous, creative way to live.

I
EARLY YEARS

All the world's a stage, and all the men and women merely players; they have their exits and their entrances; and one man in his time plays many parts, his acts being seven ages.

—William Shakespeare, *As You Like It*

Cynthia Pennick and Nigel Pennick in Gordon Square, London, 1948.
Photo by Rupert Pennick.

I was born in Guildford, Surrey, in October 1946 and was transported, at the age of three weeks, by my mother on the Southern Railway to London. We lived in a flat converted from a few rooms on the second floor of a large house in a Georgian terrace by Gordon Square in Bloomsbury. Today this sounds like a posh area, associated with the early twentieth-century Bloomsbury set of artists, literati, and the creativity of the Omega Workshop and other local art movements. But in the 1940s, there was no longer any trace of this bohemian world of the past. World War II had scarred the area with bombsites and the houses were poorly maintained and divided up into small flats after years of austerity. Bloomsbury was mostly home to working-class Londoners and war refugees.

Of course, as an infant struggling against the cold and polluted air of the 1946–47 winter (which was the coldest in decades), I had no awareness of any of this. I was told later that my parents had me baptised in a church around the corner on Woburn Square with a hot-water bottle. The church was eventually torn down by London University and the inhabitants of these squares were replaced by administrative departments—although in 1947, I am sure nobody could have imagined this. Naturally, I cannot remember that winter, but clearly it was something exceptional. I was told by my mother that she wheeled me in a perambulator across the frozen lake in Regent's Park, which I still consider to be a reckless act. But she was young, and it must have been exciting to go where no one had gone before.

Born into this urban environment, when I became aware of things around me, it was my only reality. Like all children, I had no preconceptions or intellectual critique of my surroundings.

Nigel Pennick and Cynthia Pennick on a tram in London, 1952. Through the window a bombsite is visible, with beams shoring up the adjacent building. Photo by Rupert Pennick.

Indeed, the concept of "environment" did not exist to me nor, most likely, did it exist to my parents and other adults. The struggle for everyday survival in an impoverished city—where food was rationed and fuel was in short supply—was the main concern. Shopping with my mother involved a ten-minute walk to Marchmont Street. There, outside the fishmonger's, where fish lay on a slab open to the air, eels writhed around in half a barrel of water. When a customer wanted one, the fishmonger would grab it by the head, pull it out alive, and, taking it to a wooden block, chop it into pieces with a meat cleaver. At the butcher's, sides of beef and skinned, headless pigs hung on meathooks outside. Such sights and smells are no longer possible. Every purchase required coupons, which were printed in a ration book. The shopkeeper cut out the appropriate number of coupons using scissors. Of course, I didn't know then that there was also a "black market" in rationed food and other items. Those with money and contacts could get anything they wanted without coupons. Later, my paternal grandmother told me that she, who had been in London throughout the war, ate meat that was otherwise unobtainable, bought from a butcher who was part of this network. Rationing continued in Britain until 1954, nine years after the end of the war.

Everyone who could afford it burnt coal in their fireplaces. Wood was unavailable, though whenever the tram lines were torn up, the tar-impregnated wooden blocks that made up the road surface between and around the rails used in their construction were stolen for burning. London Transport had decided to do away with electric trams and replace them with diesel-engine buses. So, a new illegal and heavily polluting fuel became available to those desperate enough to steal it from the stacks in the street. Most people, however, burnt a low-grade coal called "nutty slack." It contained a lot of dust—as the best coal was reserved for export—and was delivered by a man on a flatbed, horse-drawn coal wagon. Hessian sacks stood upright, ready for delivery. The coalman, wearing a thick leather coat and a cloth over his head, hoisted a hundredweight (212-lb.) sack on his back and shot the coal down the coal hole, an aperture in the pavement in front of the house. Covered by a decorated metal plate, the coal hole allowed coal to be dropped into the coal cellar below. As the coalman was emptying his sack, his horse walked forwards of its own accord to the next delivery place.

The kitchen-window view from the Bloomsbury flat: bombsite ruins and the church where Nigel Pennick was baptised. Photo by Rupert Pennick.

Smog filled the air, sometimes becoming so thick that when I looked out of the front window, I could not see the buildings on the other side of the street. The flat had soot-stained windows at the front and the back. Those at the front overlooked the street, and at the back they gave a view of bombsite ruins and the spire of the church on Woburn Square. Luckily, my father photographed it and it is reproduced here.

The **Battersea Power Station** building in 2011. Before its decommissioning in 1975, this coal-fired facility had produced 500 tons of emissions per day for decades and ultimately killed more people in London than died in the World War II Blitz. Photo by Carlos Leiva.

Trees grew on the bombsite and when I was taken out by my mother to go to Marchment Street, I passed other areas where bombs had fallen. They largely consisted of holes in the ground with architectural remnants, divided from the pavement by low brick walls. Where there was a gap between buildings from a fallen bomb, large baulks of timber shored up the walls of the adjoining houses. Elder and other small trees grew in places on the rubble which were not too polluted for plants to grow, and wild flowers appeared in the spring. Later, I understood that the potential to be fruitful despite great difficulties was symbolised by the successful struggle of these brave plants in the hostile environment they shared with me.

In the winter of 1952, thick yellowish smog lasted for over a week. Burning low-grade coal and tar-soaked tramway woodblocks in fireplaces added to the enormous emissions of the coal-fired power stations at Battersea, Bankside, Lots Road, and Greenwich, and the coal-burning locomotives working the trains in and out of the London rail termini. I was living a third of a mile south of Euston Station and half a mile from Somers Town, St Pancras, and King's Cross, where steam trains came and went day and night. Motor vehicles, too, had no emission controls, and, although there were few cars (and those used leaded petrol), there were thousands of buses pumping out diesel fumes all over the city. These were increasing in numbers as they replaced the electric trams. Soot was everywhere, blackening the neglected buildings. The 1952 smog was only the most protracted of many. Thick smogs occurred frequently every winter and were accepted as normal. They *were* normal.

Growing up in this polluted environment led to a cascade of medical problems that I suffer from to this day. As a result, years later my boyhood best friend Stephen Clarke died of respiratory and heart conditions at the age of 53. In addition to the everyday soot and sulphur of smog and lead from motor exhausts, we were undoubtedly exposed to particulates in the dust and fragments of buildings blown apart in the Blitz a few years earlier, including asbestos and lead from paint and piping. Sometimes I wonder how many of my contemporaries at St Giles' primary school died prematurely of respiratory and circulatory disease. All of us children were exposed to cigarettes, as the majority of people smoked—and teachers even lit up in class. My parents did not use tobacco, having given it up after leaving the armed forces, but my grandfather, Charles Pennick, was a chain-smoker of Black Cat cigarettes, and I visited him frequently. He died aged 60.

Charles Pennick was a professional musician. He played the drums and xylophone. After serving for a few months in France at the end of World War I, he had joined the Metropolitan Police (his father was a sergeant), but was then seconded to the Auxiliaries, otherwise called the Black and Tans, to fight against nationalist insurgents in Ireland. "I will not persecute the Irish," he told his commander, and resigned from his position. Having played the drum in a Salvation Army Band, he became a professional drummer after seeing the African-American musicians of the Southern Syncopated Orchestra playing jazz when they toured Britain in 1920–21. For this, he was expelled from the Salvation Army.

Subsequently, he played with American and British bands, including Albert Lemaire and his Cleveland, Ohio, Orchestra,

Charles Pennick self-portrait, July 21, 1943.

and later he was a drummer and xylophonist in Jack Payne's Hotel Cecil Orchestra, which recorded several hit records in 1927. They played in the Palm Court of the Hotel Cecil. It was then the largest hotel in the world, on London's Thames Embankment next to the Savoy Hotel, until it fell on hard times and was demolished in 1930. Later, he played in the house band of the Hungaria Restaurant. A photograph of him there in 1931 shows him playing xylophone. In his drum kit there was a tom-tom made by Kee Wo, a drum maker in Fatshan, Canton, China. It has a hand-painted dragon on one side and a phoenix on the other. At the time of this writing, it is still in my collection and I have played it on some of my recordings.

My great-grandmother Louisa Robinson, widowed in 1947, lived in a spartan tenement block ten minutes' walk away in Herbrand Street, which ran parallel with Marchmont Street where the shops were. It was a mid-Victorian building erected for working-class people and at that time was a great improvement on the slums that had been there before. We called it the Peabody Buildings, but I am not sure now if it had been erected by the philanthropic Peabody Trust. By 1950 it was certainly substandard, as the tenements did not have their own toilets, but communal ones that had to serve a whole floor of eight or ten families. There was no hot water, and no bath. As in the flat where I lived, hot water was provided in the kitchen by a gas-powered geyser which burst into flame and emitted scalding-hot water when the tap was turned. Clearly, this was an improvement on what the inhabitants had for the first seventy years in those grim, sooty tenements. My great-grandmother made wonderful caraway-seed cakes, which she gave me when I visited. She was an expert at spotting coins people had dropped, and one time she gave me, as a lucky charm, a silver three-pence piece she had found. Later, when I inherited the military identity tags her husband Charles Robinson had worn through World War I while serving with the Royal Fusiliers, I saw his lucky three-pence piece attached to the string.

I was very aware of sound from my earliest times. I remember being awakened at midnight one year by steam locomotive whistles. The drivers at Euston Station only a third of a mile away were marking the New Year. There was not much traffic noise at night in those years and in the daytime I could hear the clip-clop of horses pulling coal wagons and milk floats. The noisiest vehicle was the occasional motorcycle. But it was music that interested me. We attended the church around the corner, so of course I heard the organ, though it was not pleasing to my ear. Outside in the streets I listened to the "barrel organs," street pianos cranked by men who wheeled them from place to place, collecting donations from passersby every time they played. Echoing in almost traffic-free roadways, they played mainly music-hall tunes from half a century earlier. There were also many street musicians playing various instruments, from penny whistles and mouth organs to banjos and accordions. Other buskers further afield included men in old army uniforms wearing black-lensed, round-framed glasses who played banjo tunes for pennies. A man with a white stick holding a tin with a slot in the top collected donations. They were, I was told, ex-servicemen blinded in the war that had ended only a year before I was born, eking out a living by performing on the streets.

At other times I remember an old Irish man standing at a street corner playing beautiful spirited tunes on the fiddle. Decades later, I would play these same traditional tunes with Irish musicians in pub sessions. "South Wind" must have been in his repertoire, as it has always been a favourite of mine. I remember hearing people sing songs, such as the archetypal London tune "Knees Up Mother Brown" and the Irish ballad "The Rose of Tralee." There was a rich and diverse culture of what would now be called "live music." Occasionally, I encountered other buskers such as a one-man band with a drum on his back, playing a ukulele and banjo attached to his front. All the buskers I remember were men. There was a man who, with two bones in each hand, step-danced to their rhythm. Guitars appeared only later with the emergence of skiffle.

I remember certain musical incidents, though when they happened precisely, I cannot say. One is particularly etched in my memory. On a summer lunchtime, I was with my mother and we were going somewhere. We passed the open door of a public house. It was one of those pubs at the junction of two streets with a door set diagonally on the corner. As we passed, I stopped to listen. Coming from the crowded, smoky interior, I heard a pianist playing a spirited boogie-woogie. I was enraptured—but not for long. My mother snatched me by one arm and dragged me away, oblivious to my transport of delight as she scolded me for not keeping up with her. It is often one's lot to be misunderstood by those who do not share one's sensibilities. Most of my later schooling was in that mode. Outside Russell Square underground station sat a man playing a one-string fiddle. I know now that it was a Strohviol, or Stroh violin, from its dull aluminium horn. I do not remember what music he played, but I was fascinated that someone could play tunes on a single string with a bow. As my mother took me to the station on fine afternoons to meet my father after work, I had time to listen to the fiddler.

My repertoire of song-knowledge started early. Somewhere I remember hearing on the radio a record of the calypso song "Cricket, Lovely Cricket!" that commemorated a West Indian victory over the English cricket team at Lords in 1950. My father used to listen to programmes on the American Forces Network radio station, so I heard everything from swing and boogie-woogie to cowboy songs, Tin Pan Alley, and bebop.

When my parents dropped me off to visit my grandparents at their apartment, they would read to me, sing, and play records. My grandfather sang me old soldiers' songs from the First World War like "Pack Up Your Troubles in Your Old Kit-Bag," and played records of bands he had performed with, including a song with the chorus *"You die if you worry, / you die if you don't, / so why worry at all?"* "Cement Mixer" by Slim Gaillard was one of my favourites. My grandmother also amused me with songs including "The Wind Blew Through His Whiskers" and "Chick, Chick, Chick, Chick, Chicken (Lay a Little Egg for Me)." She also used to take me to see Strelsky's Cossack Orchestra perform in the Embankment Gardens in Central London. The open-air stage on which Strelsky's men performed was located close to the site of the former Hotel Cecil, where my grandfather had often played as a musician.[1]

In addition to the musicians, other street people I saw as I was taken shopping or visiting included men in sharp suits selling items. They were "spivs," I was told, who sold things that

---

1. The balalaikas in Strelsky's Orchestra intrigued me and thirty years later I bought one, which I sometimes played at folk clubs and once in a Plough Monday procession (see the section "Northstow Mummers," pp. 307–12).

otherwise were unavailable or rationed—and probably stolen. A man who lived in the flat above us was a spiv. Later he opened a shop selling women's clothes. Similar men, perhaps not so well dressed as the spivs, stood around surrounded by pieces of paper thrown on the ground, talking to other men and taking money from them. I was puzzled about these characters and my questions about them were fobbed off. Later I found that they were illegal bookmakers taking bets and paying out winnings to lucky punters. Horse racing was the source of their business. Off-course bookmaking was banned in Victorian times and only telephone bets on account to "turf accountants," as they were known, were permitted. This meant only well-to-do clients could bet outside the racecourses, and working-class men were a lucrative captive audience for the street bookies.

I found out later that these illicit street activities were controlled by gangsters, but of course then, as now, such things were not to be talked about. Like the bookies, we all had to be careful. Sometimes a bookie would take to his heels and run, tipped off by an inconspicuous lookout who had spotted a policeman on his beat. Occasionally, someone would set up an old fruit box and perform the three-card trick, or the pea under the cups. It was a game the punters could not win. Those who did win at the beginning were the operator's accomplices. The whole thing was rigged by sleight of hand. Later, in the early 1960s, in a crowded market in Soho on a Cup Final day, I saw visiting football supporters who were not Londoners betting £5 and £10 notes—large sums at the time—on a three-card trick set up on an upturned cardboard box. Suddenly, there was a shout, the punters turned round to look at what was going on, and the trickster snatched up well over £50 and ran off. Perhaps there was a policeman coming, or maybe that was the *modus operandi* of the racketeers all along. Having seen such things since childhood, it is no wonder I always observe the useful advice given to me by my grandfather: "Trust no one and always watch your back." Less pernicious pavement artists occupied strategic pitches and drew artistic works in coloured chalk.

I lived in an area which, though run-down and impoverished,

The Egyptian goddess Sekhmet in the British Museum. Photo by Nigel Pennick.

had a diverse richness of architectural features, and the great cultural gem that is the British Museum was just a few minutes' walk away. My mother took me there on occasion and I saw wonderful antiquities. I remember certain artefacts from ancient Egypt and China that I always wanted to see again. Parts of the museum were closed off as they had been bombed in World War II and were not then accessible. Only later did I see the ravishing illumination of the Lindisfarne Gospels and the runes of the Franks Casket and the Thames Scramasax, but knowing that there had been wonderfully skilled people thousands of years ago gave me a perspective on life that has never left me. Sometimes, my mother would take me on the Piccadilly Line tube from Russell Square to South Kensington. There I would visit the Natural History Museum to marvel at the stuffed and mounted specimens of exotic animals and birds.

As well as the British Museum, the whole local area possessed an astonishing richness of material culture. Although the cast-iron railings around squares and parks had been sawn off in the war for recycling as armaments, leaving rough stumps of iron protruding from low stone walls, wrought-iron metalwork remained in buildings. Now I know that it ranged in style from Georgian and Regency to Arts and Crafts, Art Nouveau, and Art Deco. As a small boy, I had my hair cut sitting in the chrome-and-leather chair of my Italian barber, Mr Falcone, whose Art Deco shop was lined with black geometric glass and chrome. Other wonderful Art Deco buildings I knew included Lyons' Corner House cafés and the Strand Palace hotel. These buildings, soon to be demolished as "old fashioned," were outstanding examples which would today be listed as "historic." Too late now—they are history themselves.

My local underground station, Russell Square, had its own Art Nouveau metalwork above the lift doors with ornate numbers on small shields. The Imperial Hotel nearby, facing Russell Square itself, also retained its turn-of-the-century railings with "IH" monograms on burgundy-coloured enamel. High up on the facade was a large mosaic of the sun with a gilded, full-sized metal figure of Father Time with his scythe. Niches contained statues, including a king who must have been Edward VII. This remarkable building was torn down in 1966. But the most impressive building of all, visible to the right and down the street from my front doorstep, was the Passmore Edwards Settlement, now the Mary Ward Centre. A striking structure, then just over fifty years old, its main entrance was capped by two giant stone eggs and the end-gable brickwork was made in the form of three stylised trees. Later I learnt that the eggs symbolised the Cosmic Egg from which all existence emerged, and the trees were the Tree of Life, a symbol common to many cultures. Like the Father Time sundial on the Imperial Hotel, this symbolic architecture was a formative influence on my personal studies and writing. Now I know the history and details of what I saw and experienced as a boy and can write about them in this memoir. Occasionally, I went inside the Passmore Edwards Settlement when my father was teaching there, and I saw on a window sill a yellow and orange Art Nouveau vase which struck me as interesting. Fifty years later, I bought an identical one in an antique shop. Perhaps it is the same one.

I remember being taken to meet my father coming back from

The Passmore Edwards Settlement entrance, with cosmic eggs. Architects: Dunbar Smith and Cecil Brewer, 1897–98. Photo by Nigel Pennick.

East London where he was a teacher. My mother and I waited outside Russell Square station by the lift doors, which were heavy panelled wood with metal plates in the upper part and featured stylised tulip cut-outs. When light appeared through these cut-outs, the lift had arrived from below and the doors would open. People were always standing around outside the station, news vendors selling the three London evening papers, and sometimes the one-string fiddle player going through his repertoire. When I was taken on the underground to go somewhere, Russell Square station was the entry-point to the vast unknown and mysterious network of tunnels beneath the city. The adventure of going underground began when I was taken past the ruby-red tiled entrance arch to the green-tiled fare window, where my father paid the fare and we went to wait for the lift. The lift came up from underground and the doors on the outside opened with a crash to let out the passengers. Then the doors on the inside opened and we entered past the uniformed lift attendant.

When everyone was in the lift, the diamond-like folding

Russell Square tube station exterior lettering, London. Photo by Nigel Pennick.

gates would slam shut and the lift descended down the shaft, the ribs of which could be seen through the lattice. The sound of the lift in the shaft had a deep rumbling echo with occasional reverberating concussions. I can still recall this unique set of sounds, though of course it is elusive, because all London underground lifts have been rebuilt and it is unlikely that anyone ever made a recording of it. When the lift reached the bottom of the shaft, the door opposite to the one we had entered by opened and we walked along circular tunnels. Stepping down to one of the two platforms to wait for the train, the walls were lined with the coloured tiles and festooned with colourful advertising posters. The name "Russell Square" in unusual lettering was amid the tile pattern, but the main station names were in the red-white-and-blue roundels of London Transport. Today this is a closely guarded trademark.

With a rumbling noise that increased in intensity, several white lights on the front of the train emerged from the darkness of the tunnel into the station. The red-painted train decelerated and stopped, the sliding doors opened, and people pushed their way out past those attempting to get on. The train had a section at the front and back where passengers could not ride. Once all were aboard and inside the green interior, the door closed and the train proceeded into the tunnel. Sometimes there was a bang before the train gained speed. Later I discovered that this was a "Metpop" circuit breaker blowing because the driver had accelerated too fast. To a small child, it was just another interesting sound like the whine of the motors and the clatter over special trackwork in the tunnel, though I had no idea at the time what the noises actually meant.

On one occasion in an underground train I had the realization that I was travelling beneath things I could not see, and yet were there up above. It was a shocking revelation. Unlike being on the surface, where I was aware of where I was, being down in the tube was a *no-place*. Looking back upon it, going down a lift, travelling in a train, and coming up into the street at another location was a bizarre form of existence: made mundane through repetition, yet disturbing in an undefined way. I attempted to compensate for this sense of dislocation by visualising what direction I was turning in the tunnels in relation to the entrance of the station.

When I was about six, I was given a compass as a present and took it with me down the underground so that I could maintain some sense of direction. I was scolded for looking at it when I should have been hurrying for the train. The first time I looked at my compass on a tube train, I found it was useless because the needle kept spinning. I was sitting with my parents on a transverse seat and noticed a meter on the solid support beneath it whose needle moved when the train accelerated. We must have been riding in a tube car with motors, and the magnetic field was spinning my compass. After that, I gave up trying to use it underground. But I did learn something about magnetism and electricity. Later, when I flew extensively, I felt the same disturbing sense of dislocation. Instead of being in a red electric train speeding beneath grand hotels and slums, I was precariously ensconced in a jet aircraft high above places I had never been such as the North Pole, Lake Balaton, and Chicago. Luckily, I only experienced two near misses in the two hundred and fourteen flights I made.

At some point when I was four years old, I remember a

steel scaffolding pole falling from a building site across my feet, smashing them. I was taken to hospital, but my memories of it are hazy. All I remember is pain and terror. Even now when I hear the metallic ring of a scaffolding pole, it sends a chill through me. My injuries were treated, and I was able to walk again after a period. I was sent home from hospital without the physiotherapy and rehabilitation one would receive today. As a result, I could never run as fast as other children, and this would have serious consequences for me in school. Teachers always abused and sometimes punished me for "not trying" during physical education and sports activities. I just could not do it, however hard I tried, but there was no understanding that I had suffered a serious injury when very young. The adults in charge of me could not be bothered to find out; they viewed my inability as laziness or intransigence.

School: Sunday and Weekday

Before I was sent to school proper, I attended Sunday school, where they attempted to indoctrinate us with Biblical beliefs. The Sunday school was on Kingsway next to a church opposite Holborn underground station. I remember little of it except one significant moment of realization that this place unwittingly evoked in me. It was a particularly gloomy midwinter afternoon. My mother collected me from Sunday school and we went out into the already darkened wintry street. It was very cold, and the streetlights were already on. The smog was thick, yellowish with sulphur, and ice was on the ground. I looked at a card I had just been given on which a Biblical scene was depicted. It showed a palm tree and a camel led by a man in a long robe. They were in a desert, or so it seemed. Lit-up buses loomed on the street, crawling slowly in the smog, and the headlights of cars had fuzzy haloes around them. I wondered how the scene from ancient Palestine that I held in my hands had anything to do with where I was. I could see no connection whatever. I had ridden on a camel at the London Zoo, but that was a real living animal. I could not relate to a picture of a desert. There was no point of contact.

I had to walk about three-quarters of a mile through the streets to school at St Giles', Monday to Friday, despite my damaged feet. My mother walked with me for a while, but later, aged six, I walked alone, including crossing a main street which even then had a stream of buses, lorries, vans, taxis, and cars roaring past. On many occasions, people who did not come from London have been surprised at how quickly I can cross a street amid traffic. It was out of necessity. I had to learn to gauge the speed and spacing of vehicles—there were no school crossing patrols in those days.

Primary school was an unkind place, with informal and formal corporal punishment meted out continuously and much violence between the boys. This was tolerated by uninterested adults. Smacked by teachers and assaulted by other children, one had to learn to resist and fight—or go under. Verbal abuse was the constant norm from pupils, and one could not get through a single day without being hit by someone. Unwittingly, these teachers taught dislocation and disobedience by their own obvious failure to adhere to the standards of humaneness and fairness they were supposed to uphold.

In socialist Britain we were given free bottles of milk to drink at break time, and free orange juice that came in bottles with screw-tops made of soft aluminium. Sometimes we had to stand in line while a spoonful of malt was administered to each child. Periodically, a nurse would come round with a comb to see if we had nits in our hair. Those that did were sent home. There was no playing field for pupils of this inner-city school. The playground was on the roof and ball games were not allowed. We had to throw bean-bags to each other instead. Every day, we were forced to do drill like soldiers: to line up, stand at correct spacing, march in step swinging our arms, and do military-style physical training. At a later school that had a playing field, there was no drill, but I was punished by teachers who did not know or care about my damaged feet and who viewed my inability to run as a form of "dumb insolence" (a military term for those who did not obey orders). "Orders must be obeyed at all times without question" is a phrase I remember well.

Forcefully still in my memory is an occasion around the Coronation in 1953 when the new Queen was supposed to be driven in her car along the street past the school. In the pouring rain we were led out to stand by the roadside to get drenched for what seemed like hours until a police car, followed by a large black vehicle with curtained windows, shot past at speed. Then we were all marched back in. Even as a young lad, I felt outrage at being forced to participate in such a meaningless event, while the teachers were telling us how wonderful it was.

I am still aware today of much of the futile ritual that now, different in form, but the same in essence, has become the norm in public displays of "virtue." By then my experiences had given me some critical faculty, even if I could not express it—and of course, this was not something that was taught, encouraged, or allowed. I had learnt from the structural way schooling operated, and understood that everything that was not actual information, such as basic scientific or geographical data, must be subjected to sceptical analysis. The necessity to ask *Cui bono?* (Who profits?) of any ideological assertion, whether religious or political, is never taught in schools. Knowledge of this sort was of a different order from what they expected. My experience of school taught me lessons diametrically opposed to the ones they were trying to teach me. I learnt to never respect people or institutions that were not worthy of respect, and never to obey instructions blindly or without question.

Visions of Above and Below

There are a number of memories of experiences which at the time were not planned, but proved seminal in awakening my awareness. In 1952, my mother took me to King's Cross Station, half a mile away, to see an exhibition of trains to celebrate the centenary of the station. I had never seen steam locomotives from a ground perspective, only from station platforms. Most of the trains I had ridden on were electric, on the Underground and also on the Southern Region, either to my grandmother's at Guildford or to the seaside at Brighton. Standing there in King's Cross yard, resplendent in Brunswick Green livery, was

Woodcock, Mallard's sister locomotive, King's Cross, London, 1961.
Photo by Nigel Pennick.

the streamlined locomotive *Mallard*, which held and still holds the world speed record for steam traction. The whole locomotive was spotless. It had a cast metal nameplate, and the wheels were polished an equally bright silver. There was also a circular plate announcing that this was the fastest of all. Behind the locomotive was a massive, slab-sided, eight-wheeled tender filled with coal. On its side was the proud lion-and-wheel emblem of the British Railways. Inside the tender was a narrow passage that enabled the crew to walk through a corridor connexion into the train so crews could exchange during the journey. This enabled nonstop runs from London to Scotland.

We climbed up a set of wooden steps that had been provided, and entered the cab of the mighty locomotive. *Mallard* was not in steam, so there was no fire glowing red behind the firebox door. But the brightly polished brass piping, dials, and levers fascinated me. I was placed upon the driver's padded leather bucket seat. He told of the exploits of this famous locomotive and how it still ran from London to Edinburgh, pulling the fastest trains. Even as a small boy, I could sense his pride in his job and his steel steed. The name of the designer, Sir Nigel Gresley, was mentioned. *Nigel*, my name—now I knew that Nigels had achieved great things! It was a good feeling, as my name was rare then and a subject of mockery for sounding "upper class"—which I certainly was not. In later years, several Nigels excelled in their chosen fields: Nigel Mansell, Formula One racing car world champion; Nigel Benn, champion boxer; and Nigel Kennedy, virtuoso violinist.

A bronze statue of Sir Nigel Gresley was installed in King's Cross Station in 2016. The sculptor intended to have a bronze mallard duck standing next to him, as Sir Nigel reputedly liked ducks, but the Gresley family rejected it as undignified. Seeing his wonderful piece of engineering made a great impression upon me. In later years, I often visited stations to view steam locomotives, and in 1962 I had the pleasure to ride in a train behind *Mallard*.[2] After withdrawal, it was preserved in the National Railway Museum in York, where again, over sixty years later in 2013, I entered the cab and sat in the driver's seat. But the corridor tender I walked through in 1952 had been replaced in the museum by one with no corridor.

On occasion my mother would take me to Guildford to visit her mother, Elizabeth Austin. We rode there southwesterly from Waterloo Station on the green electric trains of the Southern Region. When they stopped at stations, they stood silent until a compressor started up with a rumbling, chattering sound, replenishing the air-brake reservoirs.

My grandmother would tell me stories about her girlhood in 1880s Kent, some of them with a supernatural element. It seemed that some people thought her a superstitious old woman, as once she had thrown a peacock-feather fan straight into the fire when given it as a present. (The "eyes" on peacock feathers were associated with the "evil eye," so they were considered unlucky and not allowed in the house.) Her one-eyed dog, Winkie, also had a strange air about him. One of her recollections stuck in my mind. I understand why it was meaningful now, but then it was almost a fairy tale of magic with modern elements. One day, a farmer who always treated his workers badly was travelling in a trap pulled by a horse. When it reached a level crossing across a railway line, the horse stopped on the tracks. Despite the farmer's

---

2. See the section "If in Doubt . . ." on p. 52.

attempts, the horse would not move. Then horse, trap, and farmer were run down by an express train. It was the Granville Special Express, a fast boat train between London and Dover, which carried passengers for the cross-channel ferry to France. This was not an accident, my grandmother told me. The workers had stopped the horse there by magic, with the intention of killing the farmer. This story impressed me. It was a true account, yet I wondered how it was possible. A decade or more later, in East Anglia, I found out the answer.

At St Giles' School we sometimes traipsed along the street past the Angel public house to the church of St Giles-in-the-Fields. This was a baroque church designed by Henry Flitcroft and built in 1734 on the site of an older structure. We went there for a Church of England service where we had to sing hymns and listen to the vicar's sermon from some Biblical text. Then back to school. On one occasion, I was ill and did not feel well. I was in some kind of reverie while an old hymn about the transcendence of god was being sung, but when I heard the line "his canopy, space," suddenly the interior of the church appeared to me to expand into a manifestation of the infinite Cosmos (which is probably what Flitcroft intended). Like later such experiences at the edge of death, I did not feel the presence of the aged human father-creator I had been taught about, but a majestic continuum of space and time infinitely greater than it was possible to imagine, let alone understand. After this experience, I staggered back to school almost in a daze and was punished for not paying attention to whatever mundane task lay before me.

When I was nine, my father took me to St Paul's Cathedral, Sir Christopher Wren's masterpiece built after the Great Fire of 1666. We had been there before to buy paper and notebooks. A remnant of the old London Booksellers' Quarter, St Paul's Churchyard, it had been largely destroyed by bombs in the war. There were stalls where one could buy military surplus notebooks, sketchbooks, and austere pencils made of unpainted wood. For some reason on that day, my father decided to take me inside the cathedral—not just inside, but to the top. We climbed the stairs and entered the "whispering gallery" high up in the dome, where we looked down past a precarious balustrade into the cathedral's gilded baroque interior.

Then we passed through another door and continued to climb. We came onto an open balustraded walkway around the base of the dome. London lay in view below, but this was still not the top. From a ladder, I ascended to the great gilded cross that crowns the cathedral. Now at 365 feet above street level, I poked my head out into the cold air. I could see the remaining spires and towers of the baroque churches built after the Great Fire that appeared above the war ruins which lay all around. It seemed to me to be providential that the cathedral had not been blown apart by the enemy bombs that had wrought such destruction all around. I feel lucky to have seen the spires in their proper relationship—though many were damaged—before the commercial tide of concrete-and-glass offices dwarfed them and hemmed them in between faceless walls of rectilinear banality. This was a moment when it was still possible to experience an earlier world, which, having survived one bout of ruin, was about to suffer another—more permanent—type of destruction.

Although I was the son of a country mother and an urban father, my connexion with actual nature came late. In inner London, the natural world was constrained to squares and parks, where it was regimented and regulated, or bombsites, where it eked out an impoverished life in the polluted rubble. There were fine plane trees in Russell Square with their golden balls of seeds hanging in the autumn. St James's Park had a beautiful bevy of exotic ducks and even a pelican, but they were essentially captives. Freer nature manifested herself in the feral pigeons, starlings, and sparrows in the street and park, an occasional rat glimpsed upon a bombsite, and the mice and flies that plagued us in our flat. The remedy for this inner nature had been mousetraps, and when they failed to exterminate the rodents, a cat to hunt them down. As for the flies, one day my father came home with a brown paper bag. Unwrapping it, he showed me a pump with a can-like reservoir at the end, about the size of a modern beverage can. He opened a metal container and said, triumphantly: "DDT!" He

Nigel Pennick and friend, 1958. Photo by Rupert Pennick.

filled the reservoir and then proceeded to spray this poisonous insecticide. The flies dropped like flies. Periodically, my father would utter the magic word "DDT!" and hand me the pump to renew our toxic war against insects. Later, DDT was discovered to have a serious deleterious effect on nature and humans alike. But the damage had been done.

One day, my father took me on a long trolleybus ride out into the eastern fringes of London to Epping Forest. I was probably eight years of age. Sitting upstairs at the front, I saw streets thronged with people and traffic and watched the overhead wires that powered the trolleybus weave round corners and through complex junctions of overhead metalwork. Soon the large, six-wheeled, silent and fume-free electric trolleybuses were replaced by smaller, four-wheeled, diesel-engine buses that pumped out toxic emissions straight into the street. Then the fascinating overhead wires were torn down. Another part of my everyday lived experience was obliterated, and the change—vaunted as progress—was not for the better.

At the end of the trolleybus line, in quite rural surroundings, we somehow got into the forest. I had never been in a forest before.

Huge, gnarled, and ancient hornbeam trees loomed menacingly, almost blocking out the light. They had been pollarded for centuries and their misshapen bulk was anthropomorphic. I knew, of course, that trees were alive, but the life of these trees was of a different order. I felt that we were intruders in a place we should not have gone. It was overwhelming to be in such a space of terror and delight: a *locus terribilis*. Perhaps since then I have sought to reconcile my dual heritage of urban and rural, traditional and modern.

Frequently during this part of my childhood I was struck down with diseases. I suffered—though not necessarily in this order—from measles, chicken pox, German measles, mumps, glandular fever, and the Asian flu. I also injured a foot by treading on a plank with a nail through it whilst trespassing with other boys on a building site. It went straight through the sole of my rubber boot and halfway through my foot. I was off from school for a while, and this injury compounded my inability to run. When I was ten I suffered a major infection of my ears which affected my brain. I was treated with penicillin injections, but during the week the infection lasted, I suffered terrifying experiences. Deaf with infection, I hallucinated coloured spheres which pulsated. I felt myself floating in the top corner of the room, looking down on my body lying in bed; I was whisked out of the room through the ceiling and roof, and upwards above the streets and houses and into the clouds. I also descended through the bed, through the lower floors and cellars, and deep into the earth and rocks below. There I was encased in a series of granite and metallic shells like the chrysalis of a hawk moth. I stayed for aeons of time, or at least so it seemed, until I regained normal consciousness. My hearing had returned, and I was "back to normal."

But of course, I was *not* back to normal. I could remember everything that had happened to me "somewhere else." I had no idea whether there was any meaning in this ordeal. But I could never tell anyone about it, and nobody around me had any idea that I had experienced such a traumatic dislocation from "familiar reality" (to quote Dr. John). Such things are communicable in words, or I would not be able to write about them, but the actual first-hand experience is impossible to convey. Today a child undergoing something similar would get "therapy" to reintegrate with familiar reality and the experiences would be dismissed as aberrations caused by illness. But that did not happen, and I was profoundly altered as a result.

My father was a part-time member of Civil Defence, and he was told to prepare for the forthcoming nuclear war. He terrified me with a map of London showing in concentric rings how much would be destroyed by Soviet bombs of increasing megaton ratings. The largest of these bombs, which I think was over one hundred megatons, promised devastation as far as Brighton on the south coast and Cambridge to the north, a circle about 110 miles in diameter. He also showed me pictures of Hiroshima, which was hit by an atomic bomb a fraction of that size. One photograph showed the polished granite wall of a building where someone had been sitting as the bomb exploded. As his body had shielded the wall for a fraction of a second before vaporising, it had left a permanent image, a shadow of an annihilated person. It was a chilling thing to see, and it haunted me.

Although the biggest bomb would have blown a quarter of southern England off the map, my father thought we should move far away from Central London in the hope that when it was nuked we would survive. So we travelled from inner London further north to a house where we had a garden. I grew my own potatoes there. I went from the urban to the near-rural. School was less fraught, and it was easy to walk in fields and lanes which (at that time, at least) had not been devastated by traffic and agribusiness chemicals. I never saw the stars until I was eight— Central London was too polluted with smog and streetlights. Yet now I could see the constellations, which I looked out for at night. For the first time, I saw Venus rising and the red light of Mars; bright Jupiter, and the phases of the Moon. The canopy of space was opened to me. There were unpolluted water meadows with springtime carpets of flowers, streams with frogs and newts, and toads and lizards on sandy banks. I became familiar with

Nigel Pennick with rescued rook, 1957. Photo by Rupert Pennick.

the names of plants and was able to identify the various species of birds. I even rescued a sick rook and nursed it back to health. At that time children were allowed out to wander where they would, returning only for mealtimes or bed. So I walked alone in woods and by the riverbank and experienced the passing of the seasons. Later, it proved a liberation from the hell of the school I was then sent to. I still regularly returned to London to see my grandparents, and so my central connexion to the city was not broken.

Secondary School

At the age of eleven I was sent to a boys' school, a "grammar school" with pretensions of being a "public school," though it was not fee-paying. It had been established in the 1580s and in the late 1950s corporal punishment was still being meted out with all the zeal of the Elizabethan Puritans who founded it. Most of the teachers—who were exclusively male—had served in some capacity in World War II and had been brutalised by their experiences. Many had a "sergeant-major" attitude to the boys, treating us like troublesome conscripts—which in some ways we were. We were always called only by our surnames, which made school feel more like the army or prison. Apart from official corporal punishment administered by the headmaster, we were routinely grabbed and manhandled by teachers; smacked on the rear by a tennis shoe or wooden ruler in front of class for laughing or some similar misdemeanour; rapped across the knuckles with said wooden ruler; sometimes hit on the head by a wood-handled eraser used to wipe the blackboard of chalk; or thrown across the classroom by a grown man who should have known better. A friend of mine had a lifelong perforated eardrum from being punched in the head by a teacher. No wonder we hated them.

Mostly, the violence was meted out to those who had transgressed only mildly. Collective punishment was reserved for times when a teacher did not know who had perpetrated the offence. On more than one occasion, a whole class of thirty boys had to suffer being beaten on their bottoms with a tennis shoe, one by one in front of the class, because no one would "grass" upon the culprit. The code of silence that every boy followed actually protected some of the more vicious characters who did genuine harm. To "grass" was to invite retribution. This casual violence by teachers tended to be carried out on the younger boys. After about the age of fifteen, the only form of official corporal punishment was the cane.

The cane was the discipline of last resort (although the worst cases were expelled from school entirely). Sometimes the youth would be struck on his upturned palm several times, six strokes being usual. Alternatively—and I never found out what the grounds for the distinction were—the boy would bend over and have six strokes of the cane on his buttocks (clothed, of course), or "six of the best" as it was known. For the worst transgressors, this was done upon the stage of the assembly hall in front of all the boys in the school, arranged in ranks, class by class, with the youngest at the front. It had the ritualistic feel of a public execution, eliciting ridicule and glee from some pupils, and sympathy from others. Of course, everyone stood there deadpan, for to laugh at the plight of the punished would bring down punishment upon oneself. Most of the lads subjected to this public humiliation were from the harder stratum and endured it as a badge of honour. To endure "six of the best" with fortitude was considered admirable.

But formal punishment was rare. Outside classes, the teachers turned a blind eye to teasing, abuse, and bullying. Sons of teachers and policemen were especially targeted by the more violent element of the school and were bullied with verbal abuse and physical violence. The abuse culture was part of the teachers' *modus operandi*, too, and they often called their charges by belittling names such as "four-eyes" for a boy wearing spectacles, or "fatso" for a more stout lad. Among the pupils, insults were not so mild. The less athletic were labelled "spastic" or "spazzo," and those whose dexterity was not so good were "cacks." If someone missed what was being said, he was called "deaf school." A person suspected of telling an untruth was a "lying toad" or a "lying Arab" (there were no real Arabs at my school). More generally, one could be an "arsehole," a "shit," a "cunt," or—more threateningly—a "fucking cunt," which was usually an overture for a punch or a kick.

The teachers kept talking about "school rules," but on one occasion when I asked to see them, they were vague about where they were and I suspect there were no documented, formal rules at all. But enforcement of the nonexistent "rules" was real. When long hair became fashionable, teachers would call long-haired boys "trogs" (from "troglodyte") and pupils might call a long-haired student a "bender" or "mophrodite" if they suspected their sexuality. Any lad who grew his hair long was ordered to "get a haircut" in military tones, and sent home until he had been to the barber's for a "short back and sides." One long-haired youth I remember came back from the barbershop with a skinhead cut just short of baldness. He was then sent home for "taking the piss." Being a skinhead *avant la lettre* was also a form of defiance, and they knew it. As schooling there went until age eighteen, older pupils in the Sixth Form who grew moustaches during school holidays were forced to shave them off. "Sideboards"—as they called sideburns then—had to be shaved to a specific length, too.

Around the age of fifteen some of us used to play cards for money during breaks—pontoon (blackjack) and whist, mainly.

Someone was caught by a teacher and then we were told that the "school rules" forbade gambling in general and card playing in particular. I had been given a set of poker dice and so we started playing with them instead of cards. They were smaller and more easily concealed. Then the "school rules" suddenly contained a prohibition against possessing dice. It was all so transparent. My poker dice were confiscated, and I never saw them again. Property was never returned. Confiscation was an institutionalised form of theft by our teachers.

Perhaps this harsh regime was intended to ready us for conscription into the army, which at that time was compulsory for youths at eighteen. Girls were, for some reason, exempt from military service. I was lucky because "National Service," as conscription was euphemistically called, was abolished the year before I reached eighteen. In fact, the discipline bred resistance and transgression. In the library, we admiringly read books about the brave and resourceful French Resistance against German occupation in World War II. Tales of factories being wrecked and trains derailed by sabotage were thrilling to disaffected teenagers, so the Maquis became our role models.

There were many ways to cause disruption and not get caught. Sometimes a disgruntled pupil would go into the toilets just before the bell rang and unscrew the ball from a cistern valve so that by the next break, the floor was flooded. Some knew the secret of the cold taps. A tap could be turned off in such a way that the water continued to flow out with a vibration that increased in volume to a shriek. The pipes ran through a number of classrooms on the ground floor, and this noise would reverberate through them, with a screech louder than the teacher. Eventually, after perhaps ten minutes, the water flow would stabilise and the sound ceased. I am sure the teachers never suspected that this seemingly spontaneous failure of the plumbing was an act of sabotage. Anything vulnerable which could be tampered with was attacked. Over a number of months, someone removed screws, probably one by one, from the tables in the library until they became rickety and had to be replaced.

In the classrooms, school furniture was also deliberately

damaged. Hardware was progressively removed from the hinges of desk lids until they were loose. It was important not to do it all at once, as the teachers or caretakers would notice. The metal-framed chairs we sat on had rubber feet that could easily be removed and taken away. These were used as missiles to throw around the classroom when the teacher was absent for a while. For a few weeks my class had a broken desktop stashed in the classroom which came out and served like a bat, the batter hitting chair rubbers pitched at him across the room. This we called "Crid-Crud Cricket." Eventually, the lad caught with the "bat" had a visit to the headmaster. Queuing up to go into the hall at lunchtime, youths would use coins to grind holes in the soft red brickwork, like cup-marks on ancient megaliths.

We were compelled to assemble every morning in the hall where a pupil would read a designated text from the Bible; the head teacher would say boring, clichéd prayers; and we had to sing hymns. The school was officially Church of England, so Roman Catholics, Jews, and the rare Hindu were exempt from participating. There were no Muslims or members of other religions. They only came in at the end when the head made announcements that all had to hear. Those who professed atheism were compelled to take part in the religious portion of the assembly. On special occasions, we had to troop along the street to the local church for a service conducted by a real ordained vicar. Resistance against forcible hymn-singing involved replacing the proper words with parodies that those conducting the service could not hear. Perhaps we got this from our grandfathers and great-grandfathers who had sung ironic parodies of hymns in the trenches of World War I. Some who, against their will, knew all the hymns' words already, held their hymnals upside down and pretended to sing from them. Around then, when I first read William Blake's "Prayers plow not! Praises reap not!" I understood why I innerly objected to this forced ritual.

All teachers were called by nicknames—out of earshot! I had a teacher of English whom we called "Jack." Of course, we had to call him "sir." He was a most disagreeable man, petty and vindictive. We hated him. A hit song current at the time was

Ray Charles' "Hit the Road Jack," which we would sing behind his back. Then, one Monday morning, when we came back to the grind from the two days' glorious release of the weekend, he was not there. He had died suddenly in the interim. How we rejoiced at our delivery from torment. He was replaced by an Irishman whom we called "Denny." Denny was the total opposite, an understanding and creative man. He engaged us and made English exciting. I am a writer now because of this man's unmatched ability to communicate the essence of language. What made him different was his knowledge of great Irish writers and his unorthodoxy. He was a biker and would regale us with stories of his motorcycles. It was actually *interesting*.

There was no art teacher at the time, so Denny taught us pencil drawing and the use of perspective, light, and shade. His classes were held in the biology laboratory, and he would get down jars from the shelves containing ancient preserved specimens of squids or foetuses to draw, making comments about surrealism as he did. On one occasion, a lad sitting next to me was doodling a swastika in his sketchbook, which was not what we were supposed to draw. Denny saw it, and I thought: *Trouble now!* Any other teacher would have dragged him before the headmaster for punishment. Denny, however, held up the drawing to the class, and told us that the lad had drawn the swastika the wrong way round, and then explained that he had ridden for the Irish Free State in motorcycle races in Nazi Germany. Perhaps he was also familiar with the Swastika Laundry in Dublin, the vans of which I first saw on a visit there in 1959.[3] He was willing to allow us to indulge our curiosity, and to think for ourselves without having to conform to any particular norms, as long as we tried to write and draw according to proper principles. There are two kinds of teacher: one who crams facts that the student must know and

---

3. I was well aware that the swastika had a more venerable and spiritual history than its political use in the twentieth century. As a boy I had often passed the swastikas on the façade of the India House at Aldwych in London. It was the seat of the Indian High Commission, built in 1928–1930 by Sir Herbert Baker. The swastikas there appeared in a series of roundels with carvings of Hindu symbols. It survived World War II.

Swastika Laundry van, Dublin, 1963. Photo by Nigel Pennick.

accept without question; and the other who explains principles that the student can use to explore the world himself. Denny was the latter type, and, being a citizen of Ireland (a neutral country), had been spared the brutalization of fighting in the war that his British counterparts had not.

Despite the atmosphere of unsafe menace, some of us did manage to learn. I was taught drawing, Euclidean geometry, and Latin, as well as English, French, carpentry, metalwork, and science—all of which proved useful later in my life. When I was working in biological research in the 1970s, I had to write Latin diagnoses of the new species of marine algae I described. Without this schooling, I would have never been published in Latin, something I suspect my teacher never achieved. I was able to pass my public examinations, which finally enabled me to study for a degree. But it would have been better if I had been able to do it *because of*—rather than *in spite of*—the conditions under which I had been taught.

There was no "health and safety" in those days. Almost every teacher smoked cigarettes in class, and we breathed in the fumes.

Denny smoked a pipe sometimes, used it as a pointer, and would gently tap a pupil on the head with it to emphasise a point. On one occasion, the pipe broke in two, much to our amusement. He told us that in French "to break one's pipe" means to die, and then resumed the lesson in good humour. Most other teachers would have flown into a blind rage if this had happened. "Spud," the biology teacher, was prone to frantic rages, and some lads thought it sport to bait him by moving the tubes out of focus on his microscope. It was not destructive and could easily be remedied if approached calmly. But he lost control, ranted and raged, grew red in the face, and almost had a seizure. He was not a bad man, he did not deserve it, and it was cruel to treat him in that way. But the harsh experience of school coarsened everyone's sensibilities. At the beginning of the day, my chemistry teacher, "Harry," had three packs of Nelson cigarettes on his desk, which was raised on a dais above the laboratory. By the end of the day, all sixty cigarettes were smoked. I expect he smoked more each evening. Other teachers did not chain-smoke like Harry, but smoke they did in school.

Chemistry class was very dangerous. We had no protective equipment, no rubber gloves, masks, or goggles, only long white laboratory coats. Even when I was a government scientist ten years later, these essential items were rarely in use. We handled all manner of toxic substances, and regularly went off to lunch without washing our hands. Some disaffected students were able to seriously misuse the chemicals, which others considered amusing. In addition to our passive smoking in the laboratory, on a few occasions pupils who hated chemistry filled glass beakers with chemicals to form a fog. They called it "Operation Pea Soup" after the "pea-souper" smogs of London. On one side of the room, hydrochloric acid would be boiled over a Bunsen burner, while a student across the room boiled off ammonia. As the room became foggy with ammonium chloride, everyone began to cough and splutter, and then Harry would order us outside onto the grass. Although we were liberated from chemistry for a while, we had breathed in acid and ammonia mixed with cigarette smoke. For adolescent lungs, this could have done no good. On one occasion, someone found out how to make fulminate of mercury—and did. Fulminate of mercury is an explosive compound. We could have been blown up, but it was a minimal amount and mostly ended up on the floor. When anyone walked over it, it exploded with a small "crack."

A serious incident occurred in a public O-level examination held in the laboratory, when a lad taking the exam was carrying out a designated procedure. Someone had substituted concentrated hydrochloric acid for the dilute acid required, and it exploded all over him. His lab coat did not protect him, and he was not wearing goggles. He was taken to hospital with acid burns. I suffered a serious injury to the right hand when there was a water fight with wash bottles. These had a bent glass tube through which the water was forced. Someone spraying me slipped on the wet floor. I put my hand out and a curved broken tube was rammed into the heel of my palm. At the hospital I had the wound sewn up with seven stitches, each put in without anaesthetic. I was out of school for weeks and when I came back was forced to write notes left-handed. Later, in an art class, someone was trying to cast lead into a plaster mould. The mould was not fully dry and some splashed out, hitting the youth in the corner of his eye: another hospital case. None of these incidents or accidents—and they were frequent—were ever reported or investigated. Nothing was. Nobody cared. We had to just get on with it the best we could.

Yet, thankfully, after counting down the days to my liberation, I was freed. It was a massive relief, like being released from prison, finally to leave that school, and never to return.

Where My Photography Began

At the age of twelve, I was given a camera. My father had a primitive box camera using 120-gauge monochrome film but used it infrequently. Mine was a little better, using 127 monochrome film. It had few adjustments, and shutter speed was relatively slow. Film was expensive and had to be taken to a chemist's shop to be processed and printed, which also cost money. So, in those days, few photographs were taken. Despite this, I took my

NIGEL PENNICK

The Kingsway tramway subway (in use 1906–1952).
The first photograph Nigel Pennick had published, 1962.

camera out and took pictures of things I thought interesting. I was doing what I later found out was called "street photography." I also took photos of railway locomotives, trolleybuses, and motor buses in their natural habitats. The first photograph I ever had published was of the disused ramp of the Kingsway tramway subway in London. In 1962 it appeared in the booklet *London's Tramway Subway* by C. S. Dunbar and J. H. Price. Another of my early photographs, taken at King's Cross station in 1962, was of the steam locomotive *Royal Lancer*. This I used in my 2021 book *The Ancestral Power of Amulets, Talismans, and Mascots*. The majority of photographs in that book, monochrome and colour, were mine, all but for a few archive pictures. In the early sixties, I got a better camera, and by the mid-sixties was taking some photographs in colour. In 1966 I was able to record the demolition of the golden sundial on the Imperial Hotel at Russell Square in colour. Subsequently, I owned a single-lens reflex Pentax and Canon film cameras and then Canon digital SLRs. My latter colour photographs appeared, *inter alia*, in my 1999 book, *The Complete Illustrated Guide to Runes*, and eight pages of my colour

Street photography: Anti-European Common Market rally, Trafalgar Square London, 1964. Photo by Nigel Pennick.

photographs were featured in Claude Lecouteux's *The Tradition of Household Spirits* in 2013.[4]

Time and the Gods

At every school I attended, I was classified by the powers that be as "C of E": Church of England. In those days, it was assumed that anyone in England who was not a Roman Catholic, Jew, Hindu, or Muslim, was C of E. Baptised before I was even aware of anything, I had been induced into a national organization that claimed me as one of their own. In day school and Sunday School I was literally indoctrinated with an exoteric religion that, in addition to the mythos of the Bible, consisted of the

---

4. Colour photos of mine also appear in my books *The Ancestral Power of Amulets, Talismans, and Mascots* (Destiny, 2021) and *The Spiritual Power of Masks* (Destiny, 2022).

Thirty-Nine Articles, a dogmatic statement of its belief-system. I was expected to be conversant in all this, and to believe it without question. Those who did not or could not, I was told, would be excommunicated, and, after death, consigned to a fiery pit called Hell for ever and ever, *amen*. It was enough to give a young child nightmares. This wrathful god appeared to me to be more of a sky-dwelling version of the Bogeyman with whom my mother used to frighten me when I was little:

The Bogeyman is coming.
He's coming here today.
The Bogeyman is coming.
You can't get away.

The Bogeyman is coming.
He's coming to get you.
The Bogeyman will get you
No matter what you do.

As the Bogeyman never actually appeared, I came to realise that neither was the god whom my teachers and priests spoke of going to intervene in my activities. From a young age, however, I *was* aware that there were other, older, religions than the one I was being compelled to endure. Living a few minutes' walk from the British Museum, my mother would take me there occasionally. There were favourite things, like ancient Chinese horses and camels, shiny with brown and green glaze, and monumental Egyptian carvings, some of them of terrifying presence, depicting the lioness-headed goddess Sekhmet. I knew of Osiris and Isis, Amon-Ra, Thoth, and Anubis. I had seen their majestic images from an unimaginably archaic time. Their power was palpable, unlike the unbelievable fables I was told in Sunday School. The triumphalist stories of Israelite prophets wrecking the "idols" of other religions were a horror of wanton vandalism—the destruction of noble and sophisticated cultures by humourless, soulless fanatics. Of course, I did not put it in these terms then, but, looking back, that is how I felt. I knew

WYRD TIMES

Odin illustration from a nineteenth-century book Nigel Pennick read as a child.

that in primordial times these elemental gods emanated from the world long before the religion I was made to attend came into existence—and they *still* existed. I had *seen them* and felt their numinous presence.

Although we were taught that there was only One True Religion, which it was blasphemy to question, it was clear to me that this was not the case. As I got older, I was able to find books that told of European gods such as Zeus and Hera, Hermes and Hephaistos, and their Roman counterparts. I could see an image of Hermes with his caduceus on an office building I used to pass sometimes. It was a manifestation of an ancient god in modern London, silently presiding over commerce and communication. At Piccadilly Circus, I saw the winged image of the god Eros atop the fountain in the middle of the road, and on the courthouse of the Old Bailey, the gilded image of the goddess of justice, Iustitia, with her scales and sword. The gods were not only consigned to the inside of museums.

I was an avid book lover from the moment my mother taught me to read. At grammar school, I found a book about the gods of the North, and felt an immediate connexion with Odin, Thor, Heimdall, Freya, and Frigg. I read how the Vikings, free men flying the Raven Banner, had fought back against the Christian missionaries bent on destroying their faith. The difference between these old European gods and the ancient Egyptian ones was not great—clearly, they partook of the same spiritual current, refined according to local needs: Greek, Roman, Norse, Celtic, Slavic, or English. I found that many places in Britain are named for the ancient gods, and that their sanctuaries and temples had been destroyed by imperialist Christians. Even St Paul's Cathedral was built where a temple of Diana and, later, a Saxon holy site had once stood. These discoveries inspired my lifelong engagement with the inner nature of place—Geomancy—and the manifestations of the gods: Paganism.

Diversity

After 1960, when my paternal grandfather died, I would visit my grandmother in her London County Council flat in a block called Culverhouse on Red Lion Square. It was almost opposite the Conway Hall, where decades later I would give lectures for various esoteric organizations. Round the corner in Red Lion Street was a newsagent whose diverse publications are redolent of an open-minded age before censorship and vilification set in. The only censorship then was of pornography, most of which would not be recognised as such today. I would go there and buy two or three of the papers on offer. There were all the national daily newspapers, including the Communist Party's *Daily Worker*, and the three London evening papers: *The Evening Star*, *The Evening News*, and *The Evening Standard*. Among the weekly or monthly magazines were *Action*, the paper of Sir Oswald Mosley's Union Movement; *Freedom*, the anarchist weekly; *The Occult Gazette*, containing Gladys Spearman-Cooke's latest channellings via her spirit guide; *Combat*, the British National Party's organ sponsored by Norfolk landowner Andrew Fountaine (who was reputed to run a witches' coven there); *The Catholic Weekly*; *The Railway Magazine* for train enthusiasts; *Football Weekly*; *The Jewish Chronicle*; and pamphlets by the Campaign for Nuclear

Disarmament and other pressure groups, left, right, and centre. I was interested in finding out what all these various belief-systems were about, so, without prejudice, I bought and read these papers and magazines. In addition to this admirable newsagent, for a time the anarchist Freedom Bookshop was nearby, and, at the other end of Red Lion Square, on a narrow street where the trolleybuses turned was a communist bookshop sponsored by the Soviet Union. Its shelves were lined with grey-bound translations of the writings of Marx, Engels, and Lenin. But the books at these shops were too expensive for me. And besides, I knew I would be bored by reading Soviet "political correctness." The grey covers were a good indication of the contents.

Football

From a young age, boys began supporting their local football (soccer) team. Most actually played, but my damaged feet made me a poor footballer. My father coached in his primary school in East London and some years his under-eleven teams won a trophy in London County Council school's football competitions. He was proud when one of his schoolboy football players years later signed for Manchester United and played in First Division matches. As by far the largest city in England, London has many professional football clubs that represent their local areas. Where I lived it was an Arsenal area. If I had lived half a mile further south, my team would have been Chelsea.

My father was an Arsenal supporter and he went regularly to Highbury where the team played. He first took me there in 1954, and I have followed Arsenal ever since. From about the age of twelve I often travelled to away grounds to support the "Gunners," as we called them. Like many famous clubs, Arsenal had begun at a time in the 1880s when groups of workers in industrial plants formed amateur teams. These men came from the workforce of the Woolwich Arsenal, the main armaments factory of Britain; West Ham United originated in the Thames Ironworks shipbuilders; Manchester United in the railway workshops of the Lancashire and Yorkshire Railway Company; and so on. Professional football had a working-class origin, and

Rupert Pennick and his boys' football team, circa 1950.

the fans—short for "fanatics"—were ardent in their support.

Emotions run high at a match, especially if it is a "derby" match against a local rival, such as Arsenal versus Tottenham Hotspur. Chants and songs, taunts and jeers, and booing opponents' fouls or perceived mistakes by the referee stoke up the tension. At a goal by their own side, fans cheer wildly and jump for joy. Arsenal had its own tube station on the Piccadilly Line. I usually travelled from Russell Square, from which Arsenal was four stations northbound. Although crammed in with other supporters, it was an aesthetic experience to see the different patterns of coloured tiles on the walls of each station, all of which dated from 1906.

The tiles at Russell Square were dark green, black, and white. The next station, King's Cross, had been re-tiled in the 1940s with boring cream tiles. The station north of King's Cross, York Road, was abandoned, and the train went slower through the darkened station, making a different sound owing to the larger tunnels. The next stop, Caledonian Road, had beige, brown, and black tiles; following this, Holloway Road had dark brown, orange-brown, and cream tiles. Arsenal, my destination, was

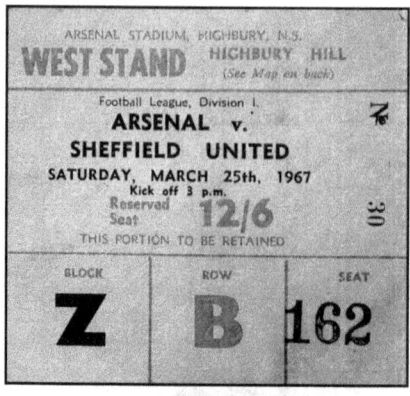

Arsenal v. Sheffield United match ticket, 1967. Final score: Arsenal 2, Sheffield United 0.

marked by mauve, white, and olive-green tiles. At Arsenal station, the line was near the surface, and there were no lifts or escalators, so it involved a long trek up a ramp in a tunnel to Avenell Road, where, through the noisy, crowded confusion, among ticket touts, pickpockets, favour and programme sellers, and men selling paper bags of "monkey nuts" (peanuts in shells) calling out "They *are* roasted!" Marshalled by mounted police and wearing our red-and-white scarves, we walked to the Art Deco magnificence of Arsenal Stadium, called by everybody "Highbury." The stadium contained almost mythical "Marble Halls" which we never saw or entered, and on each end was a giant effigy of a cannon. The cannon remains the badge of the Gunners today.

The "football tribe," as anthropologist and surrealist Desmond Morris called supporters, was composed largely of young men. Before the match, it was customary to have a few drinks at a pub, or on the train if travelling to an away match in another city. Fuelled by alcohol and adrenaline, we would march through the strange city from the station to the opponent's ground. Near the ground were police, many on horseback, to control the crowds. Nevertheless, scuffles would break out. Any stray supporter caught out alone wearing his team scarf or colours risked a severe beating, an event which still happens occasionally. The chant "We are the people—they are the cunts!" was an indication of what we thought of our opponents. Violence was always just under the surface. Not that football hooliganism was a new thing; there had been a football riot at Tottenham Hotspur's ground as early as 1910. In 2015, I wrote a song expressing this experience:

NIGEL PENNICK

When I was a football hooligan,
We used to run through town.
If anyone got in the way,
We w're sure to knock him down.

Chanting on the terraces
Songs of pride and hate;
Threw bottles at the other side,
Belonging felt real great.

We always stuck together
With our backs against the wall.
In our opponents' grounds,
We never let a comrade fall.

We were the boys in red;
We fought the boys in blue.
We'd rather end up dead
Than drop the flag we flew.

When I was a football hooligan,
We used to run through town.
If anyone got in the way,
We w're sure to knock him down.

But apart from the hardcore fanatics and the violence they wrought, in the 1960s things were not so extreme. Supporters of opposing teams were not fully segregated from each other as they are now. This sometimes led to fights, but not as many as might be imagined. I knew two lads who were West Ham supporters and we used to watch derby matches together at Highbury or Upton Park (also known as the Boleyn Ground, West Ham's stadium in East London). We stood together on the terraces, and, apart from banter and bragging rights for the winners, enjoyed the matches peacefully. Being in London, we just went there on the Underground, not *en masse* by train. So, although emotions ran high in London derbies, there was not the potential for the solidarity and violence of supporters going away to other cities.

On February 1, 1958, my father took me to see a notable match at Highbury. We did not stand on the terraces for this sell-out match. He bought seats and we sat in the famous Art Deco East Stand. Considered the most spectacular match ever played at the stadium, Arsenal lost by five goals to four to the 1957 champions, Manchester United. I was disappointed, but it was a memorable game. On the morning of February 7, I was told that most of the Manchester United team were dead, killed in a plane crash at Munich in Germany. It was horrifying to think that these fine young players—whom I had seen in a thrilling match such a short time before—were now dead in horrific circumstances. Other boys I knew were also shocked, but I was the only one who had actually been at the last match they played in England before the accident. My parents and teachers seemed unconcerned and nobody understood how traumatising it was for an eleven-year-old. They had all experienced World War II and were clearly blasé about the death of others. It was typical of the uncaring attitudes of the era. I had to deal with it as best I could.

When I went to college, I stopped travelling regularly to see Arsenal play.

If in Doubt . . .

In 1962 I travelled on an enthusiasts' train from King's Cross in London to Doncaster to visit the locomotive works there. Pulled by the celebrated world-record-holding streamliner *Mallard*, our speed topped one hundred miles an hour on the "racetrack" line near Grantham. These were the days before "health and safety" kept amateurs out of steel foundries and heavy engineering workshops. At the locomotive works we walked around in our street clothes avoiding ladles of molten steel, steamhammers, and other lethal hardware. At various places, signs on the walls admonished the workforce: "If in doubt, ask!" It was a useful lesson to me to see these signs in such a hazardous, though exciting, environment. "If in doubt, ask!" is commonsense wisdom that is all too often ignored.

II
STUDENT DAYS AND THE START OF MY CAREER IN SCIENCE

"Straight down the crooked lane,
And all round the square."

—Lewis Carroll, *A Tangled Tale*, Knot II

Cambridge "Alma Mater" who holds the Sun and a chalice, with alchemical magnesia flowing from her breasts. Sculptural ornament above the entrance to the Downing Site where the Botany School is located. Photo by Nigel Pennick.

How I Came to Cambridge

For my advanced level at grammar school, I studied Physics, Chemistry, and Biology, but soon dropped Physics and took Botany and Zoology as separate subjects. In the examinations, I took the Zoology and Botany papers without a problem, but before my Chemistry exam I began to suffer from a severe toothache which turned out to be an abscess. So I took the exam on heavy painkillers before a visit to the dentist, who extracted the tooth. I was awarded top grade with distinction for Botany, the only one awarded that year, and also a high grade in Zoology (I was not so fortunate with Chemistry). In addition, I passed an Art examination at ordinary level, and did well in the compulsory Use of English exam. Despite a distinction in Botany, my poor showing in Chemistry made it difficult for me to progress to university. The application system gave me only one interview, at Nottingham. Unfortunately, I had no coaching for the interview and did badly when I was there. The interviewer asked trick questions intended to outwit me, and I must have responded in a way he did not like. So I was not awarded a place at Nottingham University.

But I did not give up. I discovered that it was possible to take a London University degree as an external student. There were two possibilities, technical colleges at Portsmouth and Cambridge. Portsmouth was a naval dockyard city and did not attract me, so I applied to the Cambridgeshire College of Arts and Technology (colloquially, the "Tech," now rebuilt as Anglia Ruskin University) and was awarded a place there to study

Nigel Pennick and William Lyon in a defiant mood on a Tech ecological field trip to the Cambridgeshire fenland, 1966.

Botany and Zoology. So I came to Cambridge—the Town, not the University, though some University members moonlighted to give tutorials to Tech students, including me. Clearly, I made the right decision to come to Cambridge and not Portsmouth.

At the Tech

The Cambridgeshire College of Arts and Technology, or the "Tech," was considered to be part of the Town, not the Gown. Its original building from the Arts and Crafts era (late nineteenth century) was surrounded by post-WWII modernist additions and temporary structures known as "Portakabins," put down on open ground where rows of houses had been demolished. Existing streets near the Tech were partly derelict, though two public houses, the Granville and the Tiger, remained in business. Close by on East Road was the café Paul's Variety Fayre where some of us ate lunch. It was close to the abandoned tram depot, and the walls were hung with original framed photographs of

Paradise Street in the Kite Area of Cambridge, 1968. Photo by Nigel Pennick.

the horse trams that had ceased operation in 1914. The Tech was on the edge of the "Kite Area" on the other side of East Road. Its nineteenth-century buildings were decaying and derelict and awaiting demolition for roads, car parks, and shopping centres. Despite their imminent demise, these buildings had character. Though lacking the grandeur of medieval and classical University buildings, they had the honest vitality of the bricklayers, carpenters, tilers, and glaziers who had constructed them a century or more earlier.

Amid the dereliction, four other pubs—the Free Press, the Nelson, the Ancient Druids, and the Falcon (later renamed the Boat Race, then the Vine, and most recently, the Six Six Bar)—survived on the East Road side of the Kite. So there were places to get a drink, not frequented by Cambridge University types, but instead by working-class men of all ages. The poverty of the Town contrasted notably with the opulence of the University with its College Feasts and May Balls, but it was in the Granville where I would soon meet a remarkable old man who handed on to me what we were later to characterise as "ancient skills and wisdom."

WYRD TIMES

Michelle Noetzli, Nigel Pennick, and Linda Bower on holiday, Clacton-on-Sea, Essex, summer 1967.

Unlike students at the University, who were not allowed to use cars in Cambridge (Prince Charles was exempted, of course), Tech students who could afford them did run vehicles, mostly very old ones. Many students were cavalier in their attitudes to motoring law. A mature student who soon left, John Thompson, had lived in Germany and had a VW Beetle. It was registered in Germany, though its licence plate tax had long expired. He drove it around Cambridge with no tax or insurance and was never caught. There was a large car park on the rubble of where Victorian streets had existed recently. Eccles, an A-level student, was a car fanatic; he and I used to walk around looking at the old "jalopies," some of which appeared abandoned. Perhaps they were stolen vehicles, or deemed to be unroadworthy. One time, we found an abandoned Land Rover, and Eccles hotwired it and it started. Then, for several months he drove it around Cambridge without tax, insurance, or an MOT (certificate of vehicle roadworthiness). The militant atheist Sniknej had a van in which I used to ride. It finally came to an end when, on the street called Maids Causeway, the engine suddenly emitted smoke. We

NIGEL PENNICK

Poster drawing by Nigel Pennick for The New Age,
a short-lived musical group, 1967.

opened the bonnet (hood) and flames leapt high. Fortunately, another motorist pulled up and used his fire extinguisher, so the whole van was not engulfed in flames. But it was a write-off.

The Tech was quite a different place from the University. It catered to many different educational needs: vocational studies, such as mechanics' work; art; advanced-level students who were not in the Sixth Form in school (or students who had failed and were retaking the examination); and degree students in the arts and sciences under the auspices of London University. It was quite a mixture of people, and some interesting things happened. There was artistic and musical experimentation (extracurricular) and political agitation of both the mainstream and alternative variety. I soon got into producing printed material of all kinds. It seems that the projects I was involved in often ran up against both the official authorities (who usually did not understand what we were trying to do) and what we came to call the "underground establishment."

Studying for an "external" degree was never easy. Our tutors worked diligently to give us the knowledge and skills to get us through the examinations. And we worked hard, too: the first year consisted of a five-day week with six hours of lectures on three days, and nine hours on two. On the long days, there were three-hour sessions of lectures and laboratory practice in Botany, Zoology, and Geology, 9 a.m. to 12 noon, 1:30 p.m. to 4:30 p.m., and 6 p.m. to 9 p.m. Then there were notes to make and essays to write. Few passed Part 1 of the degree course; some re-took the year but most dropped out. I know for a fact that University undergraduates were not worked half as hard. In my class, only four people out of twenty-seven finally graduated after three years—three women and myself. Years two and three were not so gruelling, so I had time to participate in the activities and escapades available to me.

Glimpses through the Cracks

As Part 1 of my degree course, I had to study Geology—one academic year followed by an examination that had to be passed. Part of the course involved fieldwork, and one trip took us for a week to the Yorkshire Dales. During this excursion, as we climbed up rock faces with no ropes and no helmets, I was saved from death by another student who grabbed my arm as I slipped on a 200-foot scree slope. It was one of many providential escapes in my life, and, a few days later, led to an interesting discovery. Standing on a ledge thirty feet up on a quarry side, I broke away a fossil with my geological hammer. I climbed down to the quarry floor and showed it to my tutor. He told me that that species should not have been in that stratum. Probably I had made a significant discovery. But as, according to doctrine, the fossil should not have been there, my tutor put it in his haversack and all was forgotten. This is but one example of the well-worn maxim "Those who speak do not know."

A particular kind of oxidised siltstone (sandstone) had been quarried near Horton-in-Ribblesdale until 1850, when the quarry was exhausted. Called Moughton Whetstone, it has green and red stripes running through it, visible when wet, and was highly prized in the steel industry at Sheffield for sharpening razors. The Moughton Whetstone Hole spring can still be visited, but

NIGEL PENNICK

Moughton Whetstone image of Odin carved by Nigel Pennick, Yorkshire, England, 1967.

now it is "listed" as a Site of Special Scientific Interest and the removal of stone is illegal. Our tutor told us that the shallow river that runs through Crummackdale was reputed to contain fragments of Moughton Whetstone, and we students waded in to look. We searched for a long time, without success, and many gave up and wanted to go back to the hostel. Remembering the carved heads on the great whetstone buried in the Sutton Hoo ship burial, which I had seen many times in the British Museum, I called on Odin to give me a piece of the rare stone (my fellow students were used to this behaviour). Then, looking down, I pulled several pieces from the river. Subsequently, I carved the largest one into an image of Odin, named in Northumbrian runes.

Back from Ribblesdale, I was in the Granville pub one evening when I got into conversation with an old man, probably in his seventies, wearing the flat cap and jacket of a seasoned farm worker. He started to tell me about his experiences as a soldier on the Western Front in World War I. He probably regaled anyone who would listen with his tales of "whizz-bangs" and hand-to-hand combat with "Fritz." What would a historian today give to listen to a first-hand account of the "Great War for Civilisation"—as it says on the medals? But back then, I am sure that most University undergraduates wouldn't have given the time of day to listen to the likes of John Thorn.[1]

I often bought him a pint of beer when I could afford it, and from his tales of poison gas, storming the enemy trenches, and lost comrades, he progressed to speaking about his life with horses and then tractors on the land. For he was not a "Townie" all his life, but had been a stalwart farmhand, labouring on the black soil of the Fens. He told me of stopping horses with special oils, the mystic Toad Bone, harvest customs, and the darkness that falls during the day when a Fen Blow whips up. John Thorn was an indigenous man of the land from his cap to his boots, and he had been through hell and back to serve King and Country. It was the noble values of work and duty he embodied that contrasted so starkly with the fanatical political screechings of extremist students who knew nothing of life, yet who sought to overthrow everything people like him had defended.

Although he was a septuagenarian, a veteran in every way, he was not idly deteriorating in an old people's home but continued to live alone and grow some of his own vegetables. He asked me once to help him plant potatoes at night on an allotment at the edge of Empty Common in the south of Cambridge. It was a starry night, and the streetlights were far enough away that we could see them. He had his tools ready, and a cord wound round a small wooden stake. He tied the end of the string at one end of the allotment and gave me the other end. Then he looked at the sky, pointed out the "Nowl"—the Pole Star—and directed me in line with it to the other end, where I pushed in the stake. This, I was told, was "the rig," and I dug one row for the potatoes. Then we went for a drink. He, or someone else, must have dug the parallel rigs the next day and planted the potatoes. Clearly, this

---

1. Some pub regulars called him "Blackthorn"; I called him "Mr Thorn."

was a teaching. Years later, I grew potatoes north–south in my own gardens according to these principles.

I was not a regular at the Granville, and on one of my occasional visits I learned that no one had heard from John Thorn for some time. Nobody knew where he had gone, though the usual pub speculation was aired. Most thought he must have died, though nobody knew about any funeral. By this point, my time was fully occupied with studying for my degree. I did not encounter another practitioner of the Nameless Art until much later.

Zoology: Iguanas, Dragons, and Contraband

One Zoology tutor at the Tech lived close by in a large early nineteenth-century house that fronted on the street running along the side of the park called Parker's Piece. He liked exotic reptiles and kept a boa constrictor in a cupboard. Another, a 4-foot-long Iguana that he called "Iggy," lived on the back of a sofa visible from the street. When I went to his house for tutorials, he always made me sit on the sofa, which was stained with iguana guano, with this menacing reptile behind me. Fortunately, the reptile moved slowly and I was never attacked. Later, at a drunken party, my tutor provoked Iggy and sustained serious injuries to a finger requiring hospitalisation—much to everyone's amusement. Then to my tutor's chagrin, Iggy gained nationwide attention when a press photographer spotted the reptile through the window and the resulting image was published in a national newspaper. The iguana became a minor tourist attraction for a while. On one occasion, at the tutor's behest, a fellow student from Nigeria smuggled a monitor lizard into Britain for him. On the airline flight from Nigeria she carried the reptile in a bag secreted in her clothes and somehow got it through customs unnoticed.

Another Zoology lecturer at the Tech had contacts in China. It was the time when Mao's Red Guards were carrying out their so-called Cultural Revolution, destroying ancient monuments and persecuting those they suspected of being "bourgeois" or "intellectual." Temples were looted and vandalised; Buddhist and Daoist sacred artefacts were supposedly destroyed. However, as these were "collectible" items outside Red China, and worth a lot of money, many did not end up on the street bonfires. Instead, they were diverted into Hong Kong, where wholesalers distributed them to all parts of the world. Our lecturer became a dealer in Buddhas, dragons sawn off from the gables of temples, and other choice items of looted Chinese art. He began by selling them on a market stall. This turned out to be more lucrative than a lecturer's salary, so he gave up lecturing and became a full-time dealer in antiquities.

The Anglian Diggers

"Diggery makes politics obsolete."

—William Lyon (of Anglian Diggers)

Perhaps preparing the rig at Empty Common foreshadowed my involvement with another type of "digging": the Anglian Diggers. The Anglian Diggers attempted to emulate both the original English Diggers, or "True Levellers," of 1649; the Edinburgh Diggers of the 1920s; Diggery in the United States from 1966; and the Diggers then at Fantasio in Amsterdam. English and Welsh Diggery of the 1960s and '70s was based on localism and developed an ethos that could be called a "back-to-the-land vision of Albion." I was not in touch with Emmett Grogan at the time, but I had read about the New York "Free Frame of Reference" in an American underground newspaper I bought at the Indica Bookshop in Southampton Row, which was a five-minute walk from the flat where my grandmother, Grace Louisa Pennick, lived. Grogan ended up on the West Coast and wrote an autobiography called *Ringolevio: A Life Played for Keeps* (1972) and a novel, *Final Score* (1976); he died two years later at the age of thirty-five. In the words of fellow radical Abbie Hoffman of the Yippies: "The San Francisco Diggers combined Dada street theater with the revolutionary politics of free."

In London, I was told that a man known as Driffield ran a Digger bookshop in Coleherne Mews, but when I went there, I

Nigel Pennick with Anglian Diggers emblem, 1968. Photo by Rupert Pennick.

could not find it. Later we met the so-called King of the Hippies, Sid Rawle, who, from the London Street Commune squat at 144 Piccadilly, had set up the Hyde Park Diggers in 1967 and after 1969 the Diggers Action Movement run by John Gillatt and Barry Norcott. Rawle was later with the Tribe of the Sun, and in 1984 participated in a series of acrimonious and futile meetings regarding access to Stonehenge.

I made one visit to some Diggers who were with the group of squatters that briefly occupied my old St Giles' school, which by then had closed and was lying empty. It was a strange experience to see the interior again under such changed circumstances. Even later, the Anglian Diggers had contact with Dave Stringer of the Cornish Diggers, or Baloryon Kernow. But we were independent, and local (which is the essence of Diggery), and it was not important to be a part of something bigger. Ironically, one woman who joined us in the Anglian Diggers had been in San Francisco in the so-called Summer of Love in 1967, but she had never come across the Diggers there. Unlike the present day, when the Internet enables people (in theory, at least) to discover and connect with like-minded groups and individuals, in 1968 it was much harder.

The next year, I wrote of our experiences in the alternative newspaper *Cambridge Voice*:

> [The] Anglian Diggers began from two typewritten manifestos I pinned to a noticeboard [actually two different noticeboards] at Cambridge Tech Oct. 1968. As a result of these, a number of people contacted me and, within a week, a giveaway was arranged to coincide with the Tech societies fair. We obtained a stand at the societies fair, and, to the amazement of the people, we gave away food, drink, clothes, records, plants, books, and magazines, goods to the value of £18 to £20. The Tech Social Supervisor, having seen nothing like it, had her mind blown, and a member of the Free Front called us "fascist."

"Fascist" was in those days an all-purpose insult for anyone who was not considered a "comrade" by the cadres of left-wing groups, whether or not they followed the tenets of the original Italian *Fascisti*. Few, if any, did.

This was all a good start, but then the Anglian Diggers came up against the usual apathy combined with that hostility so redolent of entrenched organisations when faced with things they cannot understand—in this case, our critics came in the form of what I have called the "underground establishment." To resume my earlier account from *Cambridge Voice*:

> Two of us went to the Arts Lab and were shown around a complex of buildings—projected cinemas, theatres, studios, sleeping quarters, orchard café and HQ building. We were not offered any premises for our use, however. We went to the *Shilling Paper*, at that time the proclaimed organ of underground activity in Cambridge. They seemed interested, and asked for the manifesto and an article. This they got plus artwork. The

Detail from the Anglian Diggers' *postermanifestoster*, a large-format montage poster produced by Nigel Pennick, 1969.

article however never appeared. They professed interest in further artwork, which was never used.

The Anglian Diggers then obtained £10 from the social fund of the Tech, which, when added to by donations from members and sympathisers, enabled us to print the legendary *postermanifestoster*, a montage of manifesto, text, photographs, runes, and drawings in the Dada mode. Continuing my sporadic creation of posters for groups and events that began two years earlier with the founding of the Like It or Lump It Poster Company—which would later be more grandiosely renamed Galactic Intervention—this poster manifesto also ran into trouble. We were able to distribute it around Cambridge by hand through contacts in various places, but when we approached ECAL, the national "underground" poster distribution service, they refused to take it. In London, Betterbooks told us to "Come back later." Finally, the Diggers International Co-ordination took 100 copies, though they wanted 250. But as there was no further contact or feedback from them, we suspected that the posters had not been distributed. As we said on the *postermanifestoster* (*inter alia*): "We may succeed, we may collapse, but at least we have tried."

Despite this setback, the Anglian Diggers persisted. *Cambridge Voice* continues:

> Anglian Diggers attended Arts Lab open situations. Anglian Diggers provided free reading matter for the Arts Lab and the Tech. Anglian Diggers prepared the Arts Lab food. Anglian Diggers offered to run the Open Situations during the Arts Lab holidays (University Holidays), but was spurned... Anglian Diggers' offer of a free soup kitchen during the proposed Tech "Smash the Canteen" week was screwed up by the lack of moral fibre of the organisers.

This latter event was a protest against a price hike for food and drink. When the left-wing activists called off the protest for fear of the repercussions, I and seven others who were not Trotskyists held an "eat-in" where we brought our own food and drink to the canteen. I was hauled before the principal as the ringleader and given a stern warning.

Through advertisements in *Cambridge Voice*, I made contact with Har van Fulpen in Zaandam, the Netherlands. He was the organiser of *Provadya?* and *Holland Hapt*. I had first been to Amsterdam in 1967 and returned several times to participate in the activities of the "underground," where I liaised with the

Winter 1967 in Amsterdam, -14° Celsius. Photo by Nigel Pennick.

Diggers. The Human Underground Library there held a number of our publications and a short (and now lost) book I wrote while in Amsterdam, *van Gendtstraat*, which was published in a small edition. *Holland Hapt* was produced on the principle that each contributor printed 500 copies of a single double-sided page and brought them to a designated place where all the other contributors assembled. The pages were collated and each contributor took away their share of the collected "print run." *Holland Hapt's* maxim was *"Schrijf wat je schriven wil. Er is geen redactie, geen censuur"*: "Write what you want to write. There is no editing, no censorship."

The Anglian Diggers gradually faded away, as such movements do. The commune movement had put similar principles into action and was accessible nationally. Some members went to self-sufficient communes in East Anglia and Wales, while others pursued different interests. I read Emmett Grogan's book *Ringolevio* when it came out in 1972. This was probably the first Digger book since Gerrard Winstanley's *The*

True Levellers' Standard Advanced of 1649.

A coda came in 1974 when a Cambridge University undergraduate, Sue Inkster, stood for Parliament as a Digger. I contacted her, and she had no knowledge that the Diggers had existed a few years earlier in Cambridge. I assisted her campaign. The Anglian Diggers issued a new manifesto, and I spoke at one hustings, condemning all the other parties. But, as with all minuscule groups standing for election, Sue only received a few votes, lost her deposit, and that was the last of it.

Flowering Leaves

Although I was a science student, during my Tech days I collaborated with various "one-off" leaflets and ephemeral magazines, and drew or painted posters for college societies. An A-level student known only as "Ensor" produced a scandalous comic with me. He was a descendent of the Belgian symbolist artist James Ensor (1860–1949), who had been known for his scandalous art featuring masks and skeletons and a socialist Jesus entering Brussels. In 1968, we released three editions of *Fuzz-Death Comix*, which we sold to fellow Tech students.

The flowering of Tech publications came about as the result of a chance meeting in Hampstead, north London. In early 1969, I travelled there to visit an "underground" bookshop. As I came out of the depths of the tube station, I encountered the Tech poet and Free Front protagonist Simon Gould. We went to a pub for a drink together and hatched a plan to get the Tech to fund our activities. The Student Representative Council was composed of representatives from college societies. So we decided to divide our many projects into discrete units, each of which was to be a distinct society.

Back at college, we had a meeting with our friends and colleagues and set up several new societies, enough to form a majority on the SRC. They included already-existing groups such as the Anglian Diggers; the environmentalist Society Against Pollution and Waste; Simon Gould's *Jesse James* poetry magazine; *Outsider*, edited by frank edwards (*sic*—he spelled his name in lower case, like e. e. cummings); and *Catcus* ("Cat-"

Original ink drawing by Nigel Pennick for *Walrus* magazine cover, 1972.

being a reference to Cambridge Arts Technology), from a poetry collective that later published *Swastika* magazine. New societies, more or less genuine, were formed to play various board games. The Cultural Tiddlywinks Society was thought up on the spur of the moment, but, after funding, did hold actual tiddlywinks contests just for fun.

There were enough societies to outvote the existing ones, and at the finance meeting, our grouping was able to reduce their funding. The Rugby Club had the lion's share of responsibility for paying laundry bills, and we reduced this, suggesting they buy a washing machine and do their own laundry. The Anglian Diggers offered to get them one for free, but were unsuccessful. The rugby players were not happy. With our share of the money, the Anglian Diggers were able to have the London printer of *Cambridge Voice* produce the *postermanifestoster*, and to start up *Walrus* magazine, edited by Sheila Andrews (a Digger representative) and duplicated by me. *Swastika* was originally

Issues of *Walrus* with cover art by Nigel Pennick.

edited by Christopher Crutchley, and later, frank edwards. The *Tech Newsletter* and *Catastrophe* were other magazines produced around that time. *Walrus* was initially a vehicle for the Anglian Diggers, but later transmogrified into *Walrus: The Official Organ of the Non-Material World*, which was published sporadically over the next two decades. When the first issue came out, we were threatened with legal action by The Walrus Said discothèque, but when we pointed out that its name was purloined from Lewis Carroll's poem "The Walrus and the Carpenter," there was no more talk of whether pigs have wings.

But our takeover of the Student Representative Council was brought to the principal's attention, and the college authorities decided to abolish it. At the next meeting, we were ordered to take a vote dissolving the SRC. But the vote was called, and the majority voted for it to continue. Then we were told that, despite the outcome of the election, the SRC was to be dissolved regardless. Our funding dried up. *Finis*.

Inner Cambridge Violence

In late 1968, *Cambridge Voice* no. 1 carried a plea by Dr. H.

Browne, the Principal Lecturer of the Cambridgeshire College of Arts and Technology. Dated November 8, 1968, it read:

> Another of our students was very badly beaten-up last night on Midsummer Common, and I would beg all degree students both male and female not to cross the Cambridge commons after dark, but to go by the main lighted roads. There have in the past fortnight been several cases of University and Technical College students who have suffered very bad mauling at the hands of local youths.

For a young person, it was unsafe to walk across the extensive common lands of the Town at night in the dark. University students at the time had to wear academic gowns, which marked them out. Non-University students wearing college scarves also drew attention to themselves, and sometimes got a beating which they might have avoided. To the perpetrators, this activity was known as "grad bashing." Robbery was not the motive of the assailants. Many of the more snooty university undergraduates (known always as "grads" or more dismissively as "graddy boys") would not associate with students from the Tech as we were "below them." There was definitely a class element, as those who had attended more privileged schools exuded a sense of entitlement. They were just "up" at Cambridge from the so-called Public Schools which charge exorbitant fees but provide the students with essential contacts among the elite which last for life—this is known as the "old school tie."

On one occasion, I was at a party in a house on Parkside when a snooty grad insulted Tech students in his plummy, upper-class voice. He was thrown down two flights of stairs and kicked into the street for his disrespect. Some of us Tech students had been through the mill of tough neighbourhoods, violent schools, and football hooliganism, and would brook no nonsense. Another time, during a "rag" when we were parading through the street in various costumes on a flatbed truck with one of our number playing a harmonium, we were pelted with flour and water from the undergraduate rooms in Whewell's Court of Trinity College. Four of us Tech lads ran into the college, up the stairs, and pushed open the door. Two grads cowered there in fear of the worst as we trashed their room with their own flour bags and water. The grads were left unharmed. It was all over in a minute and we were back on the truck.

In a time when left-wing demonstrators were often encountered in the Town centre, the dissonance between their upper-class language and Marxist rhetoric and activism grated on Townspeople. Even left-wing "Townies" despised the grads' aura of privilege. The Free Front, a left-wing Town alliance of Peace Action, Labour Party, and Young Socialists among others, run by Frank Gawthrop and Simon Gould, would have no truck with the Anglian Diggers, but neither would they align with with university undergraduates who also espoused revolutionary socialism. But that did not mean that we had no contact, even friendship, with some of them as people. As Diggers, we valued personal connexions, seeing everyone as an individual rather than a member of some arbitrary group or other. Simon Gould was one. "What is a student revolutionary?" queried Gould in early 1969 in *Cambridge Voice* no. 5:

> He is someone who believes that revolution should be accomplished by students or at least with students as leaders. Thus the University of Cambridge, which used to produce people who arrogantly assumed they had the right ideas to impose on the country i.e. capitalism, is now producing a brand of so-called revolutionaries who think that, because they are intelligent and because they are at university, they deserve to be leaders of revolution and leaders of a new society.

Cambridge Voice no. 5 also published a letter from "Town Anarchist," which examined the divide between young people of the Town and of the University. Addressing left-wing undergraduates, the Anarchist wrote:

NIGEL PENNICK

Petty Cury, Cambridge, 1972. Drawing by Nigel Pennick.

It should not take a great effort of your agile mind to realise, that the "townie" who hits you with a bottle on Saturday night is more involved in the class struggle than the "grad" who waves his red flag, and shouts revolutionary slogans in "cultured" Eton tones, probably forgetting them as soon as his three years are up. But if, learned undergraduate, you are kicked in the balls tomorrow night, don't turn round and call your attacker "comrade"; he'll think you're taking the piss out of him, and will probably kick your head in for you.

In 1968 a bookshop opened in Mill Road, close to the Tech. Called the China Cultural Company, it was run by a Hong Kong businessman but sold Maoist propaganda like *The Little Red Book*, Chinese food products, and recordings of Chinese music, including communist Peking Operas with titles like *Sabotage on the Docks*. The front of the shop, which sported the iconic portrait of Chairman Mao, was shot up by unknown assailants shortly after it opened. Bullet-holes were visible in the wooden window frame for several years. After it was repaired, one window display featured a seven-string *guqin* and a *guzheng* with a series of bridges (both are forms of "board zither"). Being a lover of uncommon musical instruments, I was intrigued and went inside. The proprietor played me some recordings of music performed on these instruments, made me a cup of tea, and allowed me to try to play them. I bought some China Tea and when that had run out, went back and tried my hand on the *guqin* again. It was far too expensive for me to buy.

Shortly afterwards, I was waiting on Trumpingon Street next to the Botanic Garden for a friend who was coming to take me in his car to London to see a football match. A car stopped on the opposite side of the road, a window wound down, and two shots were fired at me from a handgun. Fortunately, the gunman missed at that range. I did not report it to the police—it might have been a renegade police officer for all I knew. I have no idea who it was, but I surmise that someone had been watching people who frequented the China Cultural Company. I had no interest in Maoism, seeing the obvious overdone absurdity of the propaganda photographs of the time. Every one of these, whatever the subject, was plastered with that portrait of Mao, with even more photomontaged onto the print. One picture, of a steam locomotive on a new railway, surrounded by cadres and slave labourers, had fifty-eight pictures of Mao in it. It was a salutary example of the banality of tyranny. When the shop closed, I heard that the owner had just been married and went on honeymoon to Wales, where his car was smashed off a narrow road by a truck, killing him and his bride. The driver of the truck was never identified.

The Cambridge Arts Lab

The Arts Lab movement began in London and by 1968 had a branch in Cambridge. Sometimes they called it a "Free University" but I never saw any courses offered. Clearly, this was just a delusion of grandeur. It had a hierarchical feel about it, as though the people running it were mere subordinates, answerable to a national organization that constrained their actions. The Arts Lab took over some medieval buildings in St Tibb's Row and attempted to refurbish them. I and some of the Diggers assisted in reinforcing the floors with steel beams. The Anglian Diggers, though brushed off at first, had proved useful. But the building was in the way of redevelopment, and all our work was soon dismantled by the demolition men. Where St Tibb's Row once stood, there is now a vast hole in the ground with a ramp leading to unloading bays beneath the Grand Arcade shopping centre.

For a short while I was a projectionist for 16mm sound films screened in the YMCA cellars sponsored by the Arts Lab. The Arts Lab regularly received new experimental short films from the London Film Cooperative and occasionally showed longer movies, such as the Beatles' *A Hard Day's Night*, for which the Arts Lab management charged admission. With one projector, this was hard work and required gaps when reels had to be changed. Afterwards, all the reels had to be rewound by hand—a long and tedious job.

I soon gave up projecting these multi-reel films, although I got to know a projectionist at the Victoria Cinema on Market Hill, Cambridge. On one occasion on a visit to the projection suite there, I was allowed to project two reels of a film being shown, which involved a crossover from one projector to the other. I might have become a professional projectionist, but my interest in film was not great, and I was a biology graduate by then anyway. My own career on screen consisted of an appearance as an extra in *Five Finger Spread*, directed by Tony Bomford in 1967 (and later shown at an Arts Lab event). I played a drunk in a bar scene shot in the Portland Arms pub.

I did *not* project the films shown at the national Arts Lab Conference held in St Michael's Hall in Cambridge on January 25, 1969. St Michael's Hall was actually the nave of the medieval St Michael's Church, technically still consecrated. However, only the chancel was now used for religious services. Two projectors were set up there to show the much-anticipated twin-screen version of Andy Warhol's *Chelsea Girls*. But then it was announced that this film would not be shown because the University Film Society was due to present it later that week. This was preposterous, considering that many of the conference attendees were from all over Britain and had nothing to do with Cambridge University. It was a mindless instance of Gown vs. Town disrespect *par excellence*. Instead of Warhol, the 1950 Jean

Genet film *Un Chant d'Amour* (A Song of Love) was shown. That film, which featured graphic depictions of prison inmates masturbating and engaging in sadomasochistic acts, was the subject of an American censorship case in 1966 and the U.S. Supreme Court ultimately declared it obscene. When it came on screen, some of the audience were struck with fear of an imminent police raid (such things happened back in 1969). Some walked out. The potential for prosecution, especially at a screening of *Un Chant d'Amour* in a consecrated church, was enormous. But it went unnoticed. Nothing happened, either then or later. But events like that never took place in St Michael's Hall again.

London and Cambridge 1969–70

After I graduated in summer 1969, I lived with my parents in South London for a while, unemployed. I attempted to find work in the biological sciences, but was unsuccessful that year. However, I visited Cambridge frequently and stayed for a few days with friends before going back to sign on at the "employment exchange" (dole office). I was making symbolic psychedelic paintings on plywood at the time and brought some up from London to exhibit at open art exhibitions sponsored by the City Council. Some took place in the Cambridge Corn Exchange and others were held outdoors on the fence between Christ's Pieces (a park) and the bus station. I sold several paintings—Cambridge Council took a 10% commission—and made enough to pay train fares and, on one occasion, to buy a new pair of shoes. Having to visit a South London Labour Exchange to "sign on," as a graduate, I was finally offered free emigration to Australia and a post in biological research, or, alternatively, a job as a bus conductor for London Transport.

Australia—though superficially attractive at first—in the end did not seem like a good idea. The Australian military was fighting in Vietnam, and I discovered that I would have been eligible for conscription had I emigrated there. The prospect of being in a jungle fighting the Vietcong held little appeal; I did not want my name on a war memorial in Canberra. The government of the United Kingdom wisely kept out of that war, so no British citizen had to go. I would have gone on the buses, but to become a conductor for London Transport one had to attend a ten-week training course at Chiswick in West London, so I declined. All I wanted was temporary work, not a ten-week commitment, until I could find a post in the biological sciences.

Finally, they offered me a job in a clothing factory in London's East End. I had to commute on packed slam-door trains, which were divided into compartments that seated passengers four-a-side on bench seats. By the time my train reached Albany Park station where I got on, there was standing room only. On its way to London, the train passed through Lewisham and Hither Green. I knew the names from the Lewisham Rail Crash and the Hither Green Disaster, two horrendous train crashes that took the lives of many passengers. One of Sheila Andrews's schoolmates had died at Hither Green. Fortunately, no accidents occurred during my life as a commuter. When the train reached the terminus at Cannon Street, I transferred to the underground, where I rode a District Line train to Aldgate East station.

The buildings in that district were very run-down, and the whole area spoke of poverty. It had been a largely Jewish neighbourhood for most of the twentieth century, but by 1969 there were many immigrants from other places living and working there. The owner of the factory, Mr Williams, was Jewish and his wife, Goldie, would drop in to do some admin occasionally, but the majority of his workers were black or Asian women, many of them recent immigrants. The machinists' supervisor was a black Glaswegian woman who had such a strong Scottish accent that sometimes the machinists asked me to translate her. It was all taken in a spirit of fun. I worked as a clerk, processing orders and packing them, sealing them with brown paper tape backed by glue that had to be wet on a roller machine. Each had to be the same length, and when I started I had to measure them. Then I tore off what I thought would be the right length without measuring. One morning, I tore off five strips ready for packing and the thought came into my mind to measure them. They were all the same length. I was a habituated parcel-packer.

It was a cold winter, and we laboured in poor conditions.

When I arrived at work, I clocked in, pushing my card into a machine that stamped the time on it. If we clocked in one minute late, we were docked half an hour's pay. The office heating did not take effect until about ten o'clock. Sometimes the water in the kettle I used for (instant) coffee was frozen. I had to work with my winter coat on until it warmed up. I do not know how the poor machinists, sitting in rows in the factory part, could stand such conditions. There was a woman just arrived from the Seychelles with whom I used to have lunch in a local café. She was homesick for her island, always talking about the warmth and the palm trees, and she obviously wanted to return. Once she asked me to go back there with her. I never found out if she ever made it home. Apart from invoices, orders, and packing, I sometimes had to wheel racks with clothes across the street to the shabby warehouse where they were stored before sale. It was necessary to dodge the traffic and avoid dropping new women's dresses into the slushy street.

I kept the job until March 1970 and then returned to Cambridge to be a "laboratory assistant" in the University Botany School, where I had found employment. This was the second job I had been offered at Cambridge University, but the pay in the first one was less than I was earning in the East End sweatshop, taking into account that London rail fares and living at home were less than the rent I would have to pay in Cambridge. The Botany School laboratory was a pre-WWII modern building set on the Downing Site, entered through an ornate Edwardian archway between the Archaeology and Anthropology Museum and the Sedgwick Museum of Earth Sciences. I had visited both as a student, and the site of the former St Tibb's Row was just across the street. The architect of this complex must have been a symbolist, for carved on the Sedgwick walls were dinosaurs, and on top a gilded weathervane in the form of an ichthyosaur. Over the main entrance was the sculpted stone image of Alma Mater Cantabrigiensis, the torso and head of a woman with milk—or rather, the alchemical substance magnesia—streaming

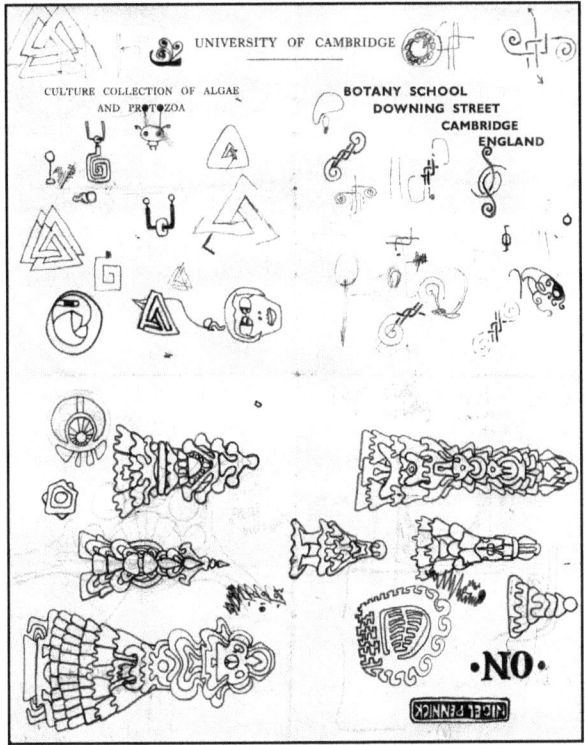

Nigel Pennick's doodles on Cambridge Botany School paper, 1970.

from her breasts.[2] In her hands she holds a chalice and the Sun, surrounded by resplendent rays.

After passing under this fantastic image of seventeenth-century alchemy every day, entering the dingy modernist block was grim. The Botany School was a hierarchical place, where "staff" and "assistants" were treated differently. At coffee breaks, the University "staff" went off to their doubtless comfortable tea room while mere assistants were sent elsewhere to two sparsely furnished rooms on another floor. The male assistants were segregated from female assistants during breaks. My work involved subculturing algal cultures in test tubes. Some of these cultures dated from the 1930s when the pioneering Prague phycologist Ernst Pringsheim, who was Jewish, had

---

2. The "milk" as magnesia was identified by Prudence Jones's researches.

fled the German occupation of Czechoslovakia and brought his cultures in a suitcase to Cambridge. This became the Culture Collection of Algae and Protozoa, and my job was to maintain the individual clones. It was repetitive work which nevertheless required knowledge and concentration.

At lunchtime, some of us assistants would go across the road to the Bun Shop public house which was the last building from St Tibb's Row still standing. It was an ancient structure with the year 1902 on the chimney, but clearly it dated from the 1600s like the now-demolished rest of the Row. The Bun Shop had a tradition of serving its customers hot cross buns every Good Friday. Reynolds, the landlord, would bewail the destruction of Cambridge. "*We* are the *real* Cambridge!" he would say, but our homes and businesses were being destroyed by University redevelopment. The Bun Shop's landlord, after fighting a commendable rearguard action against demolition, finally left in 1974, and the Bun Shop, a venerable Cambridge institution, was no more.

John, an old assistant who was a Cambridge version of Good Soldier Švejk, regaled us youngsters with tales of outwitting the "staff" and undergraduates alike. A favourite story was how, looking out of the window one day, he saw the botany professor standing below. He picked up a rubber bulb used to fill glass pipettes, attached it to a tap, and blew it up with water to the size of a football, then tied it with a rubber band. Then he dropped it onto the ground next to the professor, who was drenched. The professor never knew how or why he got wet. Another of John's tricks involved substituting a fine green plastic net for the green net-like alga that undergraduates were supposed to describe in an examination.

A few months later, a new purpose-built laboratory was opened by the government-sponsored Natural Environment Research Council, to house the culture collection. I became an employee, with better pay and conditions, and worked in the marine algae department of the new building called the Culture Centre of Algae and Protozoa (CCAP). When I left the Botany School, John remained. He had to run errands to other university

Don Yorke and Nigel Pennick. Grange-over-Sands, Cumbria, 1982.

departments and took the opportunity out of the lab to do other things, including having a drink in a pub. We agreed that I would be his contact at CCAP. If anyone telephoned, they would be put through to me and I was to say "He's just now left," even if he had never been there at all. Occasionally, he did have to cycle to CCAP to collect specimens and was there with me, but at other times I told the caller "He's just now left." What he was really up to was anyone's guess. After he died, it emerged that for years he had had two simultaneous "wives" and maintained two separate families in houses only a few streets apart.

CCAP was a system-built construction on ground that belonged to the university. Off the through street was a car park and a building dating probably from the 1920s which was accommodation for the caretaker, Don Yorke. Next to the car park were two old and fine mulberry trees, which produced copious fruit in the autumn. Like some of the younger employees, Don had a series of old cars which always needed attention. When something went wrong with one of them, he would say to me: "Nigel, cars keep us poor." We would work on them in the car park at lunchtime, changing the oil, replacing filters, adjusting brakes, tightening loose exhausts, and fixing lights.

Leaving home one day, my car's starter motor made a strange sound and the engine would not turn over. I opened the bonnet and there I saw that one of the bolts from the starter had fallen off and the motor was out of line. So I found a piece of wood and held the motor in place while my wife Ann started it for me. Getting back to CCAP, I went into the workshop and asked Don if he had a bolt that might fit. He rummaged in his box of parts and pulled out one with the name "Woden" around the top. A good omen. It did fit and was duly tightened up, fixing the problem.

When the mulberry trees were fruiting, Don collected fruit and made wine from them. He would call me from my lab on the internal telephone system asking me to go to the workshop. There, we would drink his beautiful mulberry wine. We discussed distilling it to make a brandy, and a start was made in the workshop on building an illicit still. Unfortunately, the project had to be abandoned because there was no safe place to conceal it. I am sure it would have been an outstanding liquor.

Two of Everything

In 1971, I was sent from CCAP to Belgium to be instructed in how to propagate the alga *Acetabularia* by the world expert, Professor Latour. I was given an air ticket to Brussels, and booked in at a seedy hotel, the grandly named Le Duc de Brabant et Rhin, which later burnt down with serious loss of life.

I was to commute to the campus of the Université Libre de Bruxelles and work in the French-speaking Botany department. This involved finding the place. I was told to catch a train to Rhode-Saint-Genèse station and ask for Rue des Chevaux. The train's destination was Braine l'Ailleud. So I bought a ticket at the station and looked for a train to Braine l'Ailleud. A train came in with the destination Eigenbrakkel on the front. Having been in Brussels before and navigated the place-name nightmare, I half-remembered that this was the Flemish name for my destination, so I got on the train.

After a few stops, we pulled into a station named Sint Genesius Rode, and I suddenly realized that this was where I was supposed to get off. I looked around for the university campus, and asked a couple of people in French, who refused to answer me. It dawned upon me that I was going to a French-speaking enclave in a Flemish-speaking town. So I walked around and saw the sign Paardenstraat. I understood that this meant "Horses Street" (which in French would be Rue des Chevaux) and figured that the campus entrance must be close. I found it and navigated my way to the Botany department, where I was well received and started my tuition in *Acetabularia* propagation.

At lunchtime, the students and staff in the department went to the canteen. I looked out the window of the 1960s-style modern structure and saw, about fifty yards away, an identical building where people were also eating. I was told that this was the "Flemish canteen." This led to a series of tales about the linguistic divide, including the local post office refusing to deliver letters addressed "Rue des Chevaux" and other petty aggravations over nomenclature. It transpired that there were two separate universities on the same campus, one for each language, meaning the duplication of all faculties and departments. I was shocked. Perhaps there was another expert on *Acetabularia* on the same campus, working in the Flemish Botany department. On previous visits to Brussels I had seen the dual destination blinds on buses and trams, and learnt to ask the way in English. It is better to be a total outsider than to be ranked as one of the "enemy" by asking in the wrong tongue.

To finish the story, I learnt successfully in French how to cultivate the difficult alga and never once met a Flemish-speaking academic or student on the campus. Back in Cambridge, when I told my tale to my Dada comrades, they joyfully asserted it as a living example of Dada in action. I have crossed many borders in my time, both documented and undocumented, and I have even been in sectarian-divided Belfast. But I had never before experienced a "two-of-everything" society, where the borders were a twilight zone that an outsider could never penetrate.

WYRD TIMES

Anglian Diggers representative Sheila Andrews, 1969.
Pencil drawing by Nigel Pennick.

My Career in Science, 1970–1985

The Culture Centre of Algae and Protozoa was a small unit, with only sixteen employees at its maximum. I was tasked with maintaining the cultures of unicellular marine algae inherited from the Botany School. Our holdings soon expanded. The collection of algal species from the estuaries of Essex (collected by Dr Roger Butcher in the 1950s and 1960s) was transferred from Westfield College in London, and it was my job to maintain it and work on identification. I soon became expert at identifying marine algae by light and electron microscopy, and was promoted to a higher grade and had my own assistant. This was Sheila Andrews, my Digger colleague who transferred to the better-paid CCAP from her work in the diagnostic laboratory of Addenbrooke's Hospital.

From 1971 I worked with the electron-microscopist Ken Clarke on preparing and examining algal cells, and developed techniques to highlight various identifying structures. Through this work, in 1972, I identified small scales on the unarmoured dinoflagellate *Oxhyrris marina*, and we published a paper that contained the first-ever description of scales in the dinoflagellates. I went on to make the unexpected discovery of three-dimensional scales on the outside of the "armour plating" of armoured dinoflagellates. Ken and I also worked on the

NIGEL PENNICK

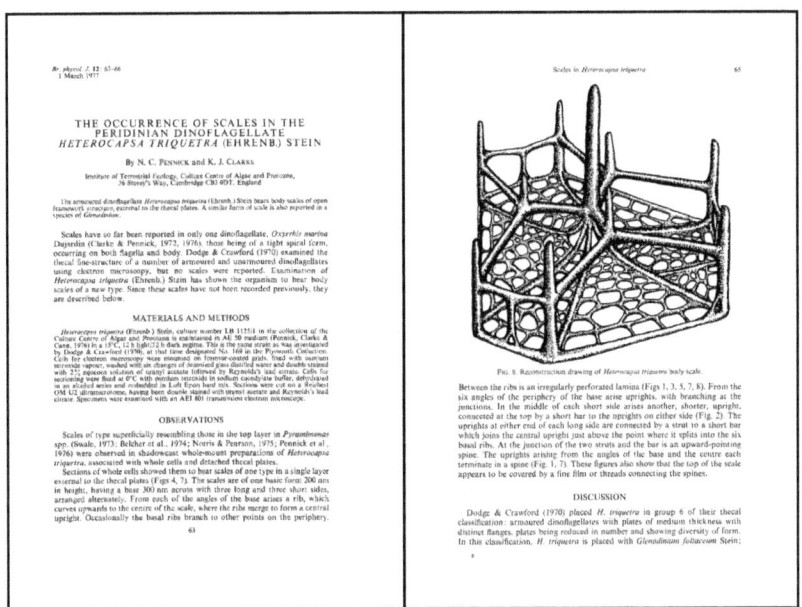

A 1977 scientific paper by Nigel Pennick and Ken Clarke published in the *British Phycological Journal*. The illustration that appears as Fig. 8 in the same article (shown in the page on the right) is also by Nigel Pennick.

genus *Pyramimonas*, of which there were many species—both identified and unidentified—in the Butcher Collection. These unicellular algae are distinguished by layers of body scales, more or less flat ones surmounted by three-dimensional, often crown-shaped ones. From our work, we published several papers, and I described in English and Latin several species new to science, including *Pyramimonas gorlestonae*, which I had collected on a Christmas Day from the sea at Gorleston-on-Sea, Norfolk, where my wife's parents lived. Another new *Pyramimonas* that I described was one collected from the North Sea by the fisheries research ship *Cirolana*. At the time, the fisheries research laboratory in Lowestoft, Suffolk, was being closed down by government cuts, and Dr John Reynolds, who came to CCAP from the east coast in his much-admired Lotus Elan sports car in its resplendent California Orange livery. So it fell to me to name it *Pyramimoas cirolanae*. In all, I was an author on around thirty published scientific papers, mainly as first author or sole

Lindsey Goodfellow and Nigel Pennick collecting marine algae
from the Blackwater Estuary, Fambridge, Essex, 1975.

author.

In 1983, I worked with Professor John Kessler from Arizona on gyrotaxis, which examined the behavior of swimming cells in a current. A thick culture of *Dunaliella salina* was flowed through a vertical glass tube at different speeds and the cells were concentrated together by their swimming motion. Various speeds produced various patterns of column, and the fluid mechanics that produced the patterns was analyzed and published in mathematical form. It was a technique that had not been utilised before. Also, in the declining years of CCAP, I corresponded with Professor Ginzburg at the Hebrew University of Jerusalem about the identity of *Dunaliella salina*, as I had amassed the largest collection of its cultures in the world. Various energy corporations were very interested in this alga, which can grow in highly saline environments and produces a substance that was viewed as a biological replacement for mineral oil. There were attempts by a certain corporation to patent a strain that they possessed, and we were concerned about both the principle of patenting a naturally occurring organism and the actual identity of the culture they held. Through documentary research, I was able to prove that the strain they intended to patent was identical with one I held in the collection. It had been collected at the Woods Hole Oceanographic Institution at La Jolla, California, in the 1960s. However, the outcome of this was not good. I heard that Professor Ginzburg had either resigned or been fired, and not long afterwards—when I was given two weeks' notice of "Premature Retirement"[3]—I was compelled to hand in all my notes and records concerning my *Dunaliella* research. Make of that what you will. I left science, never again to enter a laboratory—except as a patient at the Papworth Hospital.

---

3. For more of the background circumstances that were at play, see the section "The End of My Career in Science," pp. 181–85.

III
NOTES FROM THE UNDERGROUND

I want to make a world that doesn't exist.

—John Nicholson (1940–2021)

Mary Davenall playing one of Nigel Pennick's instruments, 1968. One of his psychedelic paintings can be seen in the background. Photo by Nigel Pennick.

Different Alternatives: A Brief Sociological Background

Because of my involvement with the "alternative" scene in England in the 1960s, I have often been asked why the British underground had a significantly different emphasis from the American one. This stems from historical and social differences. Unlike the United States, Britain has been a settled country for thousands of years, and many towns and villages were established as far back as two thousand years ago. Durolipons (later called Cambridge) was founded by the Romans around the year 47 CE, and people have lived here ever since.[1] This sense of continuity was a major factor in the nuances of the alternative cultures that emerged in the 1960s.

Conquered by the Normans in 1066, England's social structure was established under the feudal system. There are remnants of this even today, with the monarchy and the House of Lords being the most prominent examples. William the Conqueror abolished slavery in England, and the lower orders became serfs, tied to the land on which they toiled and subject to a hierarchy of lords, barons, dukes, and—at the top—the central power of the monarchy. This system disintegrated slowly in the years following the Black Death in 1349, and the decline accelerated with the Peasants' Revolt of 1381. The concept that all were created equal was promoted then by John Ball who asked: "When Adam delved and Eva span, who was then the Gentleman?" The revolt was crushed by military force. Subsequently, a freer but still hierarchical class system evolved,

---

1. Britain was part of the Roman Empire from 43 CE to 410 CE.

which developed until the English Civil War in the 1640s. Concepts of freedom emerged after the king was executed, with the Levellers and Diggers arguing that England should be a common treasury for all—the real meaning of "commonwealth." But the class system was alive and well for centuries more, throughout the expansion of the British Empire, and equally in Britain itself, where people from the lower orders had few life chances. Many who were dissatisfied went to sea or emigrated to a colony to forge a better life. From these people came the pioneering spirit of the Americans, Canadians, and Australians. Those that remained dealt with the existing situation as best they could, according to the strictures permitted by their social class. These are the people I am descended from.

During the 1960s, the British underground was driven by people (mainly men) who had been born during or just after World War II. This catastrophic event saw the destruction through aerial bombardment of large swathes of British cities, with civilian deaths and disruption of society through the mobilization of the military-age male population and evacuation of children and teenagers for safety into country towns and villages. Born into a world of upheaval and destruction, the protagonists of the underground or counterculture saw this mayhem as a systemic failing of the ruling classes. Clearly, our leaders, from the monarch downwards, had forfeited their right to rule.

Some radical contrarians took the path of "back to the land," seeking to escape the vast conurbations forged in the industrial revolution. Rural communities were seen as the solution to the modern world. Historically, one model was the Diggers and their leader Gerrard Winstanley. In 1649 they cultivated land which they did not own in an attempt to create an autonomous community with co-operative principles. The writings of William Morris were also an important theoretical basis of this movement. In addition, there were practical examples of various late nineteenth-century rural communal movements such as the Haslemere Peasant Industries in Surrey, and the Whiteway Colony in Gloucestershire. Haslemere and Whiteway had a

Collage by Nigel Pennick for *Swastika* magazine, 1969.

libertarian-spiritual ethos.[2] There was also a vegetarian imperative. A journal titled *The Herald of the New Age* promoted the principles of Haslemere and its sympathizers. There were earlier twentieth-century examples, too, including the anarchist commune of the Brotherhood Church at Stapleton in Yorkshire, and the activities of the gay anarchist Edward Carpenter in Sheffield. Another notable commune was the Bruderhof, a German Anabaptist community founded in 1920, whose members fled *en masse* in 1936 to Ashton Keynes in the Cotswolds. The community at Elmsett in Suffolk was actually founded during World War II by pacifists who were permitted to work the land as part of the war effort rather than serving in the armed forces. Findhorn, the best-known commune to survive from the counterculture era, was founded in 1962. These, and others, were more or less successful attempts to live independently of the state and society.

2. As a girl, my mother (born 1924) was taught embroidery by a woman who had been a co-worker of the Haslemere Peasant Industries.

WYRD TIMES

Those who did not see an escape to the country as the answer, and those who revelled in the electric and electrifying atmosphere of skiffle, rock 'n' roll, jazz, and blues, sought another alternative. Some in the noisy and polluted industrial cities turned to hard rock and in Birmingham forged heavy metal music from the rhythmic beat of steamhammers in the ironworks. Their music, however, carried the same contrarian ethos of the people who sat in folk clubs strumming acoustic guitars. In the British folk scene, those who did not sing American protest songs in the mould of Pete Seeger, Woody Guthrie, Buffy Sainte-Marie, or Bob Dylan explored their own indigenous traditional music with songs that told of former times in which our ancestors lived and fended for themselves and their families the best way they could. They sang of greedy farmers, cruel sea captains, highwaymen, murderers, hangings, famine, loss of loved ones, and transportation in chains to the colonies. Every aspect of human life was represented, and whether or not it was documented, it was all part of our collective *ørlög*, "Wyrd," or fate. (For example, my forbear, John Austin, was in 1783 the last man executed at Tyburn.[3] He was hanged for highway robbery and his "famous last words" are preserved.[4]) Underground artworks—including record sleeves, posters, and magazine illustrations—had a large element of the carnivalesque, harking back to the British seaside towns, with their piers, funfairs, and variety shows; the circus with its striped Big Top and garish clowns; travelling fairs with their ornate showmen's vehicles, fortune tellers' Gypsy caravans, carousels with painted horses and swirling polychrome artwork on every other ride; and even the traditional Roses and Castles painted on canal boats. The Beatles' *Sgt. Pepper's Lonely Hearts Club Band* and *Magical Mystery Tour* epitomize this current, though it was only one of many at the time.

3. Tyburn, the "triple tree," was where London's executions took place. It was in what is now the West End, close to Marble Arch.

4. "Good people, I request your prayers for the salvation of my departing soul. Let my example teach you to shun the bad ways I have followed. Keep good company, and mind the word of God. Lord have mercy on me. Jesus look down with pity on me. Christ have mercy on my poor soul!"

The counterculture also appropriated elements of "fine art." The use of photomontage, which originated in the nineteenth century and was later radicalized by Futurism, Dada, Constructivism, and Surrealism, appeared in underground newspapers (including *Cambridge Voice*). It also appeared in political posters and publications, for politics was the other component of the underground. Although 1968 was the only year in history that no member of the British armed forces was killed in combat, and despite the fact that British soldiers never went there, Vietnam became an issue. There was always tension between those who wanted peace, and those who wanted the war to end with "Victory to the Vietcong"—as many chanted and waved Vietcong flags at ostensibly antiwar demonstrations. As it turned out, the Vietcong did win. Also in 1968, student turmoil in France led first to the occupation of the university of Nanterre, then to an insurrection in Paris which threatened to become a revolution. In Cambridge, along with Vietnam, this was a trigger for left-wing radicals to stir things up. As politics poisons everything, the alliance between the politicals and the hippies was sundered, and those who did not think communism was a good idea became targets of the revolutionists.

The United States has no historical experience of having women as heads of state. Before Britain was unified as the United Kingdom in 1603, queens as well as kings had ruled the separate realms of England and Scotland. Since unification, Britain has been ruled by four queens: Mary II, Anne, Victoria, and Elizabeth II, the latter two having very long reigns. Britain has also had (at the time of writing) three female prime ministers: Margaret Thatcher, Theresa May, and Liz Truss. So, the principle that women can rule is embedded within British culture, not American. England has been a centralized state since the Norman Conquest of 1066, and centuries before that, kings such as Ecgberht and Æthelstan asserted centralized control. Consequently, since the Conquest, and despite the usual tribulations of history—civil wars, uprisings, and the deposition of kings—the status of England as a centralized nation was never in doubt. The last battle fought on British soil was in 1746.

Ownership of all British land is vested in the monarch. In English law if one owns one's own property, it is technically *freehold*, which means that the owner is free to sell it even though it is technically owned by the Crown. In the United States, this principle of the monarch owning the land, abolished in 1776, remains in the term *real estate*, which refers properly to land once part of the Spanish Empire that belonged to the king of Spain, later the state of Mexico. The expansive pioneering spirit of American settlers in the former Mexican territories and those of the native tribes unconquered by Spanish authority was impossible in Britain. All British land was already in someone's possession, mainly people from the upper classes. The common land of England had been "enclosed" progressively since the sixteenth century. It was land held for common use by local people, but greedy lords, universities, and business "adventurers" were aided by Acts of Parliament, which itself was composed of upper-class men who profited from free land.

Because there was free land in America—in reality appropriated, usually violently, from the indigenous inhabitants—the frontier between settled land and these unregulated territories became the stuff of legend. There was nothing comparable in Britain. There was nowhere to go from here, except to emigrate. It was not part of our culture, except in an uncomprehending way through the spectacle of Western movies seen in black and white on Saturday morning matinees or grainy 405-line monochrome televisions. In reality, the American experience was as alien to proper British understanding as any other exotic culture. The era in which this expansion occurred in the United States was after the Civil War, driven partly by former Confederate soldiers who did not accept "the night they drove Old Dixie down," to quote the song. There was no equivalent fratricidal civil war in Britain in the nineteenth century, and so no comparable legacy of division.

So, the cowboys on the Chisholm Trail, settlers rolling behind their oxen in Conestoga wagons, the outlaws, bushwhackers, cattle-rustlers, gun-toting lawmen who shot first and asked questions later, and the untrustworthy "other" Mexicans and

Indians, were presented to British people. Clearly, they were and are mere caricatures that began with the Wild West show of Buffalo Bill and the Hollywood movies of Tom Mix, and ended with the machismo of John Wayne and Clint Eastwood. All these characters from Western movies, and all the real people, heroic or otherwise, who strove through appalling conditions to bring the steers to the railheads, cultivate poor soil with inadequate tools, battle blizzards and drought, or fight off hostile forces in the Cherokee Outlet, had no connexion whatsoever with the British experience. The heroic American trope of the self-reliant frontiersman, Winchester rifle in hand, defending what he believed to be right, had no place here. In Britain, *collective* resistance was lionized in the World War II heroes of Dunkirk, the Battle of Britain, and D-Day.

Thus, only certain elements of the American counterculture resonated with the British underground sensibility of the time. The Vietnam War was unimportant to everyday life, and the ominous rumblings in Northern Ireland were yet to break out into violent conflict. Although Britain does not possess the "wide open spaces" of North America, travelling the roads and rails was a common theme. From Jack Kerouac's *On the Road* to the exploits of the outlaw bikers Sonny Barger, Freewheelin' Frank, and George Christie, the call of the road is universal. Beat poetry was influential early on, as were the more experimental and free exponents of rock music from the West Coast. My local record shop had a bin with the latest records labelled "West Coast, Underground." We related to the psychedelic art of San Francisco, exemplified by the poster art of Wes Wilson, Rick Griffin, Victor Moscoso, Stanley Mouse, and Alton Kelley, and the productions of the Family Dog, which were treasured possessions if one could find them. They were influential upon British underground art. My collection of many of these, including British ones by Martin Sharp, Michael English, and The Fool (Marijke Koger, Simon Posthuma, and Josje Leeger), came from a deal I made when the Indica Bookshop in London closed down. It was just round the corner from my grandmother's apartment, and I was a frequent customer. This collection would fetch a five-figure sum at auction if I still had it. But unfortunately, it was stolen in the early 1970s.

Cambridge Voice *Is Raised*

My entry into "underground journalism" came in 1968 through the aforementioned *Cambridge Voice*, of which I was a founder member. The genesis of *Cambridge Voice* and subsequent offshoot projects came about indirectly from the Town and Gown antipathy. Some of the university undergraduates connected with the Arts Lab were involved with publishing a weekly called *The 1/- Paper* (*The Shilling Paper*), which, quite naturally, sold for one shilling. Equivalent to five pence in modern money,[5] inflation has made this amount seem unimaginably small over half a century later, but at the time one could ride a long way on a bus for that fare. In late November 1968, at the end of the university's autumn term, the students running *The 1/- Paper* were going home for the Christmas vacation, and, as the publication was ostensibly for both Town and Gown, they asked "Townies" like me to take it over until they came back after the Christmas vacation.

A meeting was called and I went to it. Five of us volunteered to take it on: myself, Cecilia Boggis, Roger Furnell, Franchesca Hempstead, and John Nicholson, who was known locally as "Jesus" because of his long hair and beard (we always called him John). Born in 1940, he died in 2021. John was appointed editor and began to organise the next issue. He undertook an audit of our capital, costs, and income, and found that *The 1/- Paper* was not paying its way, and must have been supported by additional funding, namely donations. It appeared to Nicholson that the donations came mainly from dons (university college fellows and the like). In "Editor for a Day" in *Cambridge Voice* no. 2, he gave a breakdown of the unstable finances of *The 1/- Paper*, which had the potential to collapse if the supporters withdrew their subsidies. He took this up with the undergraduates running the paper and told them he intended to write an article demonstrating the paradox of student protesters being supported by dons, and

---

5. The shilling was abolished in 1971 when decimalisation was imposed in Britain.

Two issues of *Cambridge Voice* with cover art by Nigel Pennick.

gave an outline of his arguments.

What ideologues hate and fear most are analytical exposés of their belief-systems and aims. The critical techniques they use to attack their opponents must never be applied to themselves. Control is more important than discourse. So the next day the "management" decided to shut down *The 1/- Paper* for the duration of the Christmas vacation. Townies could not be trusted to follow the "party line" so it was feared they might criticise the individuals in the university whom the grads were dependent upon for funding. It was clear that the undergraduates running the paper were not in charge, as they pretended, but were the tools of anonymous dons who were using them to promote a left-wing political agenda. It was also clear that these grads were mere proxies, not agents in their own right as we were.

In *Cambridge Voice* no. 2, John detailed the genesis of the paper in a piece called "How *Cambridge Voice* Was Born." It is the only historic record of this seminal moment:

WYRD TIMES

Wed. Editor parted company with *The 1/- Paper*.
Thurs. Meeting at *1/- Paper* office. They gave their version of the story. Announced no further publication of their so-called town and gown paper until next university term.
Fri. No word of apology or explanation about the silence of *The 1/- Paper*.
Sat. I went ahead. Contacted people, suggested meeting on Sunday at the meeting convened to discuss bettering entertainment facilities in Cambridge.
Sun. Meeting 3.00 to 5.00 p.m. I was then off the map until—
Mon. 4.00 p.m. when I returned to Cambridge. That evening I began alerting, interviewing, setting up material etc.
Tues. Finally booked the printer. Wasted an entire day hunting an elusive electric typewriter. Cleared working space in my room.
Wed. Was put in touch with an electric typist (a young lady competent with electric typewriting) who did less than 2 hours of our material for a fee of 15/- [fifteen shillings = 75p in modern money]. Interviewed the landlady and her husband.
Thurs. Collected what had been typed—Afternoon spent collecting advertisements. Name "Cambridge Voice" designed [calligraphy by Andrew Kendon, embellishment by Nigel Pennick].
Fri. 12 midday: in this 14 hour period, five of us [Nicholson, Boggis, Pennick, Hemspstead, and Furnell] and Mike Shaw for 4 hours—produced "Cambridge Voice." We got it to the printer by 4.00 p.m. thanks to British Rail delays.
Note: we are not protestors, demonstrators, political agitators, undergraduates or the like—WE ARE people trying to earn a living in Cambridge.

Cambridge Voice came into being at Peabodys, John's house

NIGEL PENNICK

Jane Kirby selling *Cambridge Voice*, January, 1969. Photo by Nigel Pennick.

in Chesterton Road, a four-story late Victorian in the middle of a terrace whose garden had been converted to a road, leaving the house surrounded by incessant traffic. Looking back on the intensity of that first all-night labour of fourteen hours, we must have been driven, not by drugs (as John allowed none in Peabodys) or drink (except coffee), but by commitment. Others who helped us in different ways were dedicated to the paper's success. Simon Gould of the Free Front donated £10 worth of paper, while other supporters bought advertising or donated money. And "anyone foolhardy enough to risk selling in the street" may have met with incredulity at first, though not the persecution by the police we expected. A stalwart was Jane Kirby, shown with a friend in the above photograph taken by me outside Watches of Switzerland on the corner of Rose Crescent selling issue 2 in January 1969. Street-selling soon began to pay off. After the second issue emerged in early 1969, we hired a market stall one day a week and sold *Cambridge Voice* there. We championed Town over Gown and nonconformism (with a small "n"), and we were against all forms of dogma. Once the undergraduates returned from their long Christmas vacations (funded by left-wing dons!), *The 1/- Paper* resumed publication. Now we became their target of abuse.

Since *Cambridge Voice* was blackballed by Cambridge printers from the outset, we had to find a printer in North London: Helmut Taylor. We sent parcels of artwork by train to King's Cross station in London, where he picked them up. Once printed, he sent packages of *Cambridge Voice* by passenger train from King's Cross, and we picked them up from Cambridge railway station's parcels department. Unlike the printers in Cambridge, who feared university repercussions if they stepped out of line, Helmut's print company was not afraid to take chances. Later, he published *Jeremy*, the first legal gay magazine in Britain.

After hours in the Skyroom (attic) of Peabodys, John would play us records by the Mothers of Invention: *Freak Out, Lumpy Gravy, We're Only in It for the Money,* and *Uncle Meat.* "I hear you've been having trouble with pigs and ponies" and the like became our catchphrases. John claimed that the cry of "More!" in response to Frank Zappa's single chord on the "mighty and majestic Albert Hall organ," which appeared on a Mothers' live album, was his—and it does sound like John. In the Skyroom, whose rendered pink plastering had never been painted, we had long discussions and arguments with various visitors about all manner of subjects, and new ideas for projects emerged. Gradually, a large network of contacts was built up among local students, poets, artists, craft workers, and business-owners. The Welsh playwright Dedwydd Jones also lived at Peabodys, but he rarely participated. Later, three of his plays were published by Cokaygne Press, which succeeded *Cambridge Voice*.

The first issue of *Cambridge Voice* contained a rambling Ginsberg-esque poem written by an American Vietnam draft-dodger overstaying his three-month visa in Cambridge. It had been typed up for *The 1/- Paper*, but when we read through the first draft, we were horrified to find the phrase: "The world is doomed! ---- the Draft." "At first we were chilled," John noted, "suspecting the printer." But when we checked the artwork, we discovered that *The 1/- Paper* editorial committee had censored the poem and put "----" in place of "Fuck." In the second issue, we placed the following clarification right on the front cover:

> We apologise to the printer for wrongfully suspecting him. We apologise to you, the readers, for accidentally insulting your intelligence. In future, for ---- read "fuck."

Having "fuck" on the front of a paper sold in the street was sensational, and people bought extra copies for their friends and congratulated us on our bravery.

Cambridge Voice no. 3 came out with two-colour printing on the cover. During its existence, I produced most of the artwork in the magazine, and suggested possible experiments in printing. Number 3 was the last that used Andrew Kendon's calligraphic header. I drew the whole cover, printed in red as well as black. Among other causes, we championed Free Radio (otherwise called "pirate radio," broadcast from ships outside British territorial waters), which was then under attack and was finally suppressed completely. There were also advertisements for a tailor, secondhand clothes (including a wedding dress), furniture, and a fireguard; requests for an auburn wig; and the Anglian Diggers' attempt to procure a washing machine, which garnered no response. Nothing like this existed in *The 1/- Paper*.

Number 4, published in February 1969, again featured two colours on the cover, and was printed on yellow paper. By then, *Cambridge Voice* was stocked by the three main bookshops in the city as well as Nunn's newsagent, Record Fayre, and Jentri Boutique in Regent Street. This issue also presented the "Pennick Plan," where I suggested a radical reorganization of transport in the city centre to make it a more tolerable environment for humans:

> Cambridge is inundated with automobiles, and their associated crimes against humanity, fumes, accidents, noise and general intolerability. Most journeys by car in the city centre are unnecessary ones, causing congestion

which delays public transport, and forcing the city authorities to lay waste vast areas for the sole reason of parking the cars ... a vicious circle of reduced bus services, forcing people into cars, and cars congesting the bus routes, causing cuts in services, is the same old story, repeated again and again in Britain. That this has happened pinpoints the lack of foresight on the part of our traffic "planners."

As a remedy to this, I suggested the removal of cars from the city centre and the construction of subway routes:

Vehicles for the subway need not be London Underground style (heavy transit vehicles) but could be driverless (or at least one-man) light railcars ... Out-of-town buses would still be allowed the use of certain streets. Most other streets would be closed to traffic (except electric delivery vans, certain hours only) and all road signs, etc. could be torn up, and possibly trees planted ... the roads would be traffic-free, excepting specific roads still used by buses, and in emergency when fire, ambulance or police vehicles would traverse the streets. Those streets still used would have special one-way-only "tracks" just wide enough for the buses or electric delivery vans, and paved for people to walk in their city's streets where cars once ground their noisy fume-laden paths.

Fluorescence

My interest in experimental printing was expressed with the cover of *Cambridge Voice* no. 5, printed in red fluorescent (or "dayglo") ink with contrasting green. This we believed to be only the second time this ink was used on the cover of a publication. Fluorescent printing had appeared in 1967 on Martin Sharp's album cover for Cream's *Disraeli Gears* and then in 1968 on seminal Dutch blues band Cuby + Blizzards' *Trippin' thru a Midnight Blues*.

NIGEL PENNICK

We were aware that the Town had a history at least as ancient and interesting as the University—older, in fact. John Thorn had shown me a Cambridgeshire tradition that had nothing to do with academe. And the tile dated 1734 found in the rubble after an ancient barn was demolished in Bradmore Street was another indication that there was a local tradition of timber-frame buildings unconnected with the University. We started some serious investigation into this and came into contact with two very helpful experts: Mike Petty of the Cambridgeshire Collection at the city library, and Enid Porter, curator of the Folk Museum. We discovered that *Cambridge Voice* had precedents published by long-dead Townies, some of which used techniques which until then we imagined had been invented by the "underground press" in the 1960s.

There was *The Reformer* of 1776 (a significant date), which released seven issues in one month, while *The Snob* of 1829 had eleven issues, each printed on different coloured paper. ("Snob" was a derogatory name used by University students for Townspeople, derived from Latin *sine nobilitate*, "without nobility." The paper's name turned the insult against the insolent.) *The Individual* was also multicoloured. Various editions were printed on purple, green, yellow, and pink paper, and—in 1871—*The Lantern of the Cam* had shone out. We felt vindicated: we were carrying the same light! History is important, and we owe our gratitude to people like Petty and Porter for collecting, conserving, and making available this material that had dwindled into obscurity.

Cambridge Voice no. 6 had a "Mondrian" cover in black and dark blue. Inside, my artwork was the first of many Dada-inspired photomontages that would appear in later issues, and which continued as a style in publications like *Braingrader*. A visit to the Central Library archive turned up a 1937 issue of *The Cam*. John tracked down the editor, Rex Spalding, who was still alive and granted an interview that appeared in *CV* 6. My friend Julie Gaman and I wrote an article with maps titled "Fens," in which we described an unfolding ecological disaster: the topsoil of this former marshland was being destroyed by shrinkage, oxidation, and strong winds, the "Fen Blows" that John Thorn

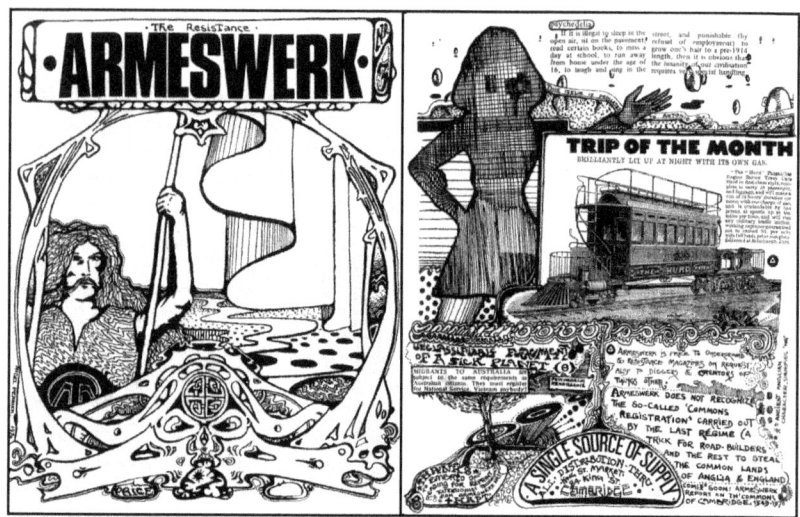

Cover art and an interior page from *Armeswerk* no. 3 (1970) by Nigel Pennick.

had described to me back at the Granville. We concluded: "So every alternative leads to the same result: the death of the fens, no arable land. They either become grazing land, a new megalopolis, or DESERT."

The Cambridge Native Press Is Founded

Issue 7 had a pastiche of the (blasphemous) Marvel comics character Thor, Mjöllnir raised, with a speech balloon that read: "By the Runes of Ragnarök—it's *Cambridge Voice* Number 7!" In this issue the formation of the Cambridge Native Press syndicate was announced, which was sponsored by *Cambridge Voice* as a series of specialty magazines. Among the publications on offer were *Little Brother*, a magazine published by school students and edited by Dave Attwood; the Anglian Diggers' *postermanifestoster*; and two poetry magazines, Simon Gould's *Jesse James* and Christopher Crutchley's *Swastika*. This latter magazine explained: "Swastika—the sign of fertility and representative of the cyclic seasons is at last rehabilitated from its Nazi misuse."[6] Later, an alternative magazine for undergraduates

---

6. On the history and widespread historic use of the swastika, see my *The Book*

called *Braingrader*, edited first by Nick Turner and later by Henry Bosanquet, and two short-lived magazines, *Bubble* and *Footnote*, were added to the CNP stable. *Walrus*, as an Anglian Diggers magazine, was never a member of the Cambridge Native Press; neither was a later offshoot, *Armeswerk*, named for the ancient Anglo-Saxon defensive earthwork formerly at the river crossing.

Folk Tradition Emerges

Cambridge Voice no. 8 was published in April of 1969. It was printed on light blue paper and my cover—a montage of photographs, drawings, and graphics—was done in black and orange ink. Inside was an article about Enid Porter and her work preserving the folk tradition of Cambridgeshire at the Folk Museum. She was the author of *Cambridgeshire Customs and Folklore*, which she had compiled from personal experience and contact over many years with craftspeople and farm workers who had lived their lives embedded in traditional life and culture.

Enid was a fount of knowledge about the local indigenous tradition. She had collaborated with the Fenman W. H. Barrett who, among other things, had participated in a traditional foundation rite in 1897. His uncle, a builder, constructed a "Primitive Methodist" Chapel at Black Horse Drove in the Cambridgeshire Fens beyond Ely, a place that remains remote even today. Barrett was sent to a knacker's yard to buy a horse's head. His uncle located the centre of the site with a stake and dug a trench, opened a bottle of beer, and placed the head in the trench. Then he poured the first glass of beer as a libation, and the men had a drink before shovelling bricks and mortar into the foundation. This story was redolent of the worldview of John Thorn, of blessed memory. Clearly, here we had a worthy traditional culture that had served our forebears well, based upon true principles that emanated from the land.

Also carrying on local knowledge in this issue was Sheila Andrews's "Kite Area Disgrace." Illustrated with my photographs,

of Primal Signs: The High Magic of Symbols (2014), 25–28, 105–16; and *The Ancestral Power of Amulets, Talismans, and Mascots* (2021), 208–10. Both titles are published by Destiny Books in Rochester, Vermont.

Paradise Cottage, Paradise Street, Cambridge, 1969. Photo by Nigel Pennick.

Sheila recounted how—for the first twelve years of her life—she had lived in this area of nineteenth-century housing and witnessed firsthand as parts of it were progressively abandoned and demolished. This process had continued apace since 1961 when her family left their home in Grafton Street. She detailed the various areas including Paradise Street, which by then had become an ironic name.

"Seek paradise" was one of the Chaldaean Oracles ascribed to Zoroaster, but in Cambridge in 1969, the tawdry and run-down Paradise Street and the windowless ruin of Paradise Cottage were dystopian reminders of the gulf between desire and reality. Three years later, the Land of Cokaygne would attain a symbolic reality in the bookshop of that name not far away in Jesus Terrace facing on to New Square. The naming of names is significant, even when their origins are all but forgotten.

The destruction of Cambridge's Town buildings contrasted with the untouched University, which—one city planner had stated—should stand "like the rock of ages." We would return to the Kite Area later.

The Arts Syndicate Comes Together

Cambridge Voice no. 9 featured my drawing of a Cambridge double-decker bus on the cover. This type of bus was technically a K5G, a Bristol-built "K" type with a five-cylinder Gardner diesel engine, the typical public transport of Cambridge at the time. With an open platform and a conductor taking fares, this type of bus was soon to be replaced with front-entrance vehicles operated only by the driver. The outline drawing of the K5G was printed in red. The main announcement in this issue was the formation of the Arts Syndicate. It was to be a group of artists, designers, and musicians, including myself, who came together at Peabodys to collaborate in projects such as staging exhibitions, producing fashion, jewellery, and furniture. Some jewellery was commissioned, and some paintings were sold, but the exhibitions were never staged owing to the difficulty Townspeople had hiring halls which were owned by the churches or University colleges. The Arts Syndicate did get some commissions for work. I painted a mural in the cellar-disco of the YMCA, but this was soon destroyed. I also painted a psychedelic fireplace for a client, which was one of three—the other two were at my parents' house in southeast London, and at Julie Gaman's house on Walnut Tree Avenue, which was later torn down for a new road and the Elizabeth Bridge over the Cam river.[7] The Arts Syndicate also sold some of my music: "Under the auspices of AS is the underground group Concrete Tapeworm, tapes of which are now available thru AS and CNP. Later, in the summer, public performances of their work are planned." Again, the impossibility of finding a venue scotched this plan as well.

Cambridge Voice no. 10 had a cover printed on light yellow paper in magenta and green. The artwork, collaboratively designed by Arts Syndicate members, depicted a faux-architectural fantasy with pseudo-classical columns and gothic-windows. In these windows were photographs of various participants, elephants, and the *Cambridge Voice* market stall. The Arts Syndicate Design logo was an Eye of Horus. (This was an allusion to the New York underground bookshop The Eye of Horus, recently visited by an AS member.) Number 10's cover bore the slogans "Peace and Freedom" and "Endurance, Value" along with the epithet: "A touch of Aristotle, a dash of Barnum." There were also several mysterious words written in Northumbrian runes: for the reader clever enough to decipher them, they read "Ragnarok" and—very small—the runic names "Odin" and "Loki." The whole cover was headed "*The Big One—Cambridge Voice.*"

Inside, the Arts Syndicate stated that it desperately needed a shop. There was an article about shenanigans in the City Council and local services, as well as my essay titled "Killer Monster Loose in City," which was about the harm wrought by air pollution from cars. Sheila Andrews reported on an exhibition concerning the City Council's plans for the Kite Area. I drew a pastiche of the sunny, idealised "artist's impression" of what it would be like, with my more realistic rendering of what it *would* become: skid row. I depicted people walking past boarded-up shops with "to let" signs, trash stacked against the boards, and—lying in the pedestrianised street—an alcoholic swigging from a bottle and a homeless person slumped against a pillar.

---

7. When Julie Gaman's house was cleared for demolition, we went onto the nearby footbridge over the Cam and ritually consigned the keys to the river. I was able to recover the Victorian ceramic number-plate (80), which is still in my collection today.

May Day demonstration. Crop marks from *Cambridge Voice* layout. Photo by Nigel Pennick.

The May Day March—On the Wrong Day

Cambridge Voice no. 10 appeared in May 1969, and that meant May Day. Our critique of undergraduate revolutionaries continued in a report Sheila and I made of what we called "May Day Rag," which actually happened from 2:30 p.m. onwards on May 3.[8] Our opener was an ironic drawing of a hammer and sickle and a clenched fist, and we reported on a gathering of University socialists and communists in the park called Christ's Pieces. The Town's Free Front had already dissociated themselves from the event, and the invited representatives of the trade unions did not come, either. We were selling *Cambridge Voice* and were threatened with violence, which, as usual, they failed to back up. What we witnessed as they gathered were young men "clutching their red or black flags" and reading various papers and magazines. We saw *The 1/- Paper, Black Dwarf, Left, Socialist*

---

8. Clearly, they didn't believe in "keeping up the day" and maintaining traditional celebrations on their proper date.

Worker, *Solidarity*, and *Morning Star*. A Saxophonist played the old German tune "Tannenbaum" (also known as "O Christmas Tree"); this was clearly meant to signify the socialist anthem "The Red Flag," which had adopted the melody, but nobody sang along to any of the words.

Then the march set off, with around 300 participants. As they marched, someone handed out song-sheets of "The Internationale" in English—and French. Playwright activist Bruce Birchall occasionally exhorted the marchers in Trinity Street through a loud hailer (bullhorn): "This is only the beginning!" was the deluded slogan. How many times have I heard that from activists of all stripes over the subsequent years? Clearly, some of the grads, remembering what had happened a year earlier in Paris, imagined that this was the beginning of a similar student insurrection. The lessons of May '68, which had been a total failure of the students' aims, had not yet sunk in. People often emulate unsuccessful movements and actions, believing that a later reenactment of the same thing will succeed "this time." There used to be a word, *mumpsimus*, that describes a person who insists on believing, against all evidence, in something that has been categorically disproven.

The wannabe revolutionists continued to march towards ultimate victory. "Outside the University Senate House, the march was halted by the constabulary in order that the traffic might flow again. An ultimatum was delivered to the Senate House, but the march soon resumed, unanswered." It then continued past the city Guildhall, where we heard some otherwise unintelligible slogans chanted containing the word *bourgeoisie*. Then finally, after a feeble rendition of "The Internationale," the march returned to Christ's Pieces, where, after a speech from a building worker who had somehow turned up, the carriers of the red flags went back to their respective colleges for tea and crumpets.

Ways and Means

Getting something for nothing is always attractive. It is a means of profiting personally, but also of "getting back" at the system.

NIGEL PENNICK

When I was at grammar school there was a scandal when some boys discovered that a chocolate machine at the railway station could be emptied of its stock. After a coin was placed in the slot, a chocolate bar could be taken from a drawer. But someone discovered a method of manipulating the drawer that allowed more than one bar to be taken at a time. So they would take three or four for themselves and their friends. Then someone got greedy, and emptied the machine, selling the chocolate bars at knock-down prices in school. Now it was obvious something illicit was going on. The culprit was caught and punished by the headmaster, though somehow he avoided prosecution for theft.

In the late 1960s in Amsterdam, there was a magazine called *Freeway to Amsterdam* that was distributed for free (of course!). With a rainbow-coloured cover,[9] it was published by one of the underground press groups and it provided examples of things that could be accessed for free in the city. It provided instructions for entering places without paying (such as an unguarded back entrance to Artis, the zoo), recommended joining tours of the Heineken Brewery to get free beer at the end, and explained a technique of hitting tram-ticket machines which would then disgorge coins.

In Britain, the newer coin-operated telephone kiosks had a receptacle where coins were returned if a call had been unsuccessful. This receptacle had a metal cover which could be pushed back to retrieve the coins. It was possible to use a matchstick to jam this cover in the open position, so coins would accumulate above it. Then the scammer would visit the box and receive free money. I did not know about this until, in a phone box in Oxford, I had my money returned but the cover was jammed. I pulled the offending matchstick away and lo!—a

---

9. In the 1960s, the rainbow had a different meaning than it took on in the twenty-first century. Then it was emblematic of universal peace and had no significance with regard to gender or sexual orientation. The rainbow flag appeared at a peace march in Perugia, Italy, in 1961. Called the "Peace Flag," it was designed by Aldo Capitani (1899–1968). Six years later, rainbows appeared prominently in the psychedelic art on the album cover of the Beatles' *Magical Mystery Tour*.

cascade of coins came tumbling out like the jackpot from a one-armed-bandit. After that, every time I passed a telephone kiosk, I checked if the matchstick scam was in operation.

Gandalf's Garden *Plants a Seed*

Cambridge Voice received exchange publications from many places. One of them was the spiritual magazine *Gandalf's Garden*. This was run out of a storefront on King's Road in the Chelsea district of London. It was right near the fashion shop Granny Takes a Trip, which had half a car sticking out of the front. In 1969 I went there and was greeted by the proprietor, Muz Murray, who gave me a free meal. This was much appreciated, as I was hard up and out of work at the time.

Muz and I talked for several hours about geomancy, astrology, meditation, and "New Age" subjects. Then he asked me if I would like to run a "seed centre" in Cambridge—a meeting-place for spiritually minded people of all pathways. I agreed. Upon returning home, I found a space for this above the Arjuna whole-food shop in Mill Road.

So once a week, I ran the Gandalf's Garden Seed Centre there, which attracted about twenty people. They included Sannyasins,[10] Buddhists, astrologers, communards, and Sufis. The communards had connexions to communes at Larling and New Buckenham in Norfolk, where I assisted with digging their land and preparing food. But the Sufis were intent on taking over. I argued with them that recruitment to their belief system was not the function of a Gandalf's Garden Seed Centre, and that they should respect others' differing pathways and go elsewhere. They became increasingly heavy towards me, and I feared that something unfortunate would occur—what in those days would hase been called a "bad scene." So I decided to close down the Seed Centre, which I did, and the "search for a perfect light" came to an end.

---

10. These were early followers of the Indian mystic Bhagwan Shree Rajneesh (aka Osho); there were several of them floating around Cambridge at that time.

NIGEL PENNICK

A New Series—Fun Supplies the Power

The tenth issue of *Cambridge Voice* was not followed by number 11, but by series 2, number 1. I had managed to get into the Cambridge Guildhall archives quite openly as a *CV* reporter, and had discovered planning documents that projected a "Main Town Road" which would have destroyed large swathes of housing. It was a link-up of roads that included the new bridge over the Cam which was already annihilating Walnut Tree Avenue. In addition to the Main Town Road were numerous roundabouts and new link roads which would have hacked their way through the Kite Area, parks, and the commons of Cambridge Town, all while leaving the University untouched. I drew a map of this, which became the cover of *Cambridge Voice*, printed in mid-blue ink on white paper. Clearly, the Town was being sacrificed for the University. It was an outrageous attack on local identity, the *sociocide* later identified by the Dutch architect Aldo van Eyck. (Van Eyck identified sociocide in an interview with William Rothuizen in the *Haagse Post* on December 14, 1974, giving as an example the destruction of the Kattenberg neighbourhood in that city: "The difference from genocide is that the people stay alive, though everything else is gone . . . all intersocial relationships vanish and the people are left sad and uprooted.")

The Fight for the Commons

Inside *Cambridge Voice* no. 2/1 was a two-page spread titled "The Siege of Cambridge." With my documentary sources from 1947 to 1969, the map showed the dereliction which had gripped parts of the Town, especially the Kite Area and Mount Pleasant, north of the river. Eight multi-deck car parks were planned, and common land was set to be obliterated by roads. This plan coincided with a government initiative to list all English common lands. The common lands were lands that could be used by the common people, a convention which dated back to the abolition of slavery in England in 1066 by William the Conqueror. Over the years, powerful lords and institutions had "enclosed" them, privatising them as their own property. Fences and ditches had been made to exclude the local residents.

WYRD TIMES

There had been many historical rebellions against enclosure. In Cambridge in 1549, Jake of the Style had led the townspeople to tear down the fences and fill in the ditches that the University had used to enclose common land. The free Digger publication *Walrus* (no. 2, December 1969) reproduced Jake's assertion of July 10, 1549:

Common to the Commons
Again I restore
Wherever it has been
Yet Common before.

Theft by the powerful of the common land of the people of England is at the heart of the Diggers' origin. Customary law and tradition should always take precedence over arbitrary rule. A century after Jake of the Style's success, in 1649, Gerrard Winstanley and his Diggers had occupied common land at St George's Hill in Surrey. They were forcibly removed by Cromwell's soldiers, but their stand for the commons, like that of Jake before them, was remembered. Like many English people of the yeoman and labouring classes, my ancestors had been driven from the land by enclosures and, without compensation, forced to work in the mills and mines of the Industrial Revolution, join the army, set out to sea, or emigrate.

On the back cover of *Cambridge Voice* no. 2/1 was "Fight for the Commons," an article in which I compiled data on the existing commons and provided a chronology I obtained from a visit to the council offices, where I perused the minutes of the Commons Committee. There, I found that, in addition to the Enclosures, pieces of the Cambridge Commons had been taken illegally over the years. Donkey's Common was illegally enclosed from 1829, when a prison was built on part of it, and in 1941 the military requisitioned the other half. (Today, in the early twenty-first century, swimming baths, a sports hall, and a multi-deck car park occupy the area.) "Fight for the Commons" detailed how various parts of the Cambridge Commons were not registered by the council, which would inevitably lead to the land being taken for other purposes. We attempted to register these parts, but we were rebuffed by the authorities and told that this was the job of Cambridge City Council.

Cambridge Voice no. 2/2 was printed on alternating sheets of mid-green and pink paper, with red ink on the green, and dark blue on the pink. On the cover was the notice that the magazine contained "Also Mystic Space Lore." This was the "spin" put on "earth mysteries" at the time, thanks to Tony Wedd's 1961 booklet *Skyways and Landmarks* and John Michell's 1967 book *The Flying Saucer Vision*. "Mystic Space Lore" appeared in a centre-page spread with images of the outer planets and an astronaut, along with a map of ancient Cambridge showing the seven churches that stand in a straight line, as well as T. C. Lethbridge's drawing of a series of chalk-cut figures he claimed to have discovered near the ancient earthwork called Wandlebury to the south of the city. These, known as the Gogmagog Hill Figures after the nearby Gog Magog Hills, were contentious landmarks that would later inspire personal interventions by John Nicholson, the Situationists, and the Institute of Geomantic Research.

Also in this issue was my article "East Anglian Wooden Architecture," which chronicled the continuing destruction of Cambridge's heritage of old barns, workshops, and the last windmill in the city. Illustrated with my photographs, the "woodens"—as we called them—were weather-boarded buildings with pantile roofs, some of them dating from the eighteenth century or even earlier. I noted that "these buildings possess more true Cambridge character than anything that could be erected in their place . . . the East Anglian Wooden Architecture is unique and may soon be no more." Indeed, soon it was all gone.

Cambridge Voice no. 2/3 was on yellow paper printed in dark green ink on the cover and black and orange inside. Headed with "Give Your Head a Holiday," the main contents were a "Buswatcher's Report January 1970" by the doyen of Cambridge bus knowledge Mark Seal (who later wrote historical booklets about Cambridge buses); more Mystic Space Lore including "Town and Gown UFOs"; and my retrospective of the Anglian

Diggers up to that time.

Cambridge Voice no. 2/4 was printed in red on white paper. Continuing the theme of Mystic Space Lore, the editor of *The Ley Hunter* magazine, Paul Screeton, wrote a piece on leys, straight lines linking sites of ancient sanctity; Mary Caine wrote about large zodiac figures in the landscape; my article described and explained the image on the issue's front cover, which showed leys across an old map of the city, including one of seven churches I had noted in 1967; and Andrew Munro, a leading Situationist, wrote about the "Gog-Magog Hill Figures." By now, dissident undergraduates like Munro had been drawn to *Cambridge Voice* by our stance against University oppression and our interest in the inner nature of place. A map, drawn by me, showed the numerous ancient earthworks, dykes, and straight roads around Wandlebury where the hill figures were. Another page featured the first appearance of Braingrader, a parody diary mocking effete undergraduate wannabe revolutionaries of the "Soc Soc" (Socialist Society) and similar groups. Soon, an actual *Braingrader* publication came into existence.

This issue also had a pullout centre section titled *The Other Britain: A Record of Pre-Doomsday Resistance*. "These are the voyages of the space planet Earth," the editorial began:

> We are all inhabitants. All under sentence of death. Death, of which the Bomb was a reminder, has gone underground. The mass death is being achieved in subtler ways: radiation, fall-out, overpopulation, poisoning of air water soil, dumping of atomic waste, leaking of killer gases, torture, massacre, human settlements in ruins, plagues, encroachments of mechanised surroundings and mechanised people ... you should know, you live in it! ... While the resources of the planet run out, more species become extinct.

The editorial continued on in a similar vein, foreshadowing the existential angst that would be seen half a century later in the writings of the environmentalist movement. The pages of the pullout section contained reportage and comment on contemporary political posturing. On the back cover of *The Other Britain* was my article titled "Geomancy," a short piece which was a forerunner of my future career of writing and lecturing about the subject.

King Street Market

Cambridge Voice no. 2/5 was captioned "The Cambridge They Try to Hide!" and had a foldout cover printed on white paper in a purple-green fade. On the front was a series of photographs of derelict Town buildings in Cambridge: a factory, a pub, shops and houses. The back cover carried advertising from a *Cambridge Voice* associate, jeweller Bill Powell's Workshop, which was a "hand-work community" in a shop on Magdalene Street next to the river; a Galactic Intervention–produced advertisement for King Street Market; and another for the place where we ate our favourite Indian food, the New Bengal restaurant. When the cover was unfolded, it revealed a Galactic Intervention poster (drawn by me) of a bird's-eye view of King Street. This was an advertisement for the new shop, King Street Market, depicted in its setting. Number 2/5 also contained another flyer for King Street Market, which I illustrated in a style influenced by the Amsterdamse School artists.

The Arts Syndicate had failed to find its own commercial premises from which to operate, but Bill Powell's Workshop and the King Street Market were independent—but connected—realizations of some of the Arts Syndicate's ambitions. King Street Market was opened early in 1970 by John Nicholson's mother, former actress Nella Greene. I did the sign lettering on the fascia of the building. English psychedelia, in art as well as music, always looked to the traditional vernacular arts of the fairground, the circus, and the seaside, and my signage reflected this tradition. King Street Market was the first shop in Cambridge to sell tarot cards, and soon became the place to go for occult books and underground newspapers from Britain and the United States. Before King Street Market, no one had had the contacts nor recognised either the "underground" or the occult

Armeswerk no. 2, 1969. Lettering and design by Nigel Pennick.

market. Shortly afterwards, all the main bookshops in Cambridge started carrying tarot cards, but King Street Market sold esoteric titles that the mainstream shops could not or would not stock. Around this time, I was commissioned to draw a cover for a book of Aleister Crowley's poems denouncing Mussolini. It was used on the limited edition which emerged.

Cambridge Voice no. 2/6 was the last. It continued the "Kite Area" theme, with a foldout map in the centre showing the streets and the derelict buildings along them. The article was compiled by Henry Bosanquet with assistance from local librarian Mike Petty, and Enid Porter, doyenne of Cambridgeshire folklore. This time around, the Mystic Space Lore consisted of an article by G. D. "Raz" Croft about the esoteric geometry and mystic meaning of the Round Church. I did not work on this issue, as we had a disagreement. Over the next few months, I produced a few issues of *The Other Cambridge*, *Armeswerk*, and *Walrus*, as well as working after hours on new discoveries in algal research. By now I had escaped from the class-and-gender divide of the Botany School and was working for the government at a new laboratory in Storey's Way. There I was the first person in the world to notice the existence of scales on an unarmoured dinoflagellate, *Oxyrrhis marina*, and—in collaboration with electron microscopist Ken Clarke—to publish an article documenting this. Subsequently, I was the author of twenty-eight scientific papers before the unit was closed in 1985 by the Thatcher government. My scientific publications included descriptions of eight heretofore unknown species of algae.

Slim Smith comic, published by the Land of Cokaygne, 1972.

Enter the Land of Cokaygne

King Street Market was still flourishing, but John Nicholson obtained better premises at Jesus Terrace on New Square in the Kite Area, so the original location was shuttered. After our disagreement, we did not see each other for a few months, until one lunchtime I was eating spaghetti bolognese in the Corner House café in King Street, and in came John. He hailed me, came over and sat down, had some lunch, and then the rift was healed over several cups of coffee. Another chapter began in Cambridge "underground" publishing: Cokaygne Bookshop took over the mantle of King Street Market and continued to be *the* place for "underground" newspapers, British and American, as well as psychedelic posters and occult books.

Neither King Street Market nor Cokaygne Bookshop were hippy "head shops" (which sold the paraphernalia of drug-taking), but genuine alternative stores. King Street Market opened at a time when we recognised no distinction between radical politics, the struggle for rights, the environment, art, local small businesses, "alternative" culture, local folklore and history, and esoteric spirituality. It was John Nicholson who coined the rubric "ancient skills and wisdom," which so aptly encapsulates the nature of the hidden heritage that underlies our culture and which we pursued along several avenues of approach. The overall business—the shop, the publishing imprint, and the printing workshop—was folded into a limited company called the Land of Cokaygne Ltd., named for the mythical English land of plenty. As John Nicholson put it: "I want to make a world which doesn't exist."

The name for this new venture was significant. I was with John Nicholson when someone asked him what Cokaygne meant—"Was it a cant version of 'cocaine'?" the drug-oriented querent asked. John replied: "No. Cokaygne is the only English paradise I know of." The Land of Cokaygne is a medieval paradise, where everything is provided without anyone having to work—food is abundant and free. Pieter Bruegel the Elder made a painting of this land of abundant pleasant idleness (the Dutch version of this earthly paradise is *Luilekkerland* ["Lazy-tasty Land"] and in Germany, *Schlaraffenland*) ["Lazy-monkey Land"]. The naming of names is significant, even when their origins are all but forgotten.

One "division" of the Land of Cokaygne Ltd. was the

Cambridge History Agency, which published guidebooks to Cambridge written by Henry Bosanquet, some of which featured my drawings. Henry also produced a booklet advocating in favour of trams in cities, deploring the destruction of twenty city tram systems in Britain between 1945 and 1962. In 1971, a new multi-deck car park opened and John greeted it with a critical pamphlet, *Tribute to Moloch*, for which I drew the cover. Also in 1971, the booklet *S.O.S. Cambridge* was published for an exhibition sponsored by *Cambridge Voice* at the Folk Museum. It detailed the major changes in the Town over recent years, including the demolition of medieval buildings along one side of Bridge Street by St John's College in 1938, and the destruction of many other fine historic non-University buildings since. The Land of Cokaygne began publishing a weekly magazine detailing all the films, theatre performances, gigs, and exhibitions in the forthcoming week. Called *Cambridge Scene*, it waxed popular and profitable. Sporadically, I would draw a cover for the magazine. *Cambridge Scene* allowed Cokaygne to fund new ventures.

Language and Words

Having heard Slim Gaillard's records at an early age, I was aware that language is a very flexible thing, and one can use it to create new words. In the mid-1940s, Gaillard devised a "hip" language, *Vout-o-Reenee*, words of which were sprinkled through his songwriting. Some of these words were current among jazz musicians at the time. Expressions such as "Groovy oroonee macvouty, mellow!" was pure Gaillard, though. In his *Vout-o-Reenee Dictionary*, he explained "Vout-o-Reen-ee" as "good performance, music," and "Vout-o-la" as "joy." "Vout-ville" was Gaillard's word for a town, and the planet Earth was "Globe-o-Vooty." Some words that prefigured later beatnik idioms played on alternative descriptions of things, like a jazz-age equivalent of ancient Northern Tradition kennings. So, a mountain was a "ground hump"; a star was a "twinkle"; something made of steel was "train track"; a door-key was a "twister"; a baker, a "wheat burner"; and a duck, a "web-stomp." "H-twenty" was water, and "H-nineteen" meant something was damp. Slim Gaillard performed an early version of the rock-'n'-roll song "Tutti Frutti," to which Little Richard added the memorable refrain "A-wop-bop-a-lup-bop, a-wop-bam-boom!"

Slightly later than Vout-o-Reenee came the beatniks, with their own patois. Beatnik comments frequently began with "like" and ended in "man," such as "Like nothing, man!" (meaning "useless") and were another alternative mode of expression I came across. Also the suffix "–ville," which Gaillard had used earlier, could be added to any word. So, for instance, death was "tombsville," and the apex of experience—the earthly paradise—"endsville." One of my early publishing ventures was called *Th'Endsville Press*, and John Nicholson's Land of Cokaygne had the same reference.

Cambridge Provocations 1970–71

Friday the thirteenth of February 1970 in Cambridge turned out to be an unlucky day for some. It happened to be the culmination of Greek Week, an event sponsored by the Greek government. At any other time, this would have been just another cultural celebration which would soon have passed into forgetfulness. However, Greece at that time was under the yoke of a military junta which had overthrown the elected government in 1967 and forced the king into exile. During Greek Week, a local cinema showed the Costa-Gavras movie Z, which depicted in graphic detail the repression of Greek citizens by agents of the junta. The letter "Z" appeared as graffiti on many walls in the city centre, and a demonstration was called for the evening of the thirteenth outside the Garden House Hotel where the Greek regime was holding a reception for the great and good of Town and Gown. The hotel was in a dead-end street next to the river, and a large group of protestors, almost exclusively students, crammed into the small space waving placards and chanting. Of course, it was obvious to everyone except the hotel staff and the police what was going to happen. I was not there, as I never participated in futile, virtue-signalling gestures.

Afterwards at Peabodys, the Situationist Andrew Munro gave us an eyewitness account, claiming that they had planned

Free England by Nigel Pennick, Rupert Pennick, and John Nicholson, 1976.

in advance how to escalate the provocation and then get away. The police were ineffective, hemmed in by the crowd on a narrow street. Everything kicked off when, according to his account, Munro evaded the police line and smashed the locked glass door of the front entrance. The demonstrators pushed the police aside and swarmed in, trashing anything they came across. Guests fled onto the lawn outside by the River Granta—the garden of the Garden House—but some were assaulted there by enraged activists. Eventually, the police received reinforcements and cleared the now-wrecked hotel, arresting a number of the activists who were then charged with various offences against the public order. The Situationists evaded arrest and escaped. They were delighted when members of the Cambridge University Socialist Society and other agitators were inept enough to be captured by the police. In those days—before the surveillance society of CCTV cameras and police bodycams—so long as one ran away, one was never caught.

Charges were brought against those arrested. The accused, aged between nineteen and twenty-five, were sent for trial and eight of them received prison sentences of between nine and eighteen months. When the verdicts and sentences were announced, the demonstrators' supporters—which included undergraduates and members of the University—staged a protest outside the Cambridge Guildhall, seat of the City Council. The Guildhall overlooks the marketplace on Market Hill, which at the time of the protest was open and trading as usual. I was there as a reporter for *Cambridge Voice*. It was not long before some angry Townspeople began to remonstrate with the demonstrators and others then pelted them with eggs, tomatoes, and vegetable waste gleefully donated by stallholders.

As reported in *Cambridge Voice* no. 2/5:

> After the "Greek Rioters" were sentenced, the routine demonstration took place outside City Hall, protesting the sentences. Unfortunately, rather than arousing sympathy for their cause, the demonstrators found themselves the subject of another demonstration. Amongst the demonstrators were the chairwoman of the Cambridge Association for Prevention of Drug Addiction, and her husband, a don and a member of the National Council for Civil Liberties. She said she would "like to make it clear that the crowd throwing things at the demonstrators was not a hostile one, neither was it made up of skinheads. It was a collection of youngsters urged on by older people." Another woman claimed: "It was all started by a man standing in the Market Square. I saw him handing eggs to a group of youths and urging them to throw them at the students. I went up to him and asked to stop it, and I told him he was inciting a riot. Then he smashed an egg on my head." Cops were called who kept things moving as egg and

tomato streamed down the front of the Guildhall. Soon the police Commander arrived and appealed to the demonstrators to keep their number down to avoid antagonising Town youth.

This was a clear example of what Townspeople thought of undergraduate wannabe revolutionaries.

The Situationists

One night towards the end of 1969, *The 1/- Paper* office was attacked by Situationist undergraduates who sympathised with *Cambridge Voice*'s psychogeographical interests. The Situationists broke in when the office was empty and trashed it completely, destroying documents and throwing an IBM Selectric typewriter through the window and into the street below, where it was smashed to pieces. When we were told about it, I was annoyed they had destroyed the typewriter—after all, they could have stolen it and given it to *Cambridge Voice*! Then we would have had a second one to prepare our offset-litho artwork for the printer.

Although small in number, the International Situationists (to give them their full title) were also active in other ways. Although the activities of Cambridge Native Press were not connected with their ideology, there were points of contact. The Situationists issued a series of provocative publications: *Hash, Gas, Period,* and *Omphalos*. They also printed a leaflet titled *The Female Fuckability Test* which listed numerous sexual techniques in graphic detail. Situationists visited the women's colleges of Newnham and Girton, and a female member put a copy in each student's pigeonhole where mail was picked up. This provocation caused an enormous scandal in the University. On the other side, a feminist magazine titled *Bloody Women* appeared around this time. Also, unconnected with the Cambridge Native Press syndicate were other short-lived "one-offs" or periodicals from various groups and individuals, both Town and Gown. Among them were *Dream, Burp, Fred, Flash, Really, Dr. Organ, Warp, Friday, Meat,* and *Nitelite*. Probably this list is incomplete. It was a time of great creativity in small publishing.

WYRD TIMES

Andrew Munro was a main activist in the Cambridge Situationists. He told me that it was he who incited and led the rioting grads into the Garden House Hotel and afterwards got away scot-free. He wouldn't always be so lucky. It emerged later that he had been manufacturing LSD at a clandestine laboratory somewhere in Cambridge. He kept it secret for obvious reasons, and none of us knew. In London he progressed to much greater things. He ran an industrial-scale manufacturing laboratory in Kingston-upon-Thames for an operation that distributed the drug at music festivals all over Britain. Caught by undercover police as part of "Operation Julie," along with his co-conspirators Richard Kemp and David Solomon, Munro was tried in 1974 and sentenced to ten years in prison. It was rumoured that he helped fund the publication of the first English edition of Raoul Vaneigem's 1967 Situationist work *Traité de savoir-vivre à l'usage des jeunes générations*.[11] Translated from the French by John Fullerton and Paul Sieveking, it was published as *The Revolution of Everyday Life* in 1975 by Practical Paradise Publications in London. But before this post-Cambridge career took off, Munro was involved in the archaeological scandal of the Gogmagog Hill Figures, a sorry tale of goodwill and rebuttal that involved John Nicholson, Sylvan Forrester, and the Institute of Geomantic Research. More on this later.

The Rise and Fall of Cambridge Dada

Cambridge Dada was an offshoot of Birkenhead Dada. Birkenhead is the city across the River Mersey from Liverpool, connected to its larger neighbour by rail and road tunnels and a ferry service.[12] Cambridge Dada came into being after notices on soup labels (not Campbell's) were posted around town announcing a Dada meeting in Lady Mitchell Hall on January 29, 1971. The hall, of course, was closed and the meeting of a few

---

11. The original French title translates to "A Treatise on Good Manners for the Younger Generations."

12. In 1860 Birkenhead was the first city in England to operate horse-drawn trams, introduced from the USA by George Francis Train. It has an electric heritage tramway that commemorates its pioneering tramline.

Dada publications, with cover art by Nigel Pennick, 1971.

people, mainly University undergraduates, took place outside and adjourned to a pub. I was there, and was a participant in most of the Dada events of the next year or so. Later, it was claimed that 700 people attended the first meeting, and that the event ended with a performance of Helmut O'Rourke's playlet *Dung*. In its pomp, Cambridge Dada consisted of Alan J. Brame, Ian J. Ireland, Thom P. Gorst, Mark A. Quigley, Keverne J. A. Smith, Ted Parton, B. Andrew Statham, Dave Townley, and myself. The "Dadators" (editors) of the newsletters which emerged were me, Parton, and Townley.

On the day that the ancient coinage of pounds, shillings, and pence was abolished and the new decimal system was introduced, a "Soirée Dada" was held in Corpus Christi College cellars. Concentrated hydrochloric acid was purloined from a University laboratory and readied for the grand finale, where the new coins would be dissolved. The Soirée had poetry readings, clog dancing, and other Dada activities, culminating in the "light-fusing ritual," Dave Townley recorded (*Dada* no. 7, published in 1971 by Cambridge Dada). What actually happened was that, after some performances, a group of anarchists attacked the event violently, fusing the lights and throwing acid around in the dark. Several participants were injured (though not seriously). On May Day, 1971, at Selwyn College Diamond, the Cambridge Dada Mixed-Media Ensemble performed "songs of the Group's own composition" as well as Simultaneous Poetry, and the Dada film shown was "hailed as a masterpiece." Cambridge Dada approached Jim Ede, doyen of the art gallery Kettle's Yard, offering an exhibition of Dada artefacts. Ede refused and so became the *bête noire* of the Dadaists, receiving in due course a parcel composed of strips of cut-up clothes accompanied by typescripts of Dada poetry.

Other Dada events took place during the year, including the Helmut O'Rourke Memorial Lecture. It was due to be read by Edgar Hornsby Nissen, a disciple who attended him on his deathbed. I was not at the event because I was in my lodgings debilitated by a virulent virus. The audience assembled and a short biography of O'Rourke was read out. Then there was a hiatus. The Dadaists on the stage nervously looked at their watches, waiting for Nissen to appear. After twenty minutes or so, another Dadaist entered the hall and ran to the front. Breathlessly, he announced that he had just received a telephone call that Nissen had died tragically in a car crash on the way to Cambridge. He called for a minute's silence, and everyone filed out, saddened. What they did not know was that Helmut O'Rourke, whose tragic life had been recounted as a preamble to Nissen's lecture—he had been a prisoner in Germany in World War I for being Irish (that is, British) and a prisoner in Britain in World War II for being German—was fictitious, and his death in a Nottingham hospital invented. Similarly, Edgar Hornsby Nissen (1936–1971) was also fictitious. The event was deemed a great success.

On Monday January 3, 1972, Birkenhead Dada set up an exhibition in the Everyman Theatre in Liverpool. Liverpool was at the time very radicalised by left-wing politics, and the theatre was dedicated to proletarian revolution. I travelled by train to attend the opening. It soon emerged that the Dada exhibition was not what the manager expected. He should have known, as Birkenhead Dada had earlier caused a stir by carrying a lavatory pan to the door of the celebrated Walker Art Gallery and demanded that it should be installed as an exhibit just like Marcel Duchamp's *Fountain* of 1917. The gallery staff called the police and the Dadaists were moved on.

Among other things, the Birkenhead Dada exhibits included a construction titled *Lucy's Lament on losing her Virginity to Sir Winston Churchill in a crowded Bus Shelter*; a framed sanitary towel titled *Period Piece*; *Turd in Jelly*, which actually was a plastic joke-shop dog mess embedded in a yellow lemon jelly; my pop art–style painting of a swastika;[13] and *The Feeding of the Five Thousand*, which consisted of loaves of bread and kippered herrings painted with red gloss paint, attached to a board. This and the jelly were intended to rot and stink during the putative three-week run of the exhibition. The contribution from the Arthur Cravan/Jacques Vaché Foundation appeared to have been lost in the post.

All was guaranteed to provoke, and the event became known as "The Banned Art Show." (In the twenty-first century this probably would all be considered mainstream—except for the swastika—and we might have won the Turner Prize.) After heated arguments, the exhibit was taken down. It had lasted three hours, but in that short time had been covered by television and local newspapers. The theatre's artistic director, Alan Dosser, deemed it too scandalous for the working class to see, though he said that the "bourgeois" might appreciate it. So we dismantled everything again and went home. It was suggested to the organiser, Alan Brame, that the exhibit should be shown again on March 29.

However, on January 5 *The Liverpool Echo* ran the headline "Art Show Won't Go On Again," stating that "the exhibition

---

13. This painting was originally made for *Swastika* magazine. It was first exhibited at an open-air art show on Christ's Pieces, Cambridge, in 1969, and subsequently—for a few hours!—at the Birkenhead Dada show in Liverpool. Later it was stolen, and today its existence and whereabouts are unknown.

which included a male contraceptive and a life-sized phallus[14] was closed by Everyman's artistic director Mr Alan Dosser." "This alleged art show will not go on," Dosser asserted. How an artistic director could have no knowledge of the notorious history of Dada beggars belief. On January 6, the newspaper stated: "Mr Harry Livermore, the Everyman Theatre chairman, is determined that the exhibition—phallic symbol and all— will never go on at the theatre." But as the plays scheduled to be performed were some sort of agit-prop performance then fashionable, the presence of Dada at any time undoubtedly would have undermined its solemn, revolutionary Marxist message.[15] Finally, on January 29, Dosser was quoted in *The Liverpool Echo* as saying: "I have already stated in a TV interview my attitude to middle-class students who spend their holidays interfering with a theatre which continually tries to make its work relevant to the people of Liverpool." I was not a student. I had taken a day off work in scientific research to travel to Liverpool, and the other contributors were not students either—one was an officer in the Royal Navy. And the theatre management had invited Birkenhead Dada to exhibit there in the first place. But the "class-war" attitude of the theatre management was clear to us all and inaccurate rhetoric was their stock-in-trade.

Back in Cambridge, the anniversary of the founding of Cambridge Dada was celebrated at the lamp in the centre of Parker's Piece, a large public park. At midnight on January 29, four Dadaists read simultaneous poetry "with percussion accompaniment" until 2:30 a.m. The lamppost long bore the

---

14. This was a reference to the aforementioned piece titled *Lucy's Lament on losing her Virginity to Sir Winston Churchill in a crowded Bus Shelter*.

15. This dour dogmatic political humourlessness at the Everyman Theatre contrasted markedly with the famous sense of humour and ironic wit of Liverpudlians. For more than a century, many nationally successful comedians came from Liverpool, including Bill Bennett, Harry Weldon, Robb Wilton, Fred Yule, Arthur Askey, Tommy Handley, Ken Dodd, Jimmy Tarbuck, Tom O'Connor, Stan Boardman, Les Dennis, Norman Vaughan, Bernie Clifton, Alexei Sayle, and Craig Charles, to name but the more famous. Politics poisons everything.

inscription "Reality Checkpoint," though it is uncertain whether it was named to commemorate this event. Subsequently, Cambridge Dada faded away, having had a brief but eventful existence. Unfortunately, the play *The Tragic Death of Helmut O'Rourke* was never staged (so far as I know). Birkenhead Dada continued for a while, producing the magazine *Square Deal* in 1972. Typed on stencils and duplicated, it had a "typewriter-art" heading, and inside an article consisting of words formed in the shape of a swastika, echoing my contribution at the Everyman Theatre.

"By Tre, Pol, and Pen . . ."

In January 1972, just after I returned from Liverpool, having participated in the banned Everyman Theatre art exhibit, I went to a social club called the Coffee Pot Club that I occasionally frequented, and there I met Ann Trevelyan, recently relocated to Cambridge from Great Yarmouth. We hit it off and were soon a couple. That year, among many other things we did together, Ann participated in the production of the Cokaygne Press publication *Arcana*.

The following year, in September 1973, we were married at the register office at Shire Hall, Cambridge.[16] We were both of Cornish descent, as our surnames showed, citing the old adage, "By Tre, Pol, and Pen, ye shall know Cornish Men" (and women). We had our honeymoon at Weston-Super-Mare on the Somerset coast.

Ann was working at the time for an estate agent, Bidwells, and the company found us a house to rent on Shelford Road close to their offices in Trumpington, south of Cambridge. The house suffered an electricity failure shortly after we moved in, caused by the wiring's rotted rubber insulation. The house had a long garden, and I planted seed potatoes oriented north–south, which was at right angles to the length of the garden. After I

---

16. As it turned out, we were married on the centenary of Alfred Jarry's birth, although this was unintentional. We only discovered the coincidence later when we were given a book on Jarry as a wedding present.

Drawing of Ann Pennick by Nigel Pennick, 1973.

planted them, I discovered they were illegal potatoes, for the Ministry of Agriculture had banned the popular King Edward variety that year. I had bought the seed potatoes legally, and now we were criminals for growing them. I let them grow anyway. Nobody noticed, as one variety's leaves look like any other, and we had a good crop.

Bidwells also had their own petrol pump, so we had subsidised fuel for our car during the petrol shortages caused by the 1973 oil crisis. Subsequently, when we had scrimped and saved enough money for a deposit, in 1974 we bought a new house in Bar Hill, a "new village" north of Cambridge. From 1975 on, our house would become the nerve-centre of the Institute of Geomantic Research, of which Ann was General Secretary, organizing many of our events and providing hospitality to our many visitors. There we started a family, and brought up three children—two sons, Martin (born 1976) and Sean (1978), and a daughter, Lindsey (1982).

Almanacks from Endsville

In 1972 I produced the first of four almanacks. The one for 1973 was titled *Pennick's Endsville Almanack*. It had an offset-litho cover with four panels showing the gradual completion of a tower on a temple that I designed. The text pages were drawn stencils printed on my mimeograph duplicating machine, with the exception of the first page—illustrated with astrological symbols, moon's signs, planetary signs, and a table of planets and houses—which was printed in purple on a spirit duplicator. The 1973 *Almanack* was published by Th'Endsville Press and printed at my parents' house in Southeast London, where my equipment resided at the time. The name *endsville* was Beatnik slang for the earthly paradise, the parallel of the English Land of Cokaygne, the Dutch *Luilekkerland*, and the German *Schlaraffenland*.

The second *Pennick's Endsville Almanack*, for 1974, had a cover showing the Earth from space, with cosmic waves and a man with outstretched arms appearing to ride the void. It was published by Megalithic Visions, Etcetera, the name I used after moving with Ann to the house in Trumpington.

Pennick's Endsville Almanack, 1974 and 1982.

There were no more almanacks produced over the next few years, but in 1979 I resumed the series and published *Pennick's Endsville Pagan Almanack* for 1980. This was issued under a new imprint name, Fenris-Wolf. It followed the format of the earlier Endsville Almanacks, but with additional material about Pagan festivals.

"Events beyond our control" in 1980 prevented a 1981 almanack from being produced. The final almanack, with the same title as the 1980 edition, was released in 1982. In the summer of 1981, *Cambridgeshire Ancient Mysteries* no. 1 appeared. An eponymous group was set up to further the local geomantic research we were involved with at that time, and the final almanack bore the imprint of the Cambridgeshire Ancient Mysteries Group. I never published another.

IV
SACRED LAND AND MEASURE

Revelation comes to those who invoke it through intense studies and a lively curiosity of Mind.

—John Michell, *The New View Over Atlantis*

Spiritual geomantic tour by horse-drawn wagons, County Kerry, Ireland, August, 1988. Diane "Seadancer" Battung at the reins, Nigel Pennick in front. Photo by Rosemarie Kirschmann.

Ley Hunting

An important element of British "alternative society" activities of the 1960s and 1970s was ley hunting. This is often overlooked by some academics who centre their studies on the counterculture of that era, for it was a peculiarly British and predominantly English phenomenon. It originated with alternative antiquarian research. In 1922 Alfred Watkins (1855–1935) published *Early British Trackways*, in which he expounded a hypothesis that ancient Britons had used straight tracks across the landscape for trading various merchandise, especially salt. These tracks, which he called *leys*, were still traceable, being marked by notable features in the landscape including mounds, standing stones, fords, sections of straight road, and churches that had been built on pre-Christian sacred sites. In 1925 Watkins followed up his *Early British Trackways* with *The Old Straight Track*, which gained a following and was reprinted many times afterwards. Ramblers who walked the land following leys were dubbed "ley hunters," much to the chagrin of professional archaeologists. An organisation was set up, and the Straight Track Club flourished until the outbreak of World War II in 1939, which put an end to rambling across the countryside.

In the 1960s, copies of *The Old Straight Track* were freely available in public libraries. Tony Wedd (1919–1980), a navy and air force veteran, came across the book in 1949. He had seen an unidentified flying object in 1941 at Thorney Island, and in the 1950s he read the early "Ufology" writings of George Adamski and Buck Nelson. In the late 1940s and 1950s Adamski published several books detailing his personal accounts of flying-saucer

Alfred Watkins. Symbolic drawing by Nigel Pennick, 1986.

sightings and alien contact. Nelson was an American farmer who claimed in his 1956 booklet *My Trip to Mars, the Moon, and Venus* to have travelled to other planets in an alien spacecraft. Wedd's organisation, the Star Fellowship, linked leys with the straight lines or "alignments" which French Ufologist Aimé Michel had described in his 1958 book *Flying Saucers and the Straight-Line Mystery*. In 1961 the Star Fellowship published *Skyways and Landmarks*, which first linked UFOs (as they had then been named) with leys. In 1961 a new Ley Hunters' Club was formed from a meeting between Tony Wedd, Philip Heselton, and Egerton Sykes, who had been a member of the original club.

In April 1965 the quarterly magazine *The Ley Hunter* appeared. Philip Heselton was editor. Like all such magazines, it was duplicated on a Roneo or Gestetner machine. Soon, Jimmy Goddard took over as acting editor, and later it passed to Paul Screeton and then in 1976 to Paul Devereux (in 1974 Paul Screeton had published a seminal earth mysteries book titled

Quicksilver Heritage: The Mystic Lays—Their Legacy of Ancient Wisdom). *The Ley Hunter* published accounts of individual leys as well as plenty of speculative material. Through these, the meaning of leys changed; they were rebranded "ley lines" and instead of providing guidance for alien space travelers, they radiated an "earth" energy which could be detected with dowsing rods. Watkins's original vision of ancient Britons traipsing from village to village with their pedlars' packs on their backs, carrying vital commodities, was overridden by more recent concerns. Pedlars—still common in Watkins's childhood—no longer roamed the country bringing necessities, so the idea of trackways for transporting merchandise no longer resonated.

These new ideas about "ley lines" began to filter through to those who had read none of the publications, and in the mid-1960s, having been told about lines on the landscape, I began to draw straight lines on maps, attempting to discover leys. In 1967 I noticed that seven medieval churches in Cambridge form a straight line—which I dubbed the "Cambridge 7-Church Ley." In 1968, in the short-lived magazine *Albion*, John Michell wrote an article entitled "UFOs and the Message from the Past." This inspired the "journey to the west" that I undertook with my girlfriend Mary to St Michael's Mount (and which I describe in the next section).[1] Michell's book *The View Over Atlantis* was published the following year and would prove to be a seminal work on geomantic matters. *Cambridge Voice* carried articles on "Mystic Space Lore" which referred to the burgeoning interest in what became known later as "earth mysteries," and in 1970, I published an article titled "Geomancy" in *The Other Britain*, a supplement to *Cambridge Voice*. Later, the Land of Cokaygne's magazine *Arcana* took this further, and subsequently, in 1975, the Institute of Geomantic Research was founded.

A Geomantic Pilgrimage

In Central London in May 1968, I bought a copy of a magazine I had not seen before. With a stylish cover printed in black,

---

1. Neither Mary nor I had read Wu Cheng'en at that time.

orange, and green inks, the last two colours of which were a fade that included a dragon, occult talismans, a pentagram, the Glastonbury Zodiac, flying saucers, and a recumbent nude woman, all influenced by or taken direct from Alfons Mucha, *Albion* no. 1 was a *must* to buy. Inside, printed over a too dark image of one of George Adamski's dubious blurred flying saucer photographs, and thus difficult to read, was an article by John Michell. I had never met him at the time. The article, titled "UFOs and the Message from the Past," described the flight of Unidentified Flying Objects in straight lines and connected them with the "ley" alignments promoted by Alfred Watkins and with the legendary landscape of England. This concept had been first put forward in 1961 by Tony Wedd in his booklet *Skyways and Landmarks*. The idea that straight lines on the landscape are connected with flying saucers was then called *orthoteny*. Michell made the analogy between the lines on the British landscape and the "dragon lines" of Imperial China, stating that they were lines of the "dragon pulse," some kind of subtle energy that—it was claimed—also provided power for the UFOs. Particularly fascinating was his description of the "most accessible and clearly defined of the English dragon lines." This line, Michell asserted, ran from St Michael's Mount in Cornwall to the East Anglian coast near Great Yarmouth, passing "directly over" a whole series of churches dedicated to Saint Michael.[2]

Back at the Tech in Cambridge, I showed this article to my girlfriend, Mary Davenall. We intended to drive to the West Country during the summer vacation, and so we decided to visit these numinous places. She owned a dark blue Ford Thames van, which I had painted in psychedelic patterns to make it so noticable that it was impossible to steal. This was because she had only the basic accident insurance and that did not include theft. When the summer came, we set out from Cambridge,

---

2. Years later, after we had set up the Institute of Geomantic Research, Michael Behrend analyzed this line mathematically and showed it was by no means as straight as had been asserted. But after this demolition, dowsers nevertheless claimed to have found it—and now, as "St Michael's Line," it has entered a certain canon of New Age belief.

Our psychedelic van, 1968. Photo by Nigel Pennick.

intending to visit most of the places John Michell had listed. We had become "seekers of the linear vision," as Paul Screeton later called "ley hunters." Michell had included the Abbey at Bury St Edmunds on his list, but that was eastwards, and so we omitted it. We went to the first site on the line, harassed by police all the way. Each time we passed into the district of another police force, a police car would pull out, follow, and stop us. Every time, we were stopped and searched, the van's tyres examined, and Mary's driving documents scrutinised closely for any possible offence. Each time, the police found nothing. It was harassment all the way in 1968 for young people in a psychedelic van.[3]

Having reached the great circular earthworks and stone circles of Avebury, we camped in a field. That evening, it began to rain. In the middle of the night we awoke, lying in several

---

3. I should note here that, although I enjoyed alcohol in all its forms, I was never a drug-taker. I didn't smoke, which precluded smoking pot, and I was enough of a chemist and botanist of the "trust no one and always watch your back" school to understand that anything one was offered in the drug line was probably not what one was told it was. My psychedelia came from real hallucinations without the intervention of drugs!

inches of water. So for the rest of the trip we slept in the van. In incessant pouring rain we detoured to Bradford-on-Avon where Mary's aunt lived. When we got there, the centre of the town was under water as the River Avon had risen far above its normal level. The bridge stood above the river, but at either end the road was deep in water. That year, massive floods hit many towns in southern England, and several people lost their lives. My grandmother in Guildford was taken from her flooded home; she died soon after. It was what would now be called "extreme weather" back in 1968.

When the flood at Bradford-on-Avon had abated somewhat, we resumed our pilgrimage to the west. In the next days we visited and climbed Burrow Mump and Glastonbury Tor. At the summit of Glastonbury Tor, I made the unwise decision to chalk the name of Thor in runes on the ruined church tower. I had just chalked the first rune, *Thurisaz* (Þ), when suddenly there was a flash of lightning. The sky opened up with torrential rain, and lightning flashed all around us. Fearing for our lives, we stumbled and slid as fast as we could down the steep hill to the refuge of the psychedelic van.

After recovering from this shock, we drove onwards to Othery, Burrow Bridge, and Brent Tor. Finally, after another night in the van, we arrived in brilliant sunshine at St Michael's Mount in Cornwall. I made several drawings of the mount, viewed from the mainland. We crossed the causeway—which is only passable at low tide—and made our way to the castle. We had achieved the goal of our geomantic pilgrimage.

Arcana

The Land of Cokaygne was set up in 1972 by John Nicholson in a shop in Jesus Terrace, on the corner of Portland Place. The shop fronted onto New Square, an asymmetrical, early nineteenth-century square with uniform terraces of weathered yellow-brick houses with a pedimented one at the centre. The square had only three sides, as the fourth adjoined on to Christ's Pieces, where a bus station had been enclosed in the 1920s. In 1972, New Square had, for some years, been concreted over to build a car park.

Arcana magazine began in 1972. It was offset-litho printed in the Land of Cokaygne's print shop in Portland Place, Cambridge. The printer was Pete Anderson. The old crew of *Cambridge Voice* was behind *Arcana*: John Nicholson, Cecilia Boggis, and myself. Slim Smith and I provided artwork. The first issues were typed by Ann Trevelyan (or Ann Pennick, after we married in 1973). A typesetting facility was soon set up in the print shop, and all further Cokaygne publications were typeset. Subtitled "A Magazine of Cambridge Occult Lore," *Arcana* had contributions from myself, Anthony (Tony) Roberts, John Michell (writing under the pen name Sylvan Forrester), Michael Behrend, David Garside, G. D. "Raz" Croft, Ken Clarke, and John Nicholson. Subjects ranged from the local sacred architecture of King's College Chapel and Ely Cathedral to landscape geometry.

The second issue of *Arcana*, 1972. The artwork shows one of the Gogmagog Hill Figures discovered by T. C. Lethbridge.

In June of 1972, the second issue carried an article by Sylvan Forrester titled "The Gods Awake: The Gogmagog Hill Figures." Hill figures are made in chalk grassland by cutting away the turf, leaving a white image. Several still exist. Usually, the hill figure is a horse, though there are two known anthropomorphic figures that are male—one of them, at Cerne Abbas, is ithyphallic. These contentious figures had been revealed in the 1950s in an archaeological investigation by T. C. (Tom) Lethbridge. He was unusual in the postwar era because, as a man of private means, he worked in the Cambridge University archaeological department as a freelancer. He was never employed there, and clearly his wealth and freedom rankled with some of the hierarchy. He had made an exemplary excavation of the War Ditches at Cherry Hinton. But now he was determined to find a hill figure at Wandlebury (an Iron Age earthwork south of Cambridge), which had been described by several medieval writers.

Lethbridge devised a unique method for locating the figure under the turf. He reckoned that where the chalk had been exposed for centuries, it would have eroded, leaving the area deeper than the surrounding surface. He rammed an iron rod repeatedly into the ground and put thin willow rods, all of the same length, into the holes. From this, he could see that in certain areas the sticks sunk deeper in the ground. Plotting these differences on a chart, he drew a figure of an "eye-goddess" riding on a horse that resembled the pre-Roman Celtic hill figure at Uffington. Under cover of night, a person or persons unknown pulled up many of the rods.

The archaeology principal, Professor Bushnell, had already pooh-poohed Lethbridge's assertions about a hill figure, and when he found it and wrote it up as a scientific paper, permission to publish in an archaeological journal was forbidden. So Lethbridge announced the discovery to *The Times* newspaper, and then wrote a popular book *Gogmagog: The Buried Gods* (1957). Since he wasn't on the University "staff" to begin with, he had not broken any protocols. But life was made difficult for him after that, and he eventually retired and went to live in Devon. Professor Bushnell became a leading light in the Cambridge Preservation Society, which took over and ran Wandlebury.

In the late sixties, Andrew Munro became interested in the Gogmagog figures, and corresponded with Tom Lethbridge. By then the site, marked "Lethbridge's Diggings" on the official plan of Wandlebury, was overgrown and small saplings had established themselves on the chalk figure, which had remained exposed. It emerged that the Cambridge Preservation Society had ordered it to be filled in with soil, but then deemed the process too expensive. With some Situationist comrades, Munro made a raid upon the site and they destroyed all the saplings.

Arcana had seven issues in all. There were many notable

articles that appeared in its pages, such as "Dragon Lines" by David Garside, for which I drew a map showing the prehistoric trackway called the Icknield Way that joins westward on to the Ridgeway through Wiltshire. This route is close to the ley line promoted by John Michell and which Mary Davenall and I had travelled in 1968. For the December 1972 issue of *Arcana*, I contributed a piece on the Cambridge seven-church alignment, King's College Chapel, and a philosophical article, "Organic Metaphysics," which examined the ideas of D'Arcy Thompson's 1917 masterpiece *On Growth and Form*. Printed in various colours, and with some text overprinted, the main illustrations were exquisite drawings of unicellular algae by the Latvian biologist Professor Heinrichs Skuja, who had died on July 19 of 1972. In two successive issues, John Nicholson published a two-parter titled "The Idol of Science," which explored the link between science, theology, and power.

The *Arcana* advertisements in 1972 and 1973 for Cokaygne Bookshop record the diverse breadth of authors available in this small independent bookseller located in a Cambridge backstreet: William Morris, Norman Cohn, John Michell, Martin Buber, Alfred Watkins, Arthur Edward Waite, Plato, George Woodcock, Francis King, Israel Regardie, William Burroughs, Georges Charpentier, Idries Shah, Heinz Höhne, Emmanuel Velikovsky, Katherine Maltwood, Louis-Ferdinand Céline, Aldous Huxley, Colin Wilson, Isidore Ducasse, T. C. Lethbridge, Alfred Rimmer, Lawrence Ambrose Hayter, Arthur Koestler, Lewis Spence, Ernst Doblhofer, Albert Camus, Black Elk, Saint Augustine, Aleister Crowley, Frances Yates, Dedwydd Jones, and Nigel Pennick.

In March of 1973, the Cokaygne Press published my influential booklet *Geomancy*.[4] Shortly afterwards, a centenary reprint of the Reverend E. J. Eitel's important 1873 work *Feng*

---

4. Later a pirated translation of my text was published in Germany, ironically helping to spur the modern German geomancy revival, in which I became a significant participant. It was reissued as part of an unauthorised collection titled *Geomantie oder die alte Kunst* (Geomancy, or The Ancient Art) by Werner Pieper's Grüner Zweig/Grüne Kraft imprint in 1993.

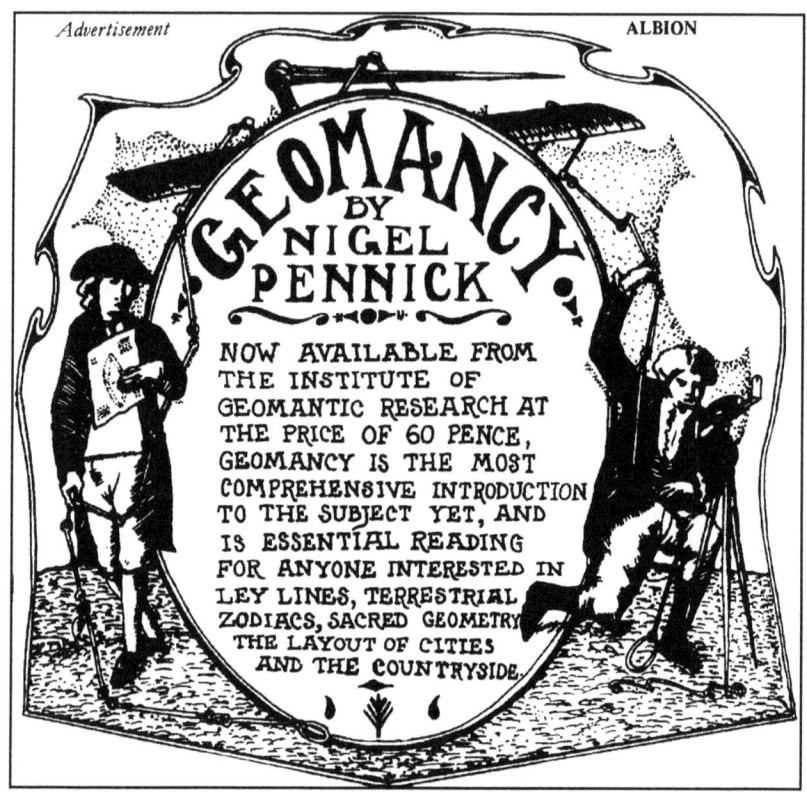

Geomancy advertisement from *Albion* magazine, 1978.

Shui, or The Rudiments of Natural Science in China was issued by Cokaygne. It was expanded with archival photographs by Ernst Borschmann and a foreword by John Michell. In the next year, my book *The Mysteries of King's College Chapel* saw the light of day, bringing the hidden esoteric roots of the chapel to public attention. It was reviewed and well received in *The Times* and the local press. *The Mysteries of King's College Chapel* appeared in 1974 and went out of print when the Land of Cokaygne ceased trading. It has subsequently been re-published several times. Cokaygne Press was also due to publish my second book, *The Mysteries of Ely Cathedral*. In 1972 I had been able to ascend the towers and walk the parapets of this great medieval building, and I had worked out the *ad quadratum* sacred geometry of the "Ship of the Fens," as it is known.

Nineteen seventy-four was a year of change. After centuries, the University's power to appoint eight unelected members to the City Council was abolished—democracy came late to Cambridge. It was also a year of political turmoil. The Conservative government under Edward Heath had challenged the coal miners, and a strike ensued. Shortages of coal, the main source of fuel for the power stations, led to shortages of electricity. Between January and March of 1974, a government edict decreed a "three-day week," meaning businesses could only use electricity on three days. This included the day when Cokaygne printed *Cambridge Scene*, a weekly detailing local gigs, exhibitions, films, public meetings, and so forth. Nothing like it had existed in Cambridge before, so it had become the main source of income for Cokaygne, and it was cut off summarily.

I was in the bookshop with John Nicholson in May 1974, when we heard on the radio that Graham Bond had died in London under mysterious circumstances. Bond was a virtuoso keyboard and saxophone player whose band the Graham Bond Organisation was prominent in the British "blues boom" of the early 1960s. The band was composed of fine musicians, all of whom later gained prominence in the rock and blues scene: Ginger Baker, Jack Bruce, and John McLaughlin, and later Jon Hiseman and Dick Heckstall-Smith. Bond's later work in the early 1970s included the albums *Holy Magick* and *We Put Our Magick on You*, which featured musical renderings of the Qabalistic Cross, Crowleyan invocations, and Druidic and Arthurian blues. Bond was enthusiastic about the Cokaygne Bookshop and recommended it at his last gig in Cambridge. We had seen him perform not long before this, and to hear that he had fallen to his death beneath a London Underground tube train at Finsbury Park was a shock—and a bad omen. The second half of 1974 saw the decline set in. Finally, the pioneering Cokaygne Bookshop and press ceased to exist after a brief but influential tenure.

Megalithic Visions and Fenris-Wolf

In 1974 I began to issue a series of publications under a

new imprint: Megalithic Visions, Etcetera. The first of the publications was my *Runic* booklet. It followed the same format as the *Endsville Almanacks*, with an offset-litho printed cover and a hand-drawn, stencil-printed (mimeographed) interior. It was printed by Janet Roberts at Zodiac House in Fulham, London, as were all the others in the series. The cover was an old engraving of a Viking ship in full sail, with oars rowing, followed by three others in its wake. The image was surrounded by a round ribbon of two dragons, with an inscription in "pointed" or "dotted" runes. All known runic rows were illustrated and described inside.

In an advertisement in the back, Megalithic Visions, Etcetera promoted the 1974 *Almanack*, back numbers of *Walrus* magazine, the Anglian Diggers' *postermanifestoster*, and my *Foulness* poster published in Southend-on-Sea, Essex. I designed this for the campaign The Defenders of Essex, led by Ron Barber, against Maplin Airport at Foulness. This offshore airport was to be built on the Maplin Sands in the Thames estuary, and would have destroyed the habitat of marine organisms and millions of migratory birds. It would have been an ecological catastrophe. The *Foulness* poster was commissioned by an activist group, the Desperate Society for a Change in Political Attitudes Towards the Environment (DSFACIPATTE). It was circulated around Southend and other coastal parts of Essex that would have been blighted by the development. The overall campaign was a success and the airport plans were scrapped.

The second of what became know as the "Megalithic Visions Antiquarian Papers" was my *Caerdroia: Ancient Turf, Stone and Pavement Mazes*. It contained a full list of recognised British turf mazes. (Later, in 1980, Jeff Saward adopted the name *Caerdroia* for his own long-running magazine about mazes and labyrinths.) Number 3 of the Antiquarian Papers was *Holy Sepulchre: The Round Churches of Britain*, also written by me. Its cover showed my drawing of the ruined round church at Ludlow Castle, Shropshire.

No more Antiquarian Papers emerged until 1975. I had been working on my first book, *The Mysteries of King's College Chapel*,

Megalithic Visions Antiquarian Papers No. 10: *The Swastika*.
Cover design by Nigel Pennick, 1975.

which was published by Cokaygne Press in 1974. We had moved from Trumpington by then, and I continued my publishing endeavours under a new rubric: Fenris-Wolf Publications. But the name Megalithic Visions Antiquarian Papers (which I'll abbreviate MVAP) continued. Number 4 of these papers was *European Metrology*, written by myself with a foreword by my father, Rupert Pennick. Numerology and metrology were his pet subjects, and in 1969 he had used numerology to win a lot of money on the football pools—enough to buy a house! *European Metrology* was released in May of 1975. It was not connected with the Anti-Metrication Board (see below). The next MVAP of 1975 was my *Leys and Zodiacs: An Introduction*. The Fenris-Wolf logo first appeared on number 5, an old engraving of a very male wolf. The next Antiquarian Paper, in August 1975, was my *Lost Towns of the Sunken Lands*, detailing the towns and territory lost to sea level rise around Great Britain in historic times.

Also appearing in August 1975 was the next Fenris-Wolf publication, my *East Anglian Geomancy*, MVAP no. 7. This detailed the landscape geometry and sacred geometry of medieval churches. It had an offset-litho printed insert of the plans of King's College Chapel and Ely cathedral, showing the *ad triangulum* geometry of the first and the *ad quadratum* geometry of the second. Also covered was Lethbridge's Gogmagog figure on a litho page showing a photograph of the original excavation and my reconstruction drawing with a facsimile of Tom Lethbridge's signature. My *Madagascar Divination* was MVAP no. 8, detailing the traditional Malagasy divination system called Sikidy as recorded in the 1890s by the Christian missionaries James Sibree and Lars Dahle. Number 9 in the series was *Dene-Holes and Subterranea* by Ann Pennick, describing the manmade chalk-cut shafts with lobed chambers in the chalk strata of Kent. It also described the chalk-mine complex known as the Chislehurst Caves. Finally, in November 1975, the final Megalithic Visions Antiquarian Paper appeared, number 10. It was my booklet *Swastika*, which had an introduction by my father. I dealt with the geometry, forms, and history of the symbol, illustrated by numerous examples drawn on the mimeograph stencils from which it was printed. This was the last Antiquarian Paper in the series.

The Anti-Metrication Board

During the early 1970s, the government began to promote the conversion of the United Kingdom's measures. In 1971 the ancient coinage of pounds, shillings, and pence was abolished and "one hundred new pence to the pound" replaced it. A fudge of the system was that a half-pence coin was introduced, but the half penny prices were soon rounded up, and it was withdrawn. New pence were referred to simply by the letter "P." Hence, a bus fare could be said to cost "ten pee." This coarsening of the value of coinage led inevitably to a "rounding-up" of prices, which is to say: inflation. (I have already recounted Cambridge Dada's response to decimalization at the Soirée Dada event.) Connected with decimalization was an attempt to convert weights and measures to the metric system. A Metrication Board was set up to oversee the transition.

In 1972 John Michell wrote a pamphlet titled *A Defence of Sacred Measures* which was published as Radical Traditionalist Paper no. 1. It was printed by Cokaygne at Portland Place, and the August 1973 issue of *Arcana* carried advertisements for Michell's works. These included his new book, *The Old Stones of Land's End*, and "two recent broadsides by a well-respected author against metrication and population control." The second of Michell's broadsides (his Radical Traditionalist Paper no. 2) was *A Defence of People and Population against the Alliance of Usurers and World-Improvers by Which They Are Now Threatened*.

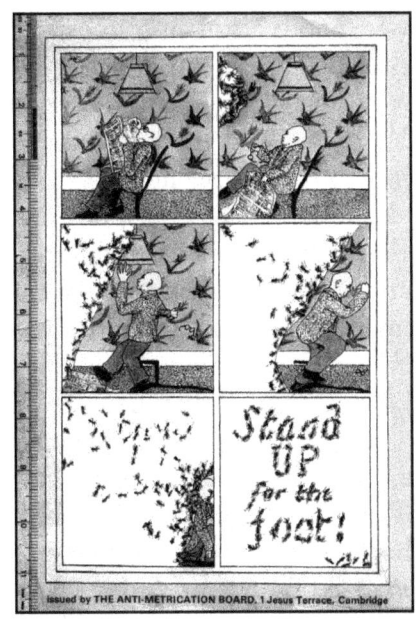

Stand Up for the Foot, 1972. Artwork by John Michell.

A Defence of Sacred Measures inspired the formation of the Anti-Metrication Board in 1973 at the Cokaygne Bookshop. A foot-long publicity card, *Stand Up for the Foot*, featured John Michell's artwork showing ants gradually eating away a man's room. Along the side of the card, like on a ruler, were the traditional graduations of the foot into inches and submultiples. The foot dated from an edict of King Edward I of England in 1306 which standardised the measure and abolished the Greek Foot, the Roman Foot, the Natural Foot, the Saxon Foot, the Welsh Foot, and the Northern Foot. The Imperial system of weights and measures was defined much later, in 1824.[5] So there

---

5. This is why the British gallon and the American gallon are different. The gallon had been originally standardised in England in 1601. In 1824 the

were 666 years of custom behind the foot, and it was for the foot that the campaign began.

On August 2, 1975, "The Grand Anti-Metrication Garden Fete" was held in the grounds of Blacklands House at Calne in Wiltshire, the home of Rupert Lycett-Green. There were alcoholic drinks, stalls, a tent selling books, the Calne Silver Band, and rides for the children. I was there with my wife, Ann, and we had come with Tony Roberts and his wife, Jan. We were in the book tent selling our works, when Tony saw a camel through a gap in the canvas. He was shocked, as though it was an hallucination. When he told us, we knew someone had brought a camel for children to ride upon. But we feigned ignorance and asserted that there were no camels in Wiltshire. Later, outside, Tony saw the camel again and realised that we had been winding him up. A play was enacted on a temporary stage with a Metric dragon that attempted to violate "Miss Foot." There was violence when some alcohol-fuelled local youths attacked the landowner and threw the bleeding Rupert Lycett-Green into the river. Shades of Town and Gown.

The Anti-Metrication Board was unsuccessful in its campaign to save the foot, but some other measures were not metricated. The Metric System was introduced to the UK in part, and then stopped before completion. The chaotic "system" in use today has Metric measures for some things, and Imperial measures for others. Milk and bottles of drink are sold in litres, but pints of beer are drunk in pubs; official maps and plans are in Metric, but miles per hour on speed limits and road-signs are in miles. The Tyne-Wear Metro in Newcastle, opened in 1980, was the first railway in the United Kingdom to be built using Metric measures rather than feet, chains, and miles, and all new road, rail, and tramway construction is now Metric. But the trams' speed limits in city streets are in miles per hour. Weather forecasts in the media give temperatures in Celsius, but wind speeds are registered in miles per hour.

British gallon was revised under the Imperial system, whereas the American gallon maintained the older measure.

NIGEL PENNICK

At the Spanish Embassy

Working at *The Times*, Tony Roberts had a press card. In September of 1975, he invited Ann and I to observe a demonstration against the Falangist dictator of Spain, Generalissmo Francisco Franco. Five rebels had been sentenced to death by garrotting, and protests were mounted in capital cities all over Western Europe. We went to London and joined Tony and Jan behind the police lines protecting the Spanish Embassy. There were several police cars and "Black Marias" (police prison vans) parked outside, some on the pavement of the closed-off street. Looking out from our safe vantage point with the other journalists, we heard chants of "*Franco assassinado!*" and saw a sea of placards and flags, including the red-and-black flag of the anarchists and the ubiquitous red flags seen at all demonstrations. Periodically, protestors surged against the police lines, which included policemen on horseback. The protestors were repulsed, sometimes with batons, and occasionally one would be dragged back to a waiting Black Maria to be taken into custody.

At one point, an unmarked car pulled up close to us and a man dressed in black got out. He was carrying a package, which he handed to one of the mounted policemen. After perhaps a quarter of an hour, another police officer came running, and called the journalists over to look. He showed us the same package, now opened. It contained theatrical fake blood, which, he told us, was being used by the protestors to pretend that the police had wounded them.

The Institute of Geomantic Research

Cokaygne Press was in terminal decline by 1975, and the print shop at Pembroke Terrace was abandoned. One day while I was at work in the laboratory, I received a telephone call. A former Cokaygne employee told me that they were stacking the remaining publications outside on the kerb, awaiting the arrival of a refuse truck, and did I want them? I took an early lunch and drove from Storey's Way across town as fast as possible. There, still being stacked, were several packages and an old tea chest stuffed with the remaining copies of my *Geomancy*

Prudence Jones, Nigel Pennick, and Michael Behrend at Institute of Geomantic Research Conference, Cambridge, 1978.

booklet. The ex-employee helped me load the books until my car was full except for the driver's seat. Most, but not all, were saved. Doubtless the remainder were trashed. I gave him my hearty thanks and a donation for his assistance. I had saved the remaining stock published by Cokaygne, and I now had copies of my own work to sell. I had never been paid for them before.

In the August 1973 issue of *Arcana* there was an announcement that the Institute of Cosmology had been "recently instituted with help from Cambridge University to promote original research into those subjects familiar to readers of *Arcana*." This was not strictly true; some undergraduates had promised to help with the project, and when they failed to honour their commitment, for whatever reasons, the Institute never materialised. Despite the failure, the concept was sound, and so in 1975 I set up the Institute of Geomantic Research (IGR), along with Prudence Jones and Michael Behrend. Tony Roberts was due to help us, but he withdrew owing to some disagreement.

Shortly after the IGR was founded, Cambridge University professor Glyn Daniel attacked us in the archaeological journal

Antiquity. He lamented such ideas existing in the "purlieus" of the University and quoted the *Oxford English Dictionary*'s entry for "Geomancy," which only dealt with the combinatorial divination systems (*geomantia, raml, Ifá*, etc.). The *OED* explained that this system was based on "lines or figures formed from the random placement of dots on paper" and so Daniel described us as "dotties at random." He also deliberately quoted the (then) obsolete form "geomants," which we adopted with alacrity, bringing the term "geomant" back into use as better than "geomancer."

But other attention was much more positive. An external account of the Institute of Geomantic Research appeared in the *Cambridge Evening News* on December 19, 1976. Journalist Dan Jackson had visited my house and interviewed us. Titled "THE ZEALOUS HUNTERS OF THE ZODIAC," and accompanied by a photograph of me holding my painting of a zodiac, the article told of a "small band of researchers," emphasising our independent and nonconformist stance. "These are no grant-cushioned university-cosseted eggheads," Jackson continued:

> Quite the reverse. They are outcasts of modern orthodox archaeology—the hardcore of the Institute of Geomantic Research.... Mainspring of the organisation is Mr Nigel Pennick, a microbiologist. In his 30s with a black mane and shaggy beard, he is intense, keyed up with enthusiasm. He spends hours, days, poring over old references, histories and plans of buildings like Ely Cathedral and King's College Chapel, compiling every scrap of fact, every hint of folklore, every minute measurement.... Mr Michael Behrend, a chemist who lives in Girton, is the mathematician of the group. His speciality is landscape geometry. He applies precise mathematical analysis to show that Britain is planned on a triangulation system. . . . He suggests sacred sites were arranged according to a grand overall plan. Prudence Jones is a truck driver who can translate medieval Latin. Her work takes her out and about and she can pursue her present exercise—to see if there is

Sheila and John Cann, 1977. Photo by Nigel Pennick.

any relationship or meaning among certain churches in East Anglia. She is looking at churches with a round tower surmounted by an octagon. Mr Pennick's wife, Ann, types the Institute's leaflets and also manages to investigate underground tunnels. Another Cambridge microbiologist, Mr John Cann, is more concerned with the local history aspect, and is currently working on plans and remains of Barnwell Priory, off Newmarket Road, Cambridge.

Jackson was very positive, though he called the men "Mr" and the women had no corresponding titles, and he was inaccurate in some points—Ann was, in fact, General Secretary of the IGR and did far more than type, and Prudence was a Cambridge University graduate as well as the first woman truck driver for the then-nationalised delivery company Roadline. The article ended with:

While the Institute's work may be scorned by some,

**IGR field trip to the maze at Hilton Huntingdonshire, 1983.
Photo by Nigel Pennick.**

their pioneer research will be useful to local historians today, and perhaps invaluable to historians tomorrow, when the only sacred buildings standing on their original sites will be cathedrals and stone circles.

Dan Jackson did recognise that we were entirely self-funded, as all my artistic work, publishing, and performing has always been—not a penny of taxpayers' money has ever been spent on any of my projects.[6] Also, as *Cambridge Voice* had pointed out earlier, architectural heritage was undergoing destruction at an alarming rate.

During its existence from 1975 to 1982, the Institute of Geomantic Research staged five symposia in Cambridge and produced the periodicals *Journal of Geomancy* and *Ancient Mysteries*, a series of "Occasional Papers," and one large-format book. We were overwhelmingly self-funding, but

---

6. In all my work—writing, publishing, art, music, and performance—I have never once received a penny from official patronage, grants, or from taxpayers' money. Everything I have done was always autonomous and self-funding, as a matter of principle.

Cambridgeshire Ancient Mysteries 1, 1981. Cover by Nigel Pennick.

naturally accepted various assistance and donations from Vince Russett, editor of *Picwinnard* magazine; my father Rupert Pennick; and Harold Wicks, the owner of a guest house in Saffron Walden for whom I drew business and advertising cards.

Our first publications were mainly duplicated with offset-litho covers and inserts. Together with Sheila Cann (*née* Andrews) and her husband John, Ann and I did all the physical work of collating copies. We also put issues in envelopes and mailed them to members and "exchange magazines," who reciprocated by sending us their own publications.[7] For the mystically inclined, a small-press magazine could join the Cosmic Circuit, which was similar to the American Underground Press Syndicate. Participants were exposed to magazines such as *Northern Earth Mysteries, The Ley Hunter, Fortean Times, The Wiccan, Magonia, Wood and Water, Quicksilver Messenger, The Cienfuegos Press Anarchist Review*, and many more British publications (not all were Cosmic Circuit members). We also exchanged with American journals such as, *inter alia*, the Californian *Stonehenge Viewpoint* and *The Pyramid Guide* (both from Santa Barbara), *Gaia* and *Spirals* (San Francisco), and *The Seven Whistlers* (Chula Vista).

We also got in contact with *Lantern* of the Borderline Science Investigation Group based in East Anglia, and I wrote articles for it and visited Ivan Bunn and Mike Burgess

---

7. Sheila, John, Ann, and I became humourously known as the "Press Gang" within the IGR (in the eighteenth and early nineteenth century, Press Gangs were the means of kidnapping people to serve in the Royal Navy).

John Cann and Nigel Pennick waiting for ghosts to appear in the middle of a cold night, Histon Manor, 1980.

in Lowestoft. I never saw the famous Rant Score Ghost there, unfortunately, although John Cann and I conducted an all-night ghost-watch at Histon Manor. I participated in another BSIG all-night ghost-watch at the site of Borley Rectory in Suffolk where, in the middle of the night, a mysterious yellow light was seen in a tree and an anomalous sound heard on our stereo tape recorder.

In 1978 and the two successive years, the IGR hired a stall in Cambridge Market Place during the City Leisure Fair. We sold publications, promoted geomancy by word of mouth, and gained some new members. We also regularly attended other organizations' moots, fairs, and conferences all over the country. Sometimes I or Prudence, or both of us, would be invited as speakers. Our most significant achievement was the recovery of material written by what we called "forgotten researchers."

In my work as a government scientist, I had access to the Cambridge University Library, with a ticket that enabled me to borrow books. During work-time it was a useful resource for scientific journals, but after hours I went there to look for geomantic material. The University Library is a small skyscraper with two six-storey wings flanking the central tower. Designed in brick by Gilbert Scott, and similar to his Battersea and Bankside power stations, it had an Art Deco feel. Modernist bronze figures could be seen above the entrance. Inside, Art Deco railings were in evidence. In the six-storey wings were the bookshelves, to which we had unlimited access. I walked around these wings, freely seeking out articles I knew of already, as well as other unknown journals that might be of interest.

On one occasion, on a dimly lit shelf, I came across a series of journals in light blue bindings. On the spine, in German black-letter type, was the title: *Germanien*. This looked promising! I took one down and opened it. It was a folklore journal, published in National Socialist Germany from the early 1930s until 1943. But it was not unmitigated political propaganda, for I found many remarkable pieces in it by obscure authors. Systematically, I borrowed volumes and went through them carefully. I photocopied what I felt was relevant and passed the articles along to Prudence Jones and Michael Behrend, who were able to translate them into proper English. They were a revelation. It emerged that the subject matter of 1970s "earth mysteries" had been preempted by a number of German writers over forty years earlier, and their work was unknown.

Germanien contained four articles by Kurt Gerlach (1889–1976), published in 1940, 1942, and 1943. Given the place and date, they had clearly never made an impact in geomantic circles. The articles were titled "Frühdeutsche Landmessungen" (Early German Land Measurements); "Böhmische Dörfer—geortet!" (Bohemian Villages—Orientated!); "'Heilige' oder zweckmäßige Linien über Böhmen" ("Sacred" or Functional Lines across Bohemia); and "'Richt'-Linien durch Deutschland" ("Straight" Lines through Germany). Straight lines on the landscape, orientation, sacred sites—all of the elements that British "ley hunters" studied were present! Gerlach's material was translated in part by Prudence Jones, and a full version of his work, translated by Michael Behrend, was published by the

IGR in 1976 as *Leys of the German Empire.*

We had already obtained a number of papers by Josef Heinsch (1886–?), including the best-known one from 1938 which Michael Behrend translated and we published as *Principles of Prehistoric Sacred Geography*. Both Zodiac House and Fenris-Wolf Publications produced editions. An issue of *Hagal* magazine from 1935 yielded another article by Heinsch, which was again translated by Michael and published as a Fenris-Wolf pamphlet titled "Find Your Local Holy Hill!" on June 28, 1979. The next day I printed the second Heinsch paper, *The Xanten Cosmographic Mosaic*. There are probably more Heinsch publications we never uncovered. In the University Library I found a run of the journal *Der Grafschafter*, which also contained relevant material. For example, in the edition of November 23, 1935, Heinsch had written an article Michael translated as "The 'Holy Mountain' Near Asperg (Moers District), 'Asciburgium'—an Old Hill of the Gods." This was published in *Ancient Mysteries* no. 17 (1980).[8]

Zodiac House edition of Heinsch translation.

Other writers I rediscovered and published were Freerk Haye Hamkens (1902–1985), who wrote an article in *Germanien* in 1934 titled "Trojaburgen" on the etymology, folklore, and traditions of the labyrinths which are called "Troy Towns" in English. In 1936, in the same journal, Siegfried Sieber wrote of "Ein Trojaburg in Pommern." This Pomeranian labyrinth is at a place called Stolp (now Słupsk, Poland), which once had

---

8. *Ancient Mysteries* was the new name of *The Journal of Geomancy*.

The Journal of Geomancy, no 3/4. Cover art by Nigel Pennick.

a Windelbahn festival connected with the local craftsmen's guilds. In a 1940 issue of *Germanien*, Friedrich Mössinger published "Baumtanz und Trojaburg" (Tree Dance and Troy Town), which connected the labyrinths with village dances around notable trees. The latter two papers were published as *Troytowns in Germany*, IGR Occasional Paper no. 10 (April 1978). All four of these papers were also published in *Trojaburgen*, jointly produced by Caerdroia and the IGR in January 1982. Wilhelm Brockpähler also wrote about the "Dorflinde," a trained linden tree found at the centre of traditional villages. In *The Journal of Geomancy* no. 3/4, we printed Michael Behrend's translation of A. Brachvogel's "The Chapel at Drüggelte on the Möhnesee" from the journal *Mannus* no. 34 (1942). Brachvogel detailed "holy lines" based upon solsticial solar lines radiating from the round medieval chapel there, which I visited in 1985.

On another shelf in the University Library, among Soviet Stalinist-era journals and American political monthlies, were bound copies of *Nationalsozialistische Monatshefte* (National Socialist Monthly). I looked through the volumes and— unsurprisingly—it was mostly records of Party meetings and propaganda. But in a 1936 edition there was one article that caught my eye: "Der Himmel über den Germanen" (The Sky over the Germanic Peoples) by Otto Sigfrid Reuter (1876– 1945). It was an exposition of ancient Germanic astronomy. In 1922, Reuter had published *Das Rätsel der Edda und der arische*

Urglaube (The Riddle of the Edda and the Aryan Primordial Belief) and in 1934 his magnum opus, *Germanische Himmelskunde* (Ancient Germanic Astronomy). I photocopied his article and in 1982 Michael Behrend translated it. In Santa Barbara, Donald Cyr, editor of *Stonehenge Viewpoint*, published the translation in his magazine. Subsequently, in 1985, Runestaff Publications produced an edition titled *Sky Lore of the North*.

In 1986, *Practical Geomancy* published a

The Welsh Temple of the Zodiac, 1986.
Cover art by Nigel Pennick.

"Commemorative" for the 110th anniversary of the birth of Otto Sigfrid (aka Siegfried, Sigfred) Reuter. I had been in touch with his daughter, Irmgard Teubert, who lived in Canada, and she wrote a piece entitled "Otto Siegfried Reuter (1876–1945): A Short Biography," which included a photograph of her father she had sent us. This was accompanied by another short piece, translated by Prudence Jones, a tribute to Reuter on his sixtieth birthday by J. Hogrebe, with another photograph.

German geomants and astroarchaeologists were not the only "forgotten researchers" I rediscovered. I had a copy of Ludovic McLellan Mann's *Archaic Sculpturings* of 1915 and Michael Behrend investigated further, successfully locating unpublished material by the Glaswegian statistician and archaeologist, who was born in 1869 and died in 1955. Through archival research and Mann's Will, Michael tracked down an unpublished typescript of Mann belonging to George Appleby in Glasgow. In his Will, Mann had waived copyright in his works, so we were able to publish it for the first time. Jack G. Scott of the

Glasgow Archaeological Society sent Michael a copy of *Craftsmen's Measures*, which was published in 1977, as part of IGR Occasional Paper no. 7, *A Forgotten Researcher: Ludovic McLellan Mann*. I also obtained an original copy from 1946 of Lewis Edwards's *The Welsh Temple of the Zodiac*, which was published as IGR Occasional Paper no. 18. Edward W. Cox's 1892 paper on the sacred geometry and dimensions of Liverpool Castle appeared in *The Journal of Geomancy* vol. 4, no. 3.

In 1982 the IGR issued a booklet *British Geomantic Pioneers 1570–1932* in a numbered, limited edition of 166 copies. It was part of the documentary material I had lectured on at the First Cambridge Geomancy Symposium on July 19, 1977. I was the editor. Its theme was lines on the landscape, the result of "several years of investigation of archival material." The earliest work was by William Lambarde who, in the 1596 edition of his *A Perambulation of Kent: Conteining the Description, Hystorie, and Customes of that Shyre* (written in 1570), had published a map showing lines-of-sight between the beacons of that county, intended to be lit as a warning in time of invasion. Next came the text of a lecture, "Boundaries and Landmarks," read by William Henry Black in Hereford on September 6, 1870—a meeting that Alfred Watkins, the discoverer of leys, had attended. Following that was "The Megalithic Antiquities of Stanton Drew" by C. W. Dymond of 1872, with an engraving of his survey of the stone circles there. Francis J. Bennett's 1904 work on the meridional position of megaliths in Kent, compared to those in Wiltshire, gave many examples of such lines. John Fraser of Orkney (1923–24) described "Antiquities in Harray Parish," and a rare paper by Alfred Watkins himself, "The Proof of Ancient Track Alinement" (*sic*—that is how Watkins spelt it) was also included. Finally, we published the work of Herbert Hudson between 1932 and 1947 in Norfolk and Suffolk, "The Meaning of Artificial Mounds and Mark-Stones," illustrated with facsimiles of his original maps.

The original hand-drawn plan by C. W. Dymond of the Stanton Drew stone circles once hung in a frame on the inside wall of Stanton Drew Church, but it was not conserved. Doubtless it had been there since the 1870s. In the mid-1970s,

Michael Behrend, Prudence Jones, Ann Pennick (and Martin Pennick), 1977. Photo by Nigel Pennick.

Tony Roberts received a telephone call from a visitor to Stanton Drew telling him he had asked the vicar of the church to preserve it, but he was rebuffed. The vicar did not care. Tony and I decided to go to Stanton Drew to steal it, as the incumbent was not fit to have it. We drove from London to Somerset, a trip of several hours, but when we entered the church we saw that Dymond's hand-drawn plan had disintegrated and was just a pile of wet, rotting paper behind the glass at the bottom of the frame. And so was lost another artefact of our heritage.

Geomantic Books of the 1970s and '80s

Technically, my first book was *van Gendtstraat*, published in Amsterdam in 1967. Whether this was a book or a booklet is a matter of taxonomic debate. My next major publication, *The Mysteries of King's College Chapel* (1974), was unquestionably a book. Like my booklet *Geomancy* (1973), it was published by Cokaygne Press. I had to wait until 1979 for my next geomantic

Nigel Pennick, Prudence Jones, and friend, Glastonbury Tor, 1978.

title to appear, *The Ancient Science of Geomancy* from Thames and Hudson. All of these geomantic books received a good press in my local newspaper, *Cambridge Evening News*. In 1987, my *Earth Harmony* was covered in an article titled "Forgotten Forces from the Earth" by Rodney Tibbs in the *Cambridge Evening News* for Friday, September 18 of that year. Tibbs began by deeming *Earth Harmony* as an "amazing new book," and proceeded to describe the principles enunciated within it. He was especially interested in what I had to say about protecting one's home from harmful influences.

About the modern house I lived in, I had told him: "There is not much you can do with these houses." Tibbs then went on to describe what I had, nevertheless, done:

An ancient emblem just above the door bell... inside the small hall a mirror on the wall deflects the forces from rushing straight up the stairs. Front doors facing stairs would not have been contemplated by the builders of homes hundreds of years ago because they knew about and took into account the forces which work with the natural order of things.... when [Pennick] was called in by some friends to protect a flat in Castle Street, Cambridge,[9] he placed a small protective mirror at a point opposite Gloucester Street because junctions are bad things.

Then the article quoted me directly:

"After that they closed Gloucester Street off. You could say 'oh well that is a coincidence,' but if you look at it at another level, that everything that occurs is part of everything else and that nothing that happens is insignificant, then you could say that perhaps the mirror, doing that function, is part of the development being constructed. To be able to work it out you would have to go back and discover when the final contracts were signed and so on. But when I told a Chinese geomant in California about this his attitude was there is nothing uncommon about that. It is a classic thing in various parts of the world. What you can say is that it made the person living there happier."

The Gogmagog Debacle

In 1978 we made a concerted effort to preserve the Gogmagog Hill Figures. Fellow geomantic researcher Paul Devereux[10] knew a former Royal Air Force pilot, Leslie Banks, who had a Cessna four-seater aircraft. Banks flew over places where Devereux

---

9. The flat belonged to Prudence Jones.

10. I later co-wrote a book with Devereux titled *Lines on the Landscape: Ley Lines and Other Linear Enigmas* (London: Hale, 1989).

could take photographs of lines on the landscape. He agreed to fly us over Wandlebury, to photograph the remains of the hill figures. I drove sixty miles to Denham airfield where the plane was kept. This flight had four "crew members" (as we were called when we later landed at Cambridge Airport): Leslie Banks, the pilot; Paul Devereux; Paul's co-author, Ian Thomson; and myself. We took off and flew in cloud all the way to Cambridgeshire. In the dazzling bright sky, we could see nothing.

Finally, the instruments informed the pilot that we were near to Wandlebury, and we descended. Coming out of the clouds, I looked at the landscape laid out below. We were not far from our destination, but I was having to transfer my ground-based knowledge into a coherent bird's-eye view. I spotted a landmark and gave the pilot instructions on which way to fly. Wandlebury was notorious because in World War II a pilot of a Wellington Bomber had flown into some trees on the high point after telling ground control that Cambridgeshire was flat. Pieces of the tail of the Wellington remained stuck in trees until they were blown down in the hurricane of 1987. I was aware of this, and we kept high enough not to repeat the bomber pilot's error. We eventually made several passes over the figures and I took some photographs. Paul's camera jammed at just the wrong time, and he remarked that this often happened: Murphy's Law in action. We then flew on to the Cambridge Airport. We were summoned to the control tower to give a weather report, then had lunch in the crewmen's canteen. Finally, we flew back and saw some landscape this time, landed at Denham, and then I drove back to Cambridge.

Later in 1978 Prudence Jones, Michael Behrend, and I went back to Wandlebury to meet with representatives of the Cambridge Preservation Society. They had almost agreed to let us clear the site. We offered to fund and erect a fence to protect the area, along with a sign for visitors to read, explaining the figures. The meeting went well, and we were given the go-ahead to do the work. We organised a working party and named the day. Ann contacted Anglia Television and they agreed to send a camera crew. But shortly before we were due to begin,

I received a telephone call from Sylvia Beamon cancelling the project. The committee had decided that nothing should be done before a resistivity survey was conducted. As no one had ever performed such a survey on a hill-figure site before, and it had not been suggested at our meeting, the whole thing appeared disingenuous. But we were stymied. All our efforts—which had begun years before and had involved the Situationists, *Cambridge Voice*, *Arcana*, and the Institute of Geomantic Research—had been for nought.

The Earth Mysteries Dome

The second Festival of Mind and Body took place at Olympia, West London, in 1978.[11] The leading lights of the English geomantic scene were invited to create a central feature, the Earth Mysteries Dome, for the festival. Paul Screeton and Philip Heselton, both former editors of *The Ley Hunter* and prolific writers on earth mysteries, were not at the dome.

Designed by architect and druid Colin Murray, the dome featured the Institute of Geomantic Research, *The Ley Hunter*, Zodiac House, the Glastonbury Group, and the Golden Section Order, in addition to John Michell, Tom Graves, and Janet Hoult. The Golden Section Order was Colin Murray's Celtic spirituality society. (Murray later committed ritual suicide in 1986 by eating yew-tree leaves two days after he had telephoned me and discussed the best day to die for a good reincarnation.) Zodiac House was Anthony and Janet Roberts's publishing venture; *The Ley Hunter* magazine was represented by Paul Devereux and his wife, Jay; the Glastonbury Group included Mary Caine, Patricia Villiers-Stuart, and others. I was also an associate of this group. The IGR was represented by Prudence Jones, Michael Behrend, myself, and my then-pregnant wife, Ann.

Opposite the IGR stand was the stall of a UFO cult. A silver

---

11. In later years, the event would come to be called the Festival of Mind, Body and Spirit, and many people mistakenly believe that this was always the name. Poor journalism often uses later terms that did not exist at the time when describing historic happenings, such as titles later granted, or nation-state names that postdate the event.

Participants at the Festival of Mind and Body, 1978. Back row (L to R): Paul Devereux, (unidentified woman), Patricia Villiers-Stuart, Nigel Pennick, Janet Hoult, Shelley Phillips, Jay Devereux, Michael Behrend, John Barnatt, Tony Roberts, (obscured woman unknown), Colin Murray, and Tom Graves. Kneeling in front: Prudence Jones, Mary Caine, and Janet Roberts.

model of an Adamski-derived flying saucer was the centrepiece of their exhibit. Grim-faced men wearing dark suits scowled and glared at us across the space between their stall and the dome. There were steel pillars between us and them, supporting the roof of the great hall. At lunchtime, when we were eating, a cultist stuck publicity posters on the pillars straight in front of our pitch. When we came back, we noticed the posters and tore them down immediately. A black-suited man then came across and threatened Ann with a curse. She received no respect from this self-styled representative of the "Interplanetary Parliament." He was hustled away by earth mysterians before violence ensued. That evening, Ann and I were at my parent's house in southeast London, where we were staying for the night. Ann started to feel unwell and feared she was having a miscarriage. We got her to hospital, where she was admitted for observation. I had to go to Olympia the next day to hold the stall, and told the others there, who were appalled at what had happened. Michael Behrend drew large eyes on papers which we stuck on the pillars facing the UFO fanatics. They were empowered to ward off the evil eye. The UFO cultists ignored us after that. When I returned to South London, Ann was discharged without miscarrying, and our son Sean was born normally in December.

The End of the IGR

The Institute of Geomantic Research was closed down in 1982. The economic situation had deteriorated for many people, an effect of the ruthless implementation of Milton Friedman's monetarist theory by Margaret Thatcher's government. Unemployment increased exponentially as businesses failed and public services were reduced. When I went to London to visit a publisher, I was shocked to see the fine park of Lincoln's Inn Fields, nearly thirty acres in extent, completely occupied by a crowded shantytown constructed from scrap wood, newspaper, cardboard, and waste plastic, where homeless unemployed people were languishing. The seventeenth-century libertarian and Leveller John Lilburne's maxim "What is done unto any one may be done unto every one" came to mind—a sentiment clearly demonstrated at Lincoln's Inn as a warning to us all. At the same time, prices of printing and paper soared, and by 1982 the IGR had been compelled to go back to duplication after a period of fully printed offset-litho publications. As a result, the quality—but not the standard!—of our output declined visibly, hammering another nail in the coffin. Because the fashion for the "earth mysteries" subjects of leys and terrestrial zodiacs was then in decline, at the demise of the IGR in 1982 I formed the Society for Symbolic Studies. I published five issues of a related journal called *The Symbol*, but this, too, ultimately proved unviable.

Research in the Library

Looking back into the 1970s and 1980s from the present day (2022) when digital media reigns supreme, and so much can be found easily with online search engines, it is salutary to remember how slow and difficult research was in the days when I had to use the Cambridge University Library to find what I was looking for. First, I had to drive to the library and find a parking place. Often the library car park was full, and so I had to find a space on the street, meaning a longer walk. Once inside, I had to go into a hall where there were hundreds of giant ledgers that contained lists of all the books and journals held by the library. They were in alphabetical order. I would find the appropriate one for the initial and second letter of the name of the author I was seeking and—provided another person was not already consulting the ledger—haul it out onto a shelf and, standing, go through it page by page until I found the name and title I needed. Then I had to tear off a piece of paper from a string by the shelf, and, with a pencil that was also attached to a string (for pens were not allowed) write down the title and its reference number, which also indicated its location. Finally, closing the ledger and returning it to its place, I would consult a list on the wall by the entrance that told me where to find the library shelves for the numbers that my book was listed under.

There were six floors of open-access shelves (known as the "stacks"), in two groups, the north and south wings of the 1930s Art Deco building. If, for example, the book I wanted was on the fifth floor in the north wing, I then had to go to the north lifts, which were some distance from the hall of ledgers, and take one to the fifth floor. Walking along the corridor beside the stacks, I located the numbers and then, hopefully, the book—unless someone had taken it out or was consulting it, in which case my journey was in vain. One advantage of the open-shelf system was that it was possible to walk through the stacks and look for interesting books and journals that I did not know about. The rediscovery of forgotten British and German geomantic researchers came about in this way. But it was a matter of serendipity.

When I had the book I was looking for, often I found new references in it—which then entailed more visits to the ground floor and more lifts and corridors. Of course, I had to write down anything I found in longhand on my notepad. There were no tablets or mobile-phone photography then. If I wanted a Xerox photocopy, I had to take the book down into the basement, fill in a form, pay a fee, and then come back in an hour or two to collect my documents. The book was left behind and was returned after hours to its correct place in the stacks. Sometimes the ledger told me that the book I required was held in the West Room, in which case I had to go there, fill in a request form, and hand it to a librarian at the desk. Then (if the book was not already being read by someone else) I had to wait for up to an hour for it to be brought out to me.

Today, so much is digitized and can be accessed without any of this time-consuming footwork and so it is much easier not to miss anything that the cumbersome old analogue system so often concealed. Of course, the downside means that it is also easier to censor and omit material which those in authority deem harmful, or which the morality police want suppressed for ideological reasons.

Dogma and Doctrine

In the early 1990s, the Institute of Geomantic Research had done its work, and was no more. Ley hunting was descending into an incompatible mix of theory and dogmatic assertion. Despite this, some seemed to assume that ley hunting was my primary concern. Turnstone Press had published my *Sacred Geometry* and a book on human-made tunnels and caves, *The Subterranean Kingdom*. Robert Hale had published my *Mazes and Labyrinths* and Aquarian Press my *Runic Astrology*. Rider had published my *Games of the Gods*, about the relationship between ancient ritual systems, divination, and board games, and also *The Secret Lore of Runes and Other Ancient Alphabets*, which appeared simultaneously in the UK, Australia, and the United States. Also, some of my transport photographs were published in national magazines at this time, including the back-cover colour spread of *Modern Tramway* for January 1991. In the Runestaff workshop, I was making Tablut and Gala boards, occasionally playing the mouth organ, and (in German-speaking countries) I was giving geomantic and runic workshops as well as teachings on European traditional spirituality under the rubric of *Der Weg der acht Winde* (*The Way of the Eight Winds*). Later I handed on my geomantic teachings to two women who continued them after I gave up travelling.

With this background, the recriminations that emerged in "earth mysteries" were not my main concern. But all movements, religions, and parties that grow large enough split into bitterly opposed factions that hold tight—like Staffordshire bull terriers—to their cherished differences. It is an observed historical process, as in the schisms of early Islam and Soviet Communism. Like the big-enders and little-enders in Jonathan Swift's satire *Gulliver's Travels*, the disputes are often over minutiae that an outsider could not even distinguish. In earth mysteries, this happened with leys. Watkins's ancient Britons' trackways had first transmogrified into UFO flight paths or "*orthotenies.*" Then they were renamed "ley lines" (a designation that the purists deplored) and seen as lines of energy akin to the *Lung Mei* "dragon lines" in Chinese feng shui. The parallel was not exact, as the flows of *qi* in feng shui rarely follow straight lines. (When *qi* is channelled in such a way, it is the "secret arrow" which is inauspicious and dangerous.)

Then *The Ley Hunter* magazine sponsored the Dragon Project, which used electronic instrumentation that attempted to find "earth energies" at and near the megalithic circle called the Rollright Stones. This was inconclusive. Nevertheless, the idea that "energies" rolled along the ley lines was reinforced by these studies—some had suggested even before this that the power of alien spacecraft was derived from these energy lines.[12] The energy-line theory was rejected by many—and even by many believers in extraterrestrial UFOs.

Dowsers then began to discover "ley lines" that had no relationship to the trackway-marker sites defined by Watkins back in 1922. By then, ley lines had become embedded in New Age lore as energy lines that could be felt by sensitives, and could be used to "heal the Earth" or quieten social disorder. Finally, the idea emerged that because the dead had traditionally been

---

12. The acronym UFO was originally coined by the United States Air Force to denote an *unidentified* flying object (my emphasis). Later many called them "yoofoes," assuming that they were alien spacecraft.

IGR sign painted by Nigel Pennick (later recovered from the ruins of his Runestaff workshop).

carried directly to the churchyards for burial, often along straight "coffin paths," folklore tales of spirit-lines were added to the ley-line mix. Around this time there were attempts by some to rein in the more outlandish claims, which were considered damaging to proper ley-hunting research.

When any movement feels itself under threat, it is not long before we see the condemnations and ostracism of those who are deemed to be "beyond the pale." In modern terms, this is known as "cancel culture"—but it has always happened. Unorthodox and dissident voices must be silenced. This does not mean that some dissident, unorthodox voices are *not* speaking nonsense, but once such a process is triggered, no one is safe from the inquisition. In the early 1990s, something like this occurred among the "earth mysteries" enthusiasts. Recriminations began to fly around in the shape of multi-page letters of accusation and I found myself on the wrong end of some of them. It was very hurtful. Today, one would be vilified instantly on Twitter. I was never sure what badmouthing I was getting, but feedback from others who were receiving similar treatment showed me that I was not the only one.

But earth mysteries were never my whole life, and I had already lost my profession under the monetarist regime, so I had nothing to prove. My ancestral tradition had always been significant to me, hence my subsequent published work for several years afterwards, inspired by my travels in Ireland, Wales, Scotland, and Cornwall. Thames and Hudson published my *Celtic Sacred Landscapes* (1996); Godsfield Press, *The Celtic Saints* (1997); and Thorsons, *The Sacred World of the Celts* (1997). My *Leylines* from Wiedenfeld and Nicolson (1997) deconstructed many of the theories that were by then the stock-in-trade of New Age belief. It was published in seven languages, including Japanese.

"Quit stallin' and get the show on the road"—or at least those are the words John Nicholson ascribed to the legendary Snake Oil Jake. They are appropriate here, as well.

Coda to the IGR

Ideas one believes, supports, or asserts at one time during one's life may later, at another time, be modified, abandoned, or repudiated. One has a right to change one's mind and not to be expected still, decades later, to be promoting notions one has long since given up, or to be persecuted for having once had those ideas. To be a *mumpsimus* is not to be true to oneself. To be a *mumpsimus* is to be untrue to oneself. One must give up belief in theories once they are proved to be false.

The Institute of Geomantic Research was set up specifically to examine the status and veracity of concepts such as ley lines, terrestrial zodiacs, earth energies, dowsing, and ancient technologies. *The Journal of Geomancy*, published between 1976 and 1981, carried articles by both believers and sceptics. One of the latter, statistician Bob Forrest, made considerable headway in demonstrating the falsehood of various metrological claims. Michael Behrend mathematically proved that many lines linking ancient sites, claimed as leys or "straight tracks," were not straight at all. Terrestrial zodiacs were shown categorically not to be intentional human artefacts, but the subjective projections of their discoverers. Today they can be viewed only as works of art, not archaeology. There were a number of other insights and debunkings in the journals. But, decades later, there are still believers and devotees of all of these disproved ideas who squabble with one another over minute differences of interpretation.

Now and again during all my activities in art, music, writing, lecturing, teaching, and performance, I have been involved in enmities, schisms, lovers' tiffs, fallings-out, fights, public quarrels, and reconciliations. Many of these in hindsight were needless, even absurd. I have been physically assaulted in Edinburgh by a Scottish writer who abused me with the racial slur "*sassenach*" just because he disagreed with my interpretation of the Ogham character *Quert*. Fortunately that time, my friend Gordon Strachan, a Church of Scotland minister and practitioner of sacred geometry, used martial arts upon him. I have been called a "member of a degenerate race" by an Austrian fanatic who took my Celtic surname as his reason why I should not teach the Germanic runes. But the present book is intended as a record and a celebration—not the miserable, unforgiving, regretful and melancholic rant of a disillusioned old man. So we will say no more of that!

The End of My Career in Science

Life is just a journey
Where you have to keep on track.
You'll soon fall by the wayside,
If you haven't got the knack.
The answer is trust no one
And always watch your back.

—from the song "Always Watch Your Back" by Nigel Pennick, 2018

Although the prime minister, Margaret Thatcher, was a scientist herself, she oversaw the reduction of funding to government science and the wholesale closure of scientific research units. When the Culture Centre of Algae and Protozoa was being run down, I lost my profession as a scientist. I was given a week to decide whether to be moved out of the taxonomic research I was conducting and become a pen-pushing civil service clerk, or to take what was laughably called "Voluntary Premature Retirement" at the age of thirty-eight. So I chose the latter. At least I got some money as a payoff. I was compelled to leave all my notes, photographs, and other documentary material behind. I was offered a job at the Medical Research Council in Cambridge, but the former CCAP Director, John Baker, refused to give me a reference because I was a Pagan. Unfortunately, he was a member of some "born-again" Christian church and had read my secret dossier.

The CCAP kept dossiers on all of us. A few years earlier, a young colleague named Lawrence had gone to the office to photocopy a document. Both the director and his secretary were off that day, and so he opened a filing cabinet which they had omitted to lock. Inside, he found folders on every member of staff. When he saw what they had written about him, he handed in a letter of resignation. Amongst other things, my dossier contained newspaper cuttings of letters I had written to the press. One was my protest to the *Cambridge Evening News* for mocking and disrespecting the veteran London anarchist Albert Meltzer. I had attended his talk at the Royal Standard pub in Mill Road to learn about his activities running an anarchist antiwar newspaper during World War II. It was a real underground paper, whose publishers could have faced the death penalty if caught. But clearly, the CCAP saw the word "anarchist" and that was all that mattered to them.

Another *Cambridge Evening News* clipping was an article and photograph of Jacky Craig and I holding our drinks outside the Mitre pub on the inaugural evening of our Pagan Moot in 1978. My letter in the scientific journal *Nature*, published on February 28, 1980, was also there. Titled "Maoist Dogma Clashes with Fair Appraisal of Science," it read:

> Sir—I deplore the descent of *Nature* into the murky realms of propaganda. A series of feature articles on Chinese science by Tong B. Tang . . . use the most blatant political jargon, something totally unsuited to

The photo that appeared in the *Cambridge Evening News* of Nigel Pennick and Jacky Craig at their inaugural Pagan Moot, 1978.

a scientific periodical. The epithet "Gang of Four," a political insult that would not be out of place in George Orwell's book *1984*, "revisionism," "capitalist roaders," and other jargon, combined with Maoist unintelligibles like "one divides into two" combine to make the articles unpalatable. Surely the peculiar outpourings of Maoist dogma clash with a fair and dispassionate appraisal of progress in Chinese science. The "ascent of deviationists" may be of interest to the changing policies of Marxist doctrinal quibblers, but such extravagant phraseology masks what really is the issue—the use of science for political ends. Like so-called Islamic science or even Christian science, these "sciences" which are oriented to some prearranged goal like "the dialectics of nature" serve only to bolster the preconceptions and prejudices of dogmatic plutocrats.

WYRD TIMES

Another *Cambridge Evening News* letter which was probably in the dossier was about "Christians and War" and dated June 15, 1982. It was written in response to an ongoing series of letters from various readers. In it, I defended Paganism, noting that over the years many Pagans had died at the hands of the Christian church, and that:

> Pagans, too, stand for the denunciation of war ... for the abolition of discrimination and persecution not only on grounds of sex, race, and class, but also on the grounds of religion, for it is with religion that fanaticism, that bane of the modern world, began.

The file also contained other documents, including some of my geomantic and Pagan leaflets. If Lawrence had told me this when he first came out of the office, I would have destroyed the dossier then and there.

So I ceased to be a scientist. I signed on as unemployed, but was given little to support my family. I was offered a course at a college in Blackpool, two hundred miles away from home, to become a professional photographer. With three children and Ann as the primary breadwinner (with a part-time job in a supermarket), family commitments meant I could not take up the offer. Weeks passed. I made and sold Runestaff artefacts and travelled to Warburg in Germany for a geomantic workshop weekend with Professor Waltraud Wagner. When I came back, I answered a newspaper advertisement for someone with the ability to paint model soldiers for Little Lead Soldiers, a company at Over, only five miles away.

In my youth, I had made model aircraft and trains and painted them, so I had some knowledge of model making. Several people turned up for the training day, and when tested, two of us were accepted. So I became a professional model-painter for a while. I painted 25mm figures of Her Majesty the Queen side-saddle on her horse for dioramas of Trooping the Colour, and red-coated, bearskin-wearing guardsmen of the various regiments of the Brigade of Guards that appear in the annual military parade in London. I also painted soldiers of Napoleon's Imperial Guard from the Battle of Waterloo. It was piece-work, time consuming, and every soldier—as in the real army—had to be immaculate. Although I never had a painted soldier rejected, I did not continue this for long.

UFOria: The UFO Sightings List

In the spirit of Dada, I created a spoof list of sightings of unidentified flying objects in the 1980s. I was receiving at that time many publications in exchange for Institute of Geomantic Research journals and Occasional Papers. We read them all, but one magazine by UFO devotees called *Viewpoint Aquarius* particularly galled us with its naïve gullibility. So we decided to test just *how* gullible the editors were. I typed up a list of purported British UFO encounters, using invented names, places, and times for the "reports." Each had a cryptic reference number, and it was made clear that this was a small segment of a much larger file. In those days, there were no word processors or personal computers, so it was produced on my electric typewriter. Put in chronological order with reference numbers, the fictional list was then entered by a friend on a computer at his place of work in the University and printed out on a perforated roll of paper. To those not familiar with computers, this would have looked official.

I printed up a micrograph of a cigar-shaped diatom and—using double exposure in a darkroom—montaged it onto a photograph of the Fenland landscape. The monochrome print looked like a "flying cigar" over field and fen. A fake rubber stamp was made for the back with an "official" number and reference, and a letter purporting to come from from an army brigadier and addressed to a top civil servant. The letter and the print were posted from a letterbox in Central London to *Viewpoint Aquarius*. It had a cover note purporting to come from an anonymous whistleblower who had supposedly intercepted the letter. It was being sent to *Viewpoint Aquarius* so they could reveal the secret to the world.

This elaborate hoax was swallowed hook, line, and sinker.

The editors of *Viewpoint Aquarius* clearly believed that they had received a classified document from a secret government agency, and they published it. We had proved that they were gullible, and shoddy journalists to boot. Clearly, they had not made the most basic checks and verifications that any journalist must make before publishing anything. How we laughed!

This was not the end of the matter. Sometime later, a debate about UFOs was called in the House of Lords by the Earl of Clancarty, who was better known as Brinsley Le Poer Trench, author of books with titles like *The Sky People* and *Mysterious Visitors*. He asserted that there were secret UFO files in existence that should be made public: "Is it not time that Her Majesty's Government informed our people of what they know about UFOs? I think it is time our people were told the truth." The lords' motion called upon the government to promote international study of the phenomenon.

In the debate that took place on the evening of October 24, 1986, several lords spoke at length on the subject. There was something Dadaistic about the whole thing, with many of the speakers appearing like caricatures of bumbling, know-nothing aristocrats. The Earl of Clancarty started the proceedings and listed supposed historic sightings of UFOs, including one reported by the army of the Egyptian Pharaoh Thutmose III around 1430 BCE. His address went on for twenty-two minutes. He was followed by Lord Trefgarne and then the Earl of Kimberley, who was evidently a keen reader on UFOs. First he made a cryptic point, clearly not intended to be humorous: "But in spite of the sceptics, such as the noble lord, Lord Wigg, the other day in a newspaper, and Sir Bernard Lovell from Jodrell Bank,[13] who says that UFOs do not exist, we must agree that they do, otherwise there would be no unidentified flying objects."

The earl's second pronouncement, however, showed he had been reading *Viewpoint Aquarius*:

---

13. Note: Jodrell Bank was the largest radio telescope then in service. There was also a model in girlie magazines who went by the name of Jodrelle Banks.

Postcard advertisement for *The House of Lords UFO Debate*.

Before I sit down, I ask the noble Lord, Lord Strabolgi, whether he will tell your Lordships why the Ministry of Defence has not informed the public of 18 contacts from 23rd May 1977 up to 22nd February 1978, numbered K5634 to K5651 inclusive? Further, what do the classification numbers 5, 3, 20, 16, 6, 8 and 23 mean for these 18 contacts? Moreover, does the noble Lord realise that 13 out of these 18 contacts were seen during the hours of daylight? There need be no fear that the people of this country may panic, since if UFOs are extra-terrestrial, their intelligence and knowledge is far ahead of our primitive understanding.

The Viscount of Oxfuird then made his maiden speech in the

House of Lords, which the following lords ritually congratulated. The next to speak was Lord Trefgarne for a second time, then Lord Davies of Leek, who said, "There is a queerness in the cosmology of the world in which we are now living," and made other mysterious pronouncements. Subsequent contributions were in a similar vein. The Lord Bishop of Norwich warned that devotees of UFOs were in danger of becoming superstitious cult members. Following Jesus was the only answer. Viscount Barrington, Lord Gladwyn, Lord King's Norton, and Lord Rakeillor said their respective pieces. Then Lord Gainsford struck a different note. He had seen a UFO in Argyll, Scotland, though on an inauspicious night, December 31—New Year's Eve. Clearly there was laughter at this and Gainsford responded: "All right, my lords, have a good laugh, it was Hogmanay."[14] He then went on to recount that people who had drunk only soft drinks had also witnessed it. The Earl of Halsbury said he had seen many things. At the age of six he had seen an angel, and later, Zeppelin airships, sun-dogs, and the green flash. It seems he was debunking UFO sightings. By now, the debate had been going on for three hours. The Earl of Cork and Orrery spoke, and finally Lord Strabolgi for the government, and then the debate was brought to an end. No vote was taken.

The transcript was published in *Hansard*, the official record of Parliament, and then as a paperback book, *The House of Lords UFO Debate*, by Open Head Press of London (1979). Brinsley Le Poer Trench wrote the preface and John Michell provided additional notes. Clearly, neither knew where the Earl of Kimberley's list had come from. The fact that it was published in the official Parliamentary record of the United Kingdom must be considered a success beyond all expectations.

A postscript to this is that, some years later, I was walking with my father in the evening on a path near the local church. This church is a modern brick box; a visitor once mistook it for a fire station because it has large red doors along one side and no churchyard. In the near twilight, we noticed a light in the sky

---

14. *Hogmanay* is the Scots term for a New Year's Eve celebration.

in front of us. It was a brilliant salmon-pink and appeared to be drifting slowly. Just then, the vicar came out of the church, and, pointing to the object, I said: "Look, a UFO!" He harrumpfed in disgust, turned round, and went back inside. The priest's reaction was just another instance of the recurring theme of "those who already know, don't see." My father reported the sighting to BUFORA, the British UFO Research Association, who, after investigation, registered it as a genuine UFO sighting (whatever a genuine *unidentification* is!). Lord Clancarty undoubtedly saw the report.

Fata Viam Invenient: *Labyrinths*

My first visit to a labyrinth was the turf maze on Saffron Walden Common around 1957. There was no information available about such mazes then, but I retained an interest until I could find more in libraries. Over the years, I visited more turf mazes, at Wing in Rutland and Alkborough near the confluence of the Rivers Trent and Ouse in Lincolnshire. My first publication exclusively devoted to labyrinths was the booklet *Caerdroia: Ancient Turf, Stone and Pavement Mazes*, published in February of 1974 in a limited edition of 200 numbered copies. Further research led to my rediscovery in archives of early photographs of the labyrinths at Sneinton in Nottingham and at Comberton in Cambridgeshire, and the design of the lost labyrinth at Temple Cowley, Oxford. With this and other new material, I wrote a book, *Mazes and Labyrinths*, which was published by Robert Hale in 1991. Labyrinths, however, are primarily physical structures, intended to be walked or danced, or, where too small for that, used for amuletic purposes.

The majority of labyrinths I made over the years were temporary ones for human use. Once constructed, they survived for the period that they were needed. Then they were destroyed or allowed to disintegrate naturally. This is the natural way of labyrinths. Starting in the late 1970s, I laid out temporary labyrinths at various places in the British Isles for particular events or teachings: in England, Wales, Cornwall, and the Republic of Ireland. My campaign to get a labyrinth constructed on New

Rupert Sheldrake at Nigel Pennick's Ojai Foundation labyrinth, 1986.
Photo by Nigel Pennick.

Square in Cambridge city centre in 1983 was unsuccessful, but I made a series of biodegradable sawdust labyrinths annually over a number of years in the "green area" at the Strawberry Fair on Midsummer Common. In mainland Europe, I laid out several temporary and permanent labyrinths in Germany between 1984 and the early twenty-first century; at Linderhof in Zürich, Switzerland, in 1985 and 1988; in Austria at Salzburg in 1988; and at Baden-bei-Wien in 1994. Materials I used included wood blocks, stones, bricks, tree bark, fir cones, and sawdust. In 1993 I designed a permanent pavement labyrinth in a private garden in a village in the Schurwald in southern Germany. It was laid by a professional paviour.

In 1986 I constructed a permanent stone labyrinth at the Ojai Foundation in California, one of the first of a new wave of spiritual labyrinths in North America. I had a number of subsequent private commissions in Great Britain and Germany, some of which were built and others of which remained as plans. In 1987 I was invited to participate in the traditional crafts section of the Art in Action festival at Waterperry House, Oxfordshire. Over a four-day period I used standard British house bricks to make a series of temporary labyrinths on the neatly mown lawn.

Labyrinth laid out by Nigel Pennick, Camp, County Kerry, Ireland, 1988. Photo by Nigel Pennick.

I employed all the common historic patterns, from the simplest three-circuit classical design to the larger Roman and medieval Christian forms.

During the event, I built labyrinths and dismantled them. While they existed, people walked through them, laughing or cursing, and when the Art in Action festival ended, the bricks were taken away. Perhaps they ended up making a wall. At one point a school party arrived, and two boys asked if they could help. They were about ten years of age and made splendid assistants. They immediately had a rapport with the process and knew where to put the next bricks. Without exception, children happily ran or skipped through my labyrinths from the entrance to the middle. If they made a false step, they resumed the path and followed it faithfully to the centre.

Many adults, however, were so self-conscious that when they stumbled or stepped over from one path to another, they uttered embarrassed laughs, commented that labyrinths were "stupid," grumbled, slinked out, or briskly walked off. It was instructive for me to watch these people's dislocated psychology in action. Not all adults behaved so immaturely; many congratulated me and discussed the labyrinths' nature and mathematics. The event was very successful, but at the evaluation meeting after it closed, I was told that because it had attracted so many people moving about, it had been out of keeping with an art festival. I was asked not to come back the next year.

I served as a geomantic guide and lecturer on a two-week coach tour of Ireland in August of 1988. Most of the participants were German or Swiss. At the village of Camp in County Kerry in the west of Ireland, the "International Labyrinth Team"—myself, Rosemarie Kirschmann, Mona Miscsicek, and Ursula Schmitz—built a large labyrinth of stones on the beach. It took three hours to make. A photograph of this, taken from a nearby clifftop, appeared in my book *Mazes and Labyrinths*. Maze-builder Adrian Fisher had proposed 1991 as the "Year of the Maze" and managed to promote a number of events in various places in Britain. In that year, I was one of the invited judges of a "design-a-maze" competition organised by the *Sunday Times* newspaper at Chenies Manor in Buckinghamshire. The prizewinning maze was built and is still there, as far as I know. In addition to walkable and danceable labyrinths, I have painted various labyrinth forms on wood and metal, and made stamps to impress ceramic tiles and polymer clay with the pattern. In 1993 I made twenty-eight paintings of labyrinths on plywood, called *The October Series*. Some were sold for geomantic purposes and may still be serving in that capacity today.

Geomantic Meetings, Lectures, and Events

I both organised and presented many lectures, slide shows, and multimedia performances in Britain between 1970 and 2019. Here are a just few of the many events, perhaps the more notable ones, demonstrating the diversity of material and interests which various experts in their fields offered those who came to listen and participate.

The Institute of Geomantic Research staged five Geomancy Symposia in Cambridge, organised by Ann Pennick and myself. A sixth was held jointly with the Caerdroia Project at Royston in Hertfordshire. The first was held at St Andrew's Hall in central

NIGEL PENNICK

Nigel Pennick speaking at the 2nd Cambridge Geomancy Symposium, September 16, 1978. Photo by John Cann.

Cambridge on July 19, 1977. This late Victorian-era hall was chosen because it was correctly oriented according to Northern Tradition geomancy, with the speaker at the north end, facing south, and the audience in the south end, facing north. Every symposium was different, and speakers dealt with diverse subjects relevant to the overall remit of the IGR. The first meeting began with my introductory words of welcome, and the first speaker was an American visitor, Donald Cyr, editor of *Stonehenge Viewpoint* magazine. His talk was on an Irish zodiac, with references to Isaac N. Vail's "canopy theory," which Cyr championed. Then Prudence Jones spoke on the complex matter of numerology, a discipline overlapping witchcraft, ritual magic, Freemasonry, and landscape geometry.

My piece was about the antiquarian pioneers I had rediscovered in archival research—the forgotten geomantic researchers. "Ley hunters" traced their origin back to a disputed "vision" of Alfred Watkins in 1921. In his writings, Watkins did not acknowledge any earlier proponents of straight lines on the landscape, and his followers lauded him as their sole discoverer.

In my talk, I debunked this hagiography, showing that there had been many before him and that Watkins himself, aged fifteen, was at a meeting at the Green Dragon Hotel in Hereford where the speaker, William Henry Black, gave a lecture on the subject. These pioneers included "forgotten researchers" such as the Reverend Duke, who had written about landscape alignments in 1846; W. H. Black, whose work the IGR rescued; and F. J. Bennett, who investigated the same landscape markers seventeen years before Watkins. I also spoke of the German school of Leugering, Heinsch, and Gerlach, some of whose forgotten geomantic writings I had rediscovered in the Cambridge University Library. I concluded with the 1950s academic dismissal of alignment researchers as "plausible hucksters," and summarised the current revival since 1961.

Kathryn Jane Preston, editor of the UFO/earth mysteries magazine *Pulsar*, then told us about a landscape zodiac in the north of England. She was followed by Mary Caine, who gave an illustrated lecture, with aerial photographs, on Katherine Maltwood's famous and disputed Glastonbury Zodiac. Next, from Hong Kong, Professor Robert Lord, with whom I co-authored a book, spoke of a zodiac around Pendle Hill in Lancashire, which he had researched. Philip Heselton—the founder (in 1965) and first editor of *The Ley Hunter*, and the then-editor of *Northern Earth Mysteries*—followed with more zodiacal material. Patricia Villiers-Stuart gave a talk on her latest geometrical experiments, especially with "odd-number" divisions of the circle related to labyrinths. Finally, another American visitor, Bill Cox, editor of *The Pyramid Guide* magazine, told us about the latest pyramid research. Overall, we had a packed schedule and Bill was forced to truncate his lecture for lack of time.

It is important to note that historians often do not have access to gatherings such as these where new discoveries or ideas are broached. They are a vernacular transmission of themes which appear later in print without reference to their genesis at meetings, lectures, and symposia. Although some have even been taped (in the days before digital recording), often these tapes are never heard or issued. Recorded on now-defunct media, they moulder in someone's attic until, at their death, they are thrown away. I know of several cases of this. Material which should have been archived is, instead, destroyed.

At the second IGR Symposium, held on September 16, 1978, I gave a lecture titled "Yggdrasil, the Omphalos, and Sanctuaries." Mike Collier talked about zodiacal landscape patterns in his native Sussex, and Prudence Jones's lecture was on "German Geomancy" of the 1930s, showing how it had an independent origin from the National Socialism with which it had become associated. In his talk titled "Some Indications of Geomantic Tradition in Tibet," Peter Martin gave a stunning slide show of the paintings of Russian mystic Nicholas Roerich, author of *Shambhala* (1930). Martin's presentation was sensational to those who had never heard of Roerich or seen his pictures before. Ivan Bunn of the Lowestoft-based Borderline Science Investigation Group; John Cann, my scientific colleague with whom I had ghost-watched through a cold night in Histon Manor and later co-wrote my final scientific paper on a new species of protozoan; Paul Devereux, current editor of *The Ley Hunter* magazine; and Bob Cowley of RILKO, the Research into Lost Knowledge Organisation, were all present. The third symposium was held on May 17, 1980, at the same venue. I gave an overview of the Cambridgeshire Ley Project, which was studying the alignments proposed by Alfred Watkins in his last book *Archaic Tracks round Cambridge* (1932). Philip Heselton talked about the work of the Northern Earth Mysteries Group, Prudence Jones spoke on Viking Geomancy, and finally, Carmen Blacker discussed Japanese holy mountains.

For some years *The Ley Hunter* magazine had an annual moot, and I spoke at several of them. Originally held in London, subsequently they took place in locations including Glastonbury, Machynlleth, Bakewell, Penzance, and Hereford. The 1978 Moot at the Highway Hall in Hampstead, North London, was opened by Paul Devereux. I spoke on the orientation of churches; Rose Heaword about the god Mercury; John Barnatt on the megalithic circles of Derbyshire's Peak District; and American dowser John Steele reported on dowsing and biofeedback techniques. Don

"Spirit of Place" lecture at the Libra Aries Bookshop, Mill Road Broadway, Cambridge. Photo by Nigel Pennick.

Robbins spoke of megalithic energies and Mike Collier about the elephantine landscape figure he claimed to have discovered in Sussex.

In 1980 the Ley Hunters' Moot was held on July 12 and 13, a Saturday and Sunday, in the Town Hall at Bakewell in Derbyshire. It was also opened by Paul Devereux. I was a speaker, as were American dowser Sig Lonegren, Jill Bruce, and Bruce Lacey. Lacey was an artist known for his surreal automata he called "robots," although (in pre-microprocessor days) they were not what we would call robots today. His claim to fame outside the artistic world was the song "Mr Lacey," which appeared in 1968 on *What We Did on Our Holidays* by the folk-rock band Fairport Convention. Recorded in 1967, this bluesy track featured in its middle three of Lacey's creations sounding suspiciously like vacuum cleaners. It was said that Lacey appeared in the recording studio wearing a spacesuit along with his automaton trio. The Pink Fairies later played a vacuum cleaner on stage at a performance I saw. Sadly, Bruce Lacey did not bring his robots to Bakewell. They would have livened up the proceedings.

On Sunday morning, some of us who got up early assembled in the Town Hall. A dowser got out his rods and dowsed some lines across the width of the building. Bored with this futile display, I called out: "This is all subjective! I shall project you a line." At least he was open to the experiment, and started again. I was sitting on a chair at the end, concentrating on producing a line running end-to-end along the middle line of the hall, as the dowser walked across it. Suddenly, as he reached the invisible centre-line, his rods twitched and he then followed the line, directly away from me to the back of the hall. He was visibly shaken as he had not found anything on the previous sweep. He *had* picked up on the line I was projecting, however, so what price the much-studied earth energy? I do not know how this experience informed his later dowsing career—but rest assured that this incident was not written up in any dowsing journal. When the others arrived, we went in our cars to Arbor Low stone circle, round which John Barnatt took us on a guided walk. The dowsers walked about in various directions, rods twitching, largely oblivious to the landscape that surrounded them. Not that I had anything against dowsing, per se. I was taught how to dowse for water by a retired British Army officer, Colonel Mirrlees, and, in *The Journal of Geomancy*, we ran advertisements for "Dowsit" divining rods made by a local company in Cottenham, Cambridgeshire.

On September 19, 1983, a meeting which had geomantic researchers as well as academic archaeologists took place at Emmanuel College in Cambridge. I was a speaker there, along with John Michell, Paul Devereux, Jeremy Harte, John Barnatt, and archaeologists Christopher Taylor, Aubrey Burl, and Leslie Grinsell. The organisers were Liz Bellamy and Tom Williamson, who had just published a critique of landscape alignments called *Ley Lines in Question*. There were heated disagreements over certain issues. One of the archaeologists even asserted to me the preposterous contention that there were no records of churches being built on the sites of Pagan temples, a completely untenable standpoint as a cursory visit to Rome would prove. Again, the recurring theme of "those who speak don't know." But the Emmanuel College event was a rare meeting point, only eight years after Glyn Daniel, the Disney Professor of Archaeology at Cambridge University, had, in the journal *Antiquity*, dismissed the Institute of Geomantic Research as "dotties at random."

In 1984, Southern Television (now defunct) made a program about Stonehenge with Professor R. J. C Atkinson, myself, and others. The illegal Stonehenge Festival was on at the time, and someone was shot in a dispute between drug dealers. Therefore, I refused to go there to be videotaped. Back in the hotel at Amesbury, I had a few drinks with Professor Atkinson, the eminent archaeologist who had excavated part of Stonehenge in the 1950s. He told me that they had used the famous dowser Guy Underwood to find certain places where stones had once stood. Underwood was not credited in the archaeological report, much to Atkinson's regret. A British media company videoed me at Wandlebury in the pouring rain, and a New York–based company, Trigon Communications, recorded me being interviewed by Paul Devereux in the tower of Great St Mary's Church in Cambridge. It appeared as *Geosophy: An Overview of Earth Mysteries*. I was described in the blurb: "Nigel Pennick is a researcher and author of numerous books including *The Ancient Science of Geomancy: Man in Harmony with the Earth*. He is world renowned for his work on 'ley lines' and 'geomancy.'" This program also featured John Michell, John Steele, Martin Brennan, and Harry Oldfield.

On August 30, 1986, an event organised by myself and Jeff Saward (editor of the labyrinths magazine *Caerdroia*) took place. Held at the Town Hall at Saffron Walden in Essex, it was billed as "Labyrinth '86." Saffron Walden was a fitting location since the town had two labyrinths of its own: one a large turf maze on the town green, dating from perhaps the 1500s, and the other a nineteenth-century hedge maze in Bridge End Gardens. Adrian Fisher of Minotaur Designs spoke on the construction of modern mazes, and John Kraft came from Sweden to tell us about ancient stone mazes in Scandinavia. Professor Peter Schmid came from the Netherlands to explain his experimental labyrinth of willow

NIGEL PENNICK

Nigel Pennick giving a runic lecture, Ludlow, Shropshire, 2009.
Photo by Linda Kelsey-Jones.

saplings at Eindhoven University. I had visited Eindhoven in 1984 to give a lecture on geomancy to his architecture students. John Bosworth described the recent restoration of the hedge maze in Bridge End Gardens, Jeff Saward talked about the Saffron Walden turf maze, and I spoke on symbolic geometry and numbers in labyrinth design. The Old Mother Redcap café provided food and drink. Afterwards, we walked to both mazes and were given guided tours around them.

"Magical Landscapes" was a four-day residential course for "environmental professionals" held by Sir George Trevelyan's Wrekin Trust at Runnings Park in Worcestershire. It took place from May 29 to June 2, 1988. Suki Pryce was the course organiser, a university lecturer in landscape management and amenity horticulture. The course leaders were John Michell, a "leading light of the earth mysteries research movement in Britain"; Jess Cormack, a holistic counsellor and workshop leader;[15] and Colin

---

15. Jess Cormack features again in the section "Christian Protests," pp. 238–43.

Bloy, who was a director of an aluminium smelting company and founder of Fountain International, an "earth-healing" dowsing society that claimed it could reduce and eventually abolish crime by sending "good vibrations" into fountains and similar structures in cities. I was described by the Wrekin Trust as a "writer and lecturer on ancient and modern mysteries, an authority on Northern European geomancy, a runemaster, practising geomant and traditional symbolic craftsman."

The event included workshops in dowsing theory and practice; principles and practice of earth harmony; and setting out a labyrinth (the latter two workshops were conducted by me). There were excursions to the Malvern Hills, local sacred springs and holy wells. Overall, it was quite an intensive four days. Later, I stayed with Colin Bloy in his opulent twenty-third-floor penthouse suite in Brighton, amid surrealist paintings by Léonor Fini. After a fine meal in an upmarket restaurant, we had returned to the penthouse when we heard sirens wailing. Looking out over the city, we could see the blue flashing lights of police cars and the flickering flames of fire at a number of locations. Brighton was a seaside city where the "good vibrations" had supposedly been activated by Fountain International to abolish crime, but we watched as Molotov cocktails were thrown and a skinhead riot rampaged through the streets below. Gradually, the hullabaloo died down, the Fire Brigade extinguished the flames, and the skinheads dispersed or were arrested. In the morning, I was relieved to find that my car, parked in the street, only had an aerial torn off.

Subterranean Worlds: The Physical Occult

Ever since I was young, underground tunnels were a normal part of my life. I was taken on the tube and sometimes watched the trams entering and leaving the Kingsway subway (tunnel) in Southampton Row. That heavily used transport link was closed in April of 1952. I was taken on one of the last trams that ever ran through it. Then it was barricaded off, though the entrance ramp with its tracks still remains at the time of writing almost seventy years later. Motor buses running above the tunnel replaced the

Russell Square Station, 1965. Photo by Nigel Pennick.

trams, adding to air pollution on the street.

From about thirteen I was allowed to travel around London by myself. London Transport offered cheap "rover" tickets that allowed unlimited travel on underground trains and buses. From Russell Square on the Piccadilly Line I rode the entire underground system from north to south and east to west. I knew every line from end to end and the subterranean topography of the interchange stations. This freedom to travel enabled me to visit museums, art galleries, bookshops, football grounds, and railway installations. At school at an end-of-term variety show with parents in attendance, I once did a "memory man" act based on the London Underground map. Almost everyone then carried a diary, and every British diary had a London Underground map in the back. So I was asked questions such as: "How do I get from Piccadilly Circus to Epping?" I would answer correctly, telling them which station they should use to change trains. No one ever caught me out.

Three of the core tube lines were built at the same time (opened 1906–1907), and so there were interchange stations between them. Some had tunnels that, although in use, were not signed. So while ordinary passengers traipsed the long way between the Bakerloo Line and the Piccadilly Line at Piccadilly Circus station, I nipped through the short passage that had no signs. Finding this out was a revelation to me, and I started to seek out other passages. It was clear that there were many hidden tunnels under London. When I went to Arsenal, the train went through an abandoned station, York Road. I could tell there had been a station there, because the trains decelerated.[16] I had noticed other mysterious dark stations on the Piccadilly Line before South Kensington and on the Central Line near Holborn. I finally found books which recounted the history of the Underground and the names of these abandoned stations. I also discovered that at least one of them, Down Street, had been used in World War II as a bunker for key workers controlling the railway system.

There had been really deep shelters constructed in World War II. Within walking distance of the place where I lived until I was eight, close to Goodge Street tube station, were two huge concrete cylinders set on heavy rectangular structures. Grey steel doors guarded access, and there was no notice or sign to tell anyone what the building was. Later I realised that a building being unlabelled was one way of telling that it held some state secret. Also, in the street where I lived at the time was a bomb site fenced off with hoardings and access for vehicles. Lorries came and went, seemingly carrying away soil or clay from an excavation. Through cracks in the hoarding, I could see a crane and what seemed to be the entrance to a shaft. The men there were building a new underground railway, I was told. Clearly, this information was false as no new line ever opened. My father,

---

16. The station tunnels had been built with an ascending gradient before them to slow the trains entering the station, and a descending gradient after them to aid acceleration. When stations were abandoned, the underground topography of the tube tunnels could not be altered.

Civil Defence volunteer that he was, speculated that it was a shelter being built for the Third World War. Even he did not know—or was not telling me. Eventually, the work stopped and a new building was erected on the site. From this, and from seeing the mysterious doors at various parts of the underground system, I surmised that there must be tunnels down there that were secret. At Holborn tube station, the next one down the line from Russell Square, were heavy thick steel gates painted grey that clearly fitted into the entrance of the escalators down to the lower level of the station. At Charing Cross was a gate on a pivot that could be used to plug the circular tube tunnel. These, I found out, were relics of World War II, installed to prevent flooding of the tunnels should a bomb destroy water mains and sewers. They were kept in place for the coming World War III.

I was fascinated by what else was underground, but (for obvious reasons) no information was available. Travelling around, I discovered other "deep tube shelters" beneath stations on the Northern Line south of the river and near to Chancery Lane Station, where there was an unmarked building with a crane attached outside. They were not normal architecture. At the other end of the station was an office block with glass doors that gave access to a lift. Looking closely through the glass, I could see buttons for several levels below the ground floor. If I had noticed, so had the Russians, as a shop selling Soviet products was on the other side of the road. I bought a clock-making kit there. Then, in 1963, an anarchist group called Spies for Peace gained access to an underground bunker at Warren Row and exposed what the government had been planning for World War III. Anthony Roberts, whom I knew a decade later in geomantic circles, was a member of the group.

It transpired that, in the event that Britain was nuked, the military top brass, key politicians, civil servants, and technocrats would be ensconced deep underground in thirteen secret bunkers inaccessible to the common citizenry. These would be the "Regional Seats of Government," from which they would rule a country laid waste. What might be left of this annihilated nuclear wasteland, no one ever stated. But the bunkers were built, and now they were public knowledge. In 1972 Peter Laurie released *Beneath the City Streets*, in which he deduced from published material and observation the network of Post Office sites and military bunkers that made up the British state's post-nuclear contingency.

Spies for Peace missed an important bunker code-named "Guardian" under central Manchester. This was revealed in 2021 in a history of the light rail system Metrolink as the reason why an underground railway was not built in the 1970s to link two of the main stations. The planners were forced to sign the Official Secrets Act (OSA), and then were told of the bunker's existence and location. They were instructed to find some excuse why not to build the railway they had planned through the site of the secret bunker. In the late 1970s and early 1980s, through the agency of Roger Morgan, I was able to access both the abandoned tram subway and the bunker at Goodge Street. The bunker, which had housed General Eisenhower's headquarters on D-Day in 1944, still had the beds and other facilities in place. It had been used as a transit camp for army conscripts until a fire in 1956 caused its closure. Exploring the tunnels, I could hear the tube trains running through Goodge Street Station above. I came across a shaft with a spiral access stair and, using my torch, entered a small circular tunnel with cables on the walls. It appeared to run in either direction for a long way, and I walked a hundred yards or so along it. Then I realised how late the time had got, and I had to turn back. I believe I had been in the secret tunnel whose construction shaft I had passed every day as a child. I did not have an opportunity to further investigate, though, so I will never know for sure.

Around that time, Electric Traction Publications was another of my publishing ventures. It has gone largely unnoticed by those interested only in my antiquarian, occult, artistic, and folkloristic work. Among my Electric Traction booklets, which were offset-litho printed, were the historical *Trams in Cambridge* (March 1983), *Early Tube Railways of London* (September 1983), and *Bunkers under London* (three editions: 1984, 1985, and 1988). A contact in the London Transport archives, who went under the pseudonym Heinrich Heineken, photocopied for me original plans of some of the "New Tube Shelters" begun in 1940 as a contingency against future German superweapons. Monty Service also located plans and maps for me, including London Transport tunnels that were never built. This material appeared in my tube and bunker publications.

After the publication of my book *The Subterranean Kingdom: A Survey of Manmade Structures beneath the Earth* by Turnstone Press in 1981, the national BBC invited me to participate in a sound experiment. I went to West Wycombe, to the Hellfire Caves dug for Sir Francis Dashwood in the eighteenth century. Down underground, I was interviewed about the history, structure, and symbolic meaning of the caves. The sound engineer used "free-space" stereo equipment which the BBC technical department had just developed. The effect was stunning. The program was aired later with several repeats and also broadcast on the BBC World Service.

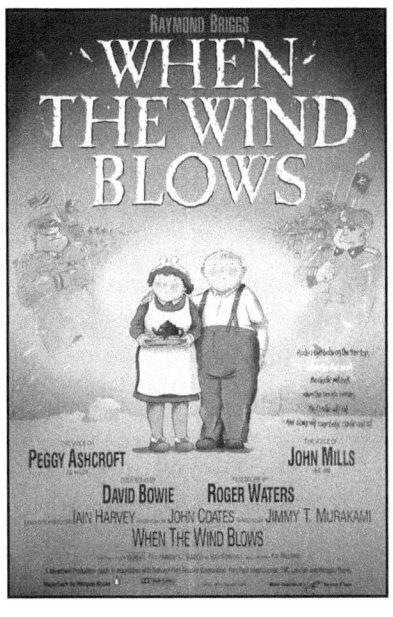

When the Wind Blows, 1986.

The animated movie *When the Wind Blows* (directed by Jimmy Murakami) premièred on October 24, 1986. Based on the cartoon book by Raymond Briggs, it detailed the decline and demise of an optimistic old couple in the days after a nuclear strike. As the author of *Bunkers under London*, I was invited to the reception that took place following the première, which was held in the "New Tube Shelter" at Goodge Street. Outside it looked just like it did when I had seen it as a child and in 1982 when I visited it with Roger Morgan, except for a guard checking entry. Down the lift I went and entered another world. Part of the bunker had been decorated with potted palms and the ambience was of an upmarket hotel. Liveried waiters and waitresses served champagne to the guests, including the director and prominent members of the film world. There I also met Monseigneur Bruce Kent, leader of the Campaign for Nuclear Disarmament (CND), who had scant knowledge of the bunkers under London when I discussed them with him. I had a wonderful time beneath the city streets. It was a great idea to have the reception in the bunker, though in reality it was no laughing matter. Not long afterwards, the company Security Archives took it over, and now it is sealed to the public.

V
THE ELDER FAITH

Unwearied Nature ruleth over the worlds and works, that the heavens drawing downward might run an eternal course, and that the other periods of the Sun, Moon, Seasons, Night and Day, might be accomplished.

—*Chaldean Oracles of Zoroaster*, 140

Motto card with Thor's Hammer by Nigel Pennick, 1998.

From the One Way to the Elder Ways

From my early visits to the British Museum I was aware that religion has taken many forms. There were images of goddesses and gods, some in animal or hybrid animal-human form; there were sacred artifacts used in shrines of various religions; and even pieces of ancient temples from Assyria, Egypt, Greece, and Rome. Some buildings close to where I lived had images of ancient gods like Neptune and Mercury, the latter appearing on banks and post offices. So when I was taught that there was only One Way, I questioned what this could mean. Clearly, there was not just One Way (even Christianity itself was divided into many competing sects). Otherwise, all the devout followers of other faiths would be punished by God. This was monstrously unjust, as we were all members of various religions by chance, according to which families we belonged to. In St Giles's primary school, some of the children were Jewish. They were exempted from going to church, while the rest of us were given no choice. Religious identity, then, was obviously just a matter of random happenstance. Living just after World War II, when millions had been done to death in horrible ways, the idea of a vindictive God thrusting well-meaning people into eternal damnation just because they happened to be born in a particular culture seemed repellent.

Because we were given lessons in "scripture" (as it was then called), I became conversant with large parts of the Bible. I was appalled at the sections in the Old Testament that told of ancient tribal wars, colonization, and genocide in Bronze Age Chaldea and Canaan. Of course, at the time I could not have

Mountaintop Goddess Apparition. Ink drawing by Nigel Pennick, 2000.

used this terminology, but I could not see why God—who in other contexts we were told "is Love"—had aided and abetted the destruction of peaceful cities, the extermination of their inhabitants, and the execution of their kings. There was a terrible cognitive dissonance between the violent and pitiless rampages of the ancient Israelites and the peaceful, compassionate, teachings of Jesus. Perhaps if the Christian religion had decided not to incorporate the Old Testament into its Bible, then it may have had a more peaceful and positive trajectory. As I got older, I read a lot of history and was saddened that the wonderful sacred images and buildings of the Greeks and Romans had been desecrated by Christian zealots, their treasures looted, and their believers put to death. In Britain, the indigenous holy places were destroyed, and Christian places of worship were erected in their place.

However, during my travels I saw that remnants of the elder faith were present in many of these ancient churches, some more than a thousand years old. Continuity had been maintained. At Great Canfield in Essex, the vicar pointed out to me a carving of a bearded man flanked by two birds and a row of swastikas. This

Odin with ravens carved in the twelfth-century church at Great Canfield Essex, England.

was, I was told, a Pagan image. To me, it represented Odin (or Woden) with his ravens, Hugin and Munin. Every time I went into a church, I looked for other archaic carvings, and saw many interesting things that had no biblical interpretation.

I also found out that many places in England had names from the elder faith, recalling their foundation by the Anglo-Saxons. Whether it was true or not, I was told that there had been a *træf* (temple site) at the ford which became Old Trafford in Manchester, where Manchester United's football ground and a cricket ground of the same name exist. So when I saw Manchester United play Arsenal there, I had an awareness that an ancient shrine had been somewhere nearby. Of course, the football ground *is* a contemporary shrine for many: the "Field of Dreams." Wednesbury, north of Birmingham, bore the name of Woden (or "Woden's Burg"), and Thundersley, near Southend, that of Thunor. Tysoe, Warwickshire, where once there was a giant horse carved in the red soil of the hillside, meant a "spur of land dedicated to the god Tig" (Tiw). In many places, I found, the names of the ancient gods remained, and their surrounding landscape retained the numinous qualities associated with them. The land of my birth was redolent with the spirit of past ages and the sacred places of the elder faith.

When I read the folklore of these places, or was told stories by local people, I learned of encounters with the wildfolk, fairies, sprites, boggarts, elves, pixies, and other impressive nature spirits and deities. All of this was far removed from the biblical worldview I had been taught at school. Sunday newspapers scurrilously ran stories about witches and magicians, satanic covens, and secret voodoo temples in which "unspeakable rites" were performed, as well as the Black Mass and sexually charged, skyclad Wiccan orgies. Stories about Rollo Ahmed, Gerald Gardner, Doreen Valiente, and others gave distorted, sensationalized accounts of their activities. Sometimes Church of England priests condemned it all, and conducted exorcisms at "infected" sites. I was never sure how much of this had any basis in reality, and how much of it came from sensationalist pulp novels. The works of Dennis Wheatley and the horror films produced by the British studio Hammer were filled with virgins tied to satanic altars, rescued "just in time" by handsome heroes.

Occasionally, some genuinely unpleasant activities were discovered. In the early 1960s, Sunday newspapers reported rituals at abandoned, deconsecrated churches and other ancient sites. In March 1963, my girlfriend Mary had her cat stolen and sacrificed in the desecrated church at Clophill, Bedfordshire. The papers made much of this event, describing the arrangement of the exhumed bones and the skull of a woman and a red cross in a circle painted on the church wall, though they wrongly described the sacrificial animal as a rooster. Also in that year, at Castle Rising in Norfolk, a black cross and a circle of soot were found on the ground near the castle door to which two clay figures and a sheep's heart pierced with hawthorn twigs were nailed.

But the people I knew were not into sacrificing cats, nailing up sheep's hearts, or otherwise trying to impress the journalists at *The News of the World*. They were countrypeople who had a relationship to the landscape, the changing of the seasons, and the subtle qualities of space and time. One could commune with

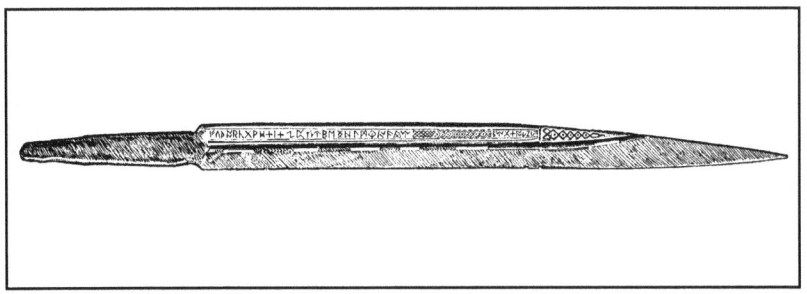

A 1923 illustration of the Thames scramasax from a British Museum guidebook.

certain trees, feel the energies of sacred wells and waters, and allow the spirits of the land to speak. This spirituality was an expression of the relationship of human beings to the world in which we live. One might call it Nature Religion, but that is an oversimplification—for to name something, is to destroy it.

How the Runes Came to Me

On my early visits to the British Museum as a youth, I had noticed artifacts with inscriptions in ancient writing systems, among them Egyptian hieroglyphics and Mesopotamian cuneiform. On display was the Rosetta Stone from Egypt, which has three inscriptions of the same text in three different writing systems—hieroglyphics, demotic script, and Greek. There were also Chinese artifacts with yet another writing system on them. So I became aware that what I had been taught to read and write was in the Roman alphabet. In the ancient British section, I saw yet other systems of writing, Ogham and runes. I was particularly attracted to the runes, as it was clear to me that they were part of my English ancestral heritage. In 1960 I noticed an Anglo-Saxon blade which had been discovered in 1857 in the River Thames—the so-called Thames scramasax. It was dated to the ninth century. On it were inlaid a row of twenty-eight runes and the maker's or owner's name in runes: *beagnoþ*. Next to it in the glass case was a drawing of the scramasax with the runes and their equivalent in Roman letters. As I always carried a notebook with me, I copied the runes in the proper order from the scramasax and wrote down their phonetic equivalents.

Nigel Pennick's rune doodles, 1963.

After that, I began to write in runic and endeavoured to find out more about these symbols. Of course there was no internet in those days, but ordinary public libraries were superb in their range then in comparison to the truncated and diminished state they fell into later after repeated cuts in funding. In a municipal library I came across the then-new book *Runes: An Introduction* by Ralph W. V. Elliott (Manchester University Press, 1959), which provided me with the wealth of information I was seeking. From that invaluable source, I was able to delve further into the mysteries of the runes, and to use them in various ways, exoteric and esoteric, including incorporating them into my artwork and artifacts. They have also been an ongoing topic of investigation for my publications and books.[1]

---

1. In 2015 I was named an honorary member of the Rune-Gild (established in 1980 by Stephen Flowers) in recognition of my extensive and life-long work in this area.

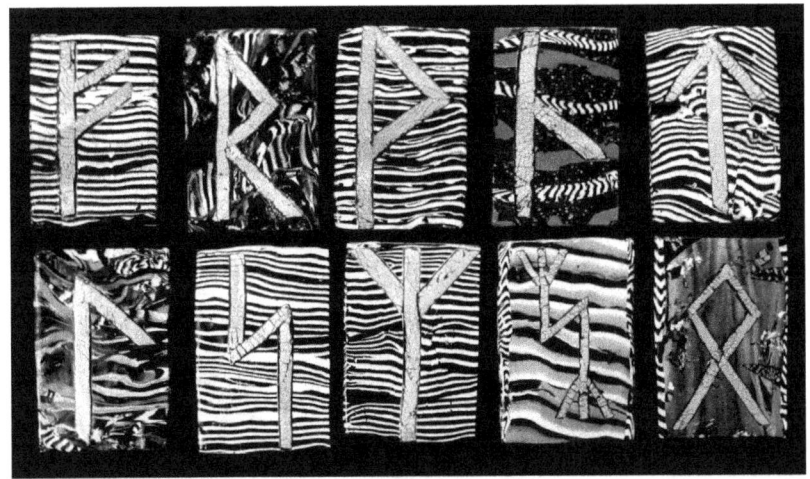

Runic plaques sculpted in polymer clay with gold, silver, and copper leaf by Nigel Pennick, 2019.

Runes on My Cup

As a student at the Tech in the mid-1960s, the college canteen was a meeting-place during lecture breaks and at lunchtime, although on occasion I preferred Paul's Variety Fayre café in East Road for sausage and chips if I was at that end of the site. Sometimes students were employed part-time by the canteen to clear up tables and take out the trash. The canteen used paper cups which were discarded after a single use. In late 1966 there was a particular student who would come round with a trolley and a bin to clear the tables once customers had left. However, he thought it amusing to pick up our half-empty cups and throw them into the bin before we could finish our coffee. As we were hard-up students, we resented this affront. One lunchtime, after he had done this to me again, I went and bought another cup of coffee. After drinking about half of the coffee, I wrote a runic formula on the outside of the cup. The trolley-pusher saw the half-empty cup standing there on the table and made a bee-line for it. But before he could pick it up, I warned him that it bore the "Curse of Loki" in runes. My companion at the table, Jennie, was startled by this, as she was a Roman Catholic who used to argue with me that any interest in the supernatural and the

Nigel Pennick's bookplate, 1965.

occult was worthless. I had not actually invoked Loki—I knew better than that—but the runic formula was real, nevertheless. He laughed, so I advised him that if he picked it up he would have "received the runes" knowingly and it would be the worse for him. He persisted in his folly and triumphantly threw my cup into the bin.

A weekend passed, I went to the canteen to drink a cup of coffee, but he was no longer clearing up. I enquired about him to the student who was doing the job, and she told me he had been expelled from the Tech. This was in consequence of his failing to attend classes and deliver his assignments. Jennie never argued with me again, saying that I had "fixed him up" with the runes in a practical demonstration she had witnessed firsthand. That was the last time I did such a thing, though the waitress in the café at Drummer Street bus station also took away the customers' half-empty cups and I was tempted!

NIGEL PENNICK

The Pagan Front

During the mid-1970s when I was deeply involved with geomancy, I almost took over the leadership of an organisation called the Pagan Front. In 1976, a few of us went to Avebury for a guided tour of the landscape around the vast ancient mound called Silbury Hill. Michael Dames, who had just had his book *The Silbury Treasure* published, speculated that the hill and surrounding ditches and earthworks had been fashioned by Neolithic people into a symbol of the Great Goddess. At the event was John Score, a practising Wiccan or, more specifically, a follower of what he called the "Old Religion of Wisecraft." John had edited a publication called *The Wiccan* since 1968 and founded the Pagan Front in 1971. After the tour of Avebury, I visited John's house and we discussed Paganism—past, present, and future. He was unwell and felt he had not long to live, so offered to hand over the Pagan Front to my safekeeping. As I was fully engaged in my scientific career as well as the IGR, I had to decline. Prudence Jones finally took it over, and it was revamped as the Pagan Federation in the wake of John Score's death some months later.

In 1978, with Jacky Craig, I founded a Pagan Moot at the Mitre pub in Bridge Street, Cambridge. The landlord was a Pagan and welcomed us. The Moot served as a focus for Cambridge Pagans and it still exists—albeit in a slightly different form—at the time of writing this memoir. Out of this came the short-lived Society for Promoting Pagan Knowledge[2] and two publications: *Basic Paganism: Four Views* (consisting of essays by Jacky Craig, Michael Howard, Chris Ogden, and myself) and *The Indestructible Castle*, a philosophical musing I wrote on Paganism.

Runestaff and Beyond

In June of 1984, with the rumours of the imminent closure of my place of work getting more credible, I set up Runestaff Crafts. I made Runestaff artefacts according to traditional principles.

---

2. The name was a play on the Society for Promoting Christian Knowledge, a religious charity founded in 1698.

Runestaff Crafts signboard designed and painted by Nigel Pennick, 1984.

Each artefact was handcrafted in keeping with British tradition, using the correct symbolic colours where apposite. As I described it at the time in a Runestaff advertisement from December of that same year, I was pursuing the "appropriate indigenous interpretation of worldwide universal principles . . . suited to the local conditions of Britain, the essential characteristic of geomancy." I was striving to embody something of the eldritch world in my handicrafts, and they came from my given heritage and environment. I aimed to utilise traditional techniques and ways-of-doing that came from the past, but yet were of our time, bypassing the mere fashionable, which comes and goes. I was practising what I later identified as the "Spiritual Arts and Crafts."

I made my Runestaff craft-works in a large shed I had built in the garden. I had no electricity, though I could run a cable out to power a small Dremel wood-turning lathe when I needed it. Otherwise I used hand tools. When it got dark, the Runestaff Workshop was lit by oil lamps burning paraffin (kerosene), a very congenial light. I bought materials and began to design geomantic artefacts. Earlier, in 1978, I had obtained some genuine *Bagua* Chinese geomantic mirrors which I offered for sale. They sold out, but I was unable to obtain any more. So I decided to make larger ones with European sigils, "eternal living signs," in place of the eight trigrams. These sold well. I also made several geomantic compasses, one of which was sold to Denmark and another to the United States. I experimented with using a photocopier to reproduce Northern Foot measuring rods (different and older in origin than the foot championed by the Anti-Metrication Board). But the paper stretched in the copy machine, so I meticulously painted them by hand.

Other items offered for sale by Runestaff were rune-boards, weathercocks, board games, and geomantic paraphernalia. They were supplied to customers in England, Scotland, West Germany, Denmark, the Netherlands, and the United States. Among the traditional northern European board games I made for Runestaff were Merels (or Nine Men's Morris), Tablut, and Gala. The boards were hand-painted on plywood and the "men" or playing-pieces were turned from wood on my lathe. Merels and Tablut "men" were stained and varnished, whilst Gala pieces were painted in colour. Runestaff Publications also came into being at that time.

Samas the Cat and the Demise of the Workshop

On top of the Runestaff Crafts workshop was a weathercock that I had made from plywood and painted gold. It measured almost two feet long and was the "luck" of the building. The usual weathercocks I made in the workshop and sold were small, about four inches long, and cut by hand from brass sheet.

In 1987 when I was attending pottery classes in Cambridge in a building that later became the Hotel Felix (now closed),

WYRD TIMES

Runestaff weathercock, 1985.
Photo by Nigel Pennick.

I was given a cat.[3] A Norwegian woman there told me she and her family had to go back to Norway, and she was not allowed to take the cat with her. She claimed that he was a friendly cat and he liked her children. In hindsight, this must have been a lie and she was trying to get rid of the animal.

I drove to the woman's apartment and was handed a box in which the cat—Samas by name—was enclosed. On the way back, he clawed at the box in a frenzied attempt to escape, yowling loudly. We already had a cat, called Felix, and when I opened the box Samas ran upstairs and hid beneath a bed. My daughter Lindsey tried to stroke him but received a slash from his claws. My son Martin then pushed a rolled-up newspaper under the bed and it was slashed to ribbons. Clearly, the cat was a berserker—not the friendly pet the woman had promised us.

Seeing that Samas was dangerous, we took him to a veterinary surgeon and had him neutered. But his rage was probably increased by what we had done to him, and after a few weeks of hiding behind furniture, he went outside and refused to come in again. So we fed and watered him outside. Occasionally, Samas had bloody fights with other local cats (but not Felix). All the bouts I witnessed saw Samas defeat his opponents, sometimes standing lordly upon their cowering bodies. He was a hard cat.

One day, working in the Runestaff workshop, I heard scuffling on the roof. I went outside and there was Samas making a furious attack on the weathercock. He ripped off part of its tail before I could shoo him away. Eventually, he disappeared and we never saw him again. The weathercock, fatally damaged, eventually fell

3. Felix, from Latin *felis* ("cat") is a common cat name. Indeed, it was the name of our own cat.

off in windy weather, and then an exceptionally violent storm tore off the roof of the workshop, whose walls collapsed into the nearly flooded garden. That was the end of it. Everything inside was irreversibly wrecked. I had someone take most of the debris away, but later I recovered some fragments in an "archaeological dig." I continued occasionally to make Runestaff Crafts artifacts, but not in a new workshop.

Odinic Rites

The Odinist Committee was founded as a Germanic Pagan religious group in 1973 by John Yeowell (Stubba) and John Gibbs-Bailey (Hoskuld). In 1980 it became the Odinic Rite and began publishing *OR Briefing*, which was an exchange magazine. On June 27, 1984, the Odinic Rite set up the Runic Guild (Odinic Rite), with Ellie Hooijschuur (aka Freya Aswynn) as Guild Master and Anthony Looker as Recorder/Treasurer. I had no connexion with this group, and never attended any of its meetings.

OR Briefing did, however, review some of my runic and Pagan publications, and through this I was invited to appear at the Odinic Rite's National Moot, which was was held in London's Conway Hall on September 18–19, 1987. Hosted by Stubba, the Director of the Court of Gothar, the Moot began before lunch with a fraternal greeting by leading members of the Rite, many of whom were addressed by their Odinic names. After lunch, the ritual Blot of Winter Finding[4] was held, which begins:

> Idunn, we hail you!
> Odin, worshipped by gods and men, who makes strong whom you choose, and who makes them holy and wise;
> Raven god, from whom comes all knowledge—
> Odin, chief ruler of the gods, all hail!

The Blot lasted an hour, after which Asbjorn gave a talk

---

4. A *blōt* (from Old English *blōt* and Old Norse *blōt*, both meaning "sacrifice") is a ritual in Pagan Germanic religious practice, usually an offering to a deity or deities.

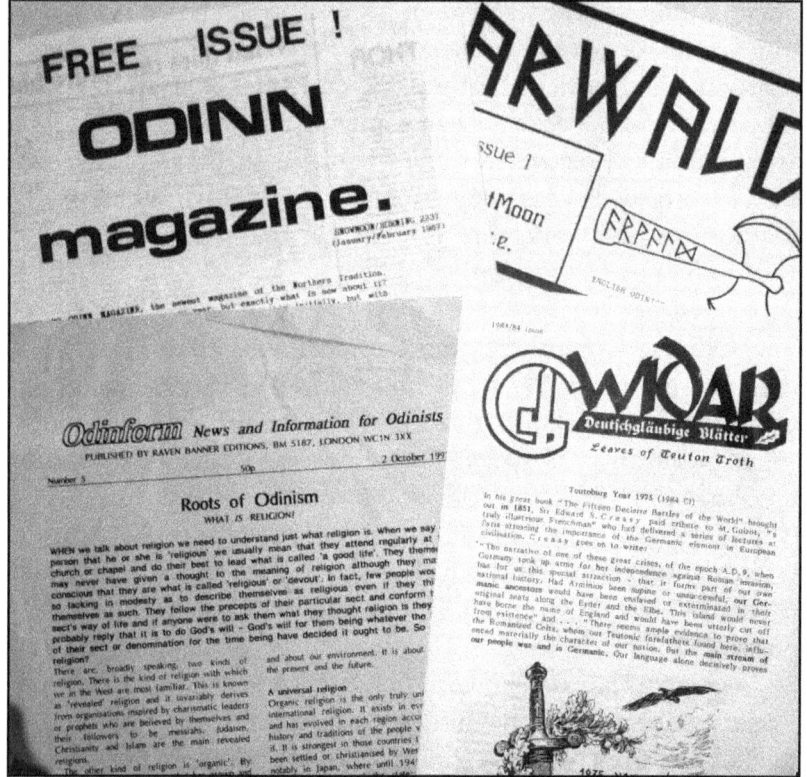

Odinist exchange magazines of the 1980s and 1990s.

on shamanism. Then it was tea-time, and at 5:30 in the afternoon, Freya Aswynn spoke on "Runes and the Calendar." At 6:30 was supper, and at 7:45 Dr Odfried Jungklaaß of the Deutschgläubiger Gemeinschaft (Teutonic Troth Community), who had come over from Germany for the event, gave a talk on "Odinism in Northern Europe." The final speaker of the day was me. I gave a lecture titled "The Sacred Grid and Board Games in the Northern Tradition."

Day two of the National Moot featured talks by Leigh Taylor on "The Holy Runes" and Richard Lawson on "Pagan Survival in English Folk Culture: Song, Dance, and Mumming." Then Wulf, Harald, and others talked about organising Odinic Hearths. The final talk was by Stubba, looking to the future. The Moot formally concluded when members of the Hearth of Wayland conducted the closing Blot, after which attendees repaired to the Smithfield Tavern, a bus ride away from the Conway Hall, for an "Odinical" pub social. I did not attend the latter event.

In 1991 Prudence Jones and I participated in an Odinic Rite memorial Blot at Maldon in Essex. It was solemnised on the one thousandth anniversary of the Battle of Maldon, where an Anglo-Saxon force was defeated by shipborne Danes. We were at the actual site of the battle. Stubba conducted the rite, and Prudence and myself did the readings as the tide came in. We had kept up the day!

I communicated with John Yeowell and a few other members of the Odinic Rite over the years. At one point Yeowell even asked me to publish his memoirs after he died, but I never received them. Like most organizations in the fields of religion, politics, and earth mysteries, the Odinic Rite subsequently had a tortuous history of schisms, resignations, and splinter groups. But I know few details, as I was never a member of the Rite nor its Runic Guild. (Indeed, the same is true of most of the other spiritual and earth mysteries groups to whom I lectured as a guest speaker.)

Keeping Up the Day

An old Fenland saying tells us: "It is necessary to keep up the day." This means that there are special days in the year that must be celebrated. Nowadays, people are used to celebrating their birthday on the correct date, but—apart from Easter Sunday, Christmas Day, and New Year's Day—other days are casually traduced by individuals and institutions alike. Those devotees who are observant of the proper sacred days of their calendar, whatever their religion, are those who "keep up the day." Ploughmen in the days of oxen and horses kept up the days of their profession, Plough Monday being their primary festival. Other rural fraternities and trade guilds also kept up their own days, celebrating with parades, food, and drink. These were held on immutable dates in the calendar, regardless of the day of the week. There were also fixed events, such as the stations of the sun

"Keeping up the Day": Leaflets for St George's Day and Lammas Scot-Ale events.

and the winter and summer solstices and equinoxes.

The exigencies of urban employees in the working week eroded the proper tradition of keeping up the day. It was considered acceptable to celebrate a festival on the nearest Saturday so that work could continue on the actual date if it did not coincide with the weekend. Even the celebration of Guy Fawkes' Night with bonfire and fireworks, recalled in the rhyme *"Please to remember, / the fifth of November / Gunpowder, treason and plot; / I see no reason why gunpowder treason / Should ever be forgot,"* is often held on the nearest Saturday. This makes a mockery of the commemoration.

Even some Pagan groups I know celebrate their rituals on the nearest Saturday. But if their tradition had any meaning to them, they would repudiate this practice and perform them on the correct days. In all the groups I have run—the Institute of Geomantic Research, the Pagan Moot, the Cambridge Pagan Fellowship, and the Way of the Eight Winds—I have always kept up the day. Not to do so is to disrespect our ancestors and the power that each day embodies. So from the late 1970s, the Pagan Moot held a gathering (jokingly called the "Mystics' Picnic") at Mutlow Hill on the ancient Fleam Dyke on each August the 1st, Lammas Day. We always kept up other significant days, and from 1986 I called a winter solstice Scot-Ale at a series of public houses. This was celebrated annually without fail until the Covid lockdown of 2020. Even then, four of us (Prudence Jones, Jon Ward, my son Martin, and myself) held an outdoor observance at midday in the Country Park at Milton, north of Cambridge. We kept up the day! The tradition was restored again in 2022 when a Scot-Ale was held at the Baron of Beef on the winter solstice. In Cambridge, the Midsummer Fair has been held annually from the year 1208 without a break until the present day. Even in 2020 and 2021 when the fair was in abeyance under orders from the City Council because of the Covid pandemic, Gypsies and Travellers still came and kept it up—so its ancient continuity remained.

Scot-Ales are an ancient tradition. A thirteenth-century prelate, Robert Grosseteste, the Bishop of Lincoln who also had hegemony over the Cambridge region, banned townspeople and villagers from performing "miracle plays, scotales, ram-raisings and athletic contests" as well as the "Festival of Fools and the Pagan *Inductio Mali sive Autumni*." A *scot-ale* was a get-together where each person played their *scot*, or toll, for their drink. Scot-Ales were held on festival days not authorised by the Church, and so were banned. But not forever!

A Ceremony of the Bardic Chair

Although the Cambridge Pagan Moot was largely a social gathering at various pubs, some members conducted rituals together as part of various groups and occasionally there was a special collective event. In the early 1980s the London druid Colin Murray, as the head of his Golden Section Order, had conferred upon the Moot the status of the Cambridge Bardic Chair. However, the rites and ceremonies we conducted at Cambridge tended to be based on the Northern Tradition and Wicca, rather than Druidism.

Nigel Pennick with runestaff and hammer
at the Bardic Chair handfasting, Cambridge, 1996.

One of the Bardic Chair's more notable events was the handfasting of Linda Catterson and Nicholas Gregory on July 20, 1996. This is the only Bardic Chair ritual of which I have a full account that has been preserved.

For the rite, a section of the hired playground of a Cambridge school was made into a sacred circle by "enhazelling" it with hazel rods driven into the ground. Prudence Jones officiated as Priestess, and I, with a consecrated hammer and a runestaff, as Priest. Members of the Bardic Chair, wearing oak leaves, played music as the participants entered in a line and circled three times around the enclosure. At the eight points of the compass stood the guardians of the airts, each a member of the Sisters of Gaia and wearing crowns of flowers. Once all was in place, each of the Sisters in turn opened her point. We did not allow photographs or videos of the ceremony, as this would have distracted the participants from a proper reverence for the ritual.

From the eight direction-points, runic blessings were called using the Anglo-Saxon rune-names, beginning in the North: "*Ger* holds the still point of the turning circle, the mystery of time." North-east: "*Eolh* offers protection—strong in earth and heaven." East: "*Beorc* brings fertility, as life springs new each morning." South-east: "*Lagu*, the waters of fruitfulness, as day flows on to noontide." South: "*Dæg* brings substance and fulfillment, the glorious flowering of will." South-west: "The *Thorn*-rune gives fierce loyalty and wild desire; channel it well." West: "*Cen*, the light of knowledge, and fruits of knowledge, value them." North-west: "*Hægl*, the hag-rune, gives us both hard storm and hearty greeting."

After this, the Priestess called upon Freya: "Freya, radiant goddess of the heavens, first chooser of the noble dead, lady of beauty, joy and delight, bless this gathering. In your Hall of Benches, women and men make merry; may we today do likewise. May these two people, marrying in your name and those of your fellow divinities, be touched by beauty, filled with joy, and blessed by delight on this day. Lady, heap your gifts upon them, may their days be filled with plenty and may their lives be long and fruitful. Hallow this gathering, encircle it with your joy, fill it with your delight. May love find her fulfillment, and true fellowship be forged."

Then the bride walked from the west and the groom from the east to the centre of the circle to face each other. Bearing the sacred hammer as priest, I challenged the bride and groom: "Do you, Linda, and you, Nicholas, call upon all here present, to the High Ones, the ancestors and your posterity, to witness that you do pledge yourselves to each other with holden hands, to finish and fulfill your whole engagement, both trusted and true?" The bride and groom each clasped the hammer and said: "I do."

Then the Priestess challenged the bride and groom: "As the head of the hammer is bound to the haft, will you be bound to each other, to take life's obstacles in your stride, to steady each other if you stumble, and to support each other along the straight?" The bride and groom answered: "I will." Then the priest and priestess bound them together with a cord, and the priestess placed a besom (broomstick) across their path. Then the bride and groom ran nine times deosil (sunwise) round the circle, jumping the broomstick at each turn, while the participants sounded rattles and clapped their hands.

Then the women sang:

> *We all come from the Goddess*
> *And to Her we will return,*
> *Like a drop of rain*
> *Going to the ocean.*

Then the men sang:

> *Hoof and horn, hoof and horn,*
> *All that dies shall be reborn.*
> *Seed and grain, seed and grain,*
> *All that falls shall rise again.*

After the final circuit, the priest and priestess unbound them. The priestess then addressed the bridegroom: "Do you, Nicholas, make a solemn vow and take the Ancient Ones who rule over all things to witness that Linda you will have as your own?" And the groom replied: "I do swear it." The priestess took the ring from a designated participant and offered it to the groom, saying: "Then get from her love like your love and give her this ring in token thereof." The groom took the ring while the priest addressed the bride with the same words, and the bride answered: "I do swear it." Then bride and groom exchanged rings, while the priest and priestess together said" "Hlin, goddess of rings, bless their union." The bride and groom kissed. The priestess said: "Freya, radiant wearer of the necklace of the Brisings, encircle their marriage with your love." Then the priest: "Frey, bless their marriage with fertility and plenty." Priestess: "Frigga, give them stability, happiness, and peace." Priest: "Tyr, guardian of oaths,

Freya from *Visions of the Goddess* by Nigel Pennick, 1993.

hold them together staunchly through thick and thin. May they grow in honour and in wisdom." They kissed once more, to the applause of the participants.

Finally, the closing, when the priestess said: "These two are handfasted, and as they are joined in fellowship, love, and honour, we stand as witness to their bond. May Freya, Frey, and all the ancient goddesses and gods bless them." And lastly, the priest invoked: "To joy and prosperity!" which was repeated by all present. The guardians of the airts gave their farewell blessings, widdershins; all participants circled deosil, and left by the north.

East Anglian Magic

Beneath the cape of concealment,
I walk out of the sight of men.
Along the crooked path I roam;
Straight paths are for the dead alone.

—from the song "The Toadman" by Nigel Pennick, 2017

In the 1980s I knew a witch named Sonny Howe. She was much older than me and lived in a cottage in Soham, Suffolk, with about fifteen cats. She was a local character with the reputation—well played up by her—of being a "black witch." Occasionally, she held parties which even the local Church of England vicar would attend. A few times a year, she would invite me over, offer me borage wine, and we would discuss herbs, astrology, witchcraft, Toadmanry, and the Nameless Art. On one occasion, I received a telephone call from her. A parcel had been delivered by registered mail (special delivery, signed for) which contained a fine crystal bowl engraved with runes. She asked me to come and read them to her. I duly obliged and made the half-hour drive across the Fens.

When I got there, I drank the customary cup of tea and, while I petted various cats, she explained that she had no knowledge of who had sent this fine and expensive present. The bowl, about ten inches in diameter, was indeed of fine crystal glass and the runes were elegantly engraved upon it by a professional. However, she was dismayed when I told her that the runes were in fact a formulaic death curse. Someone who knew what he or she was doing had gone to the effort of purchasing a valuable object, having it engraved with the runic curse, parcelling it up, and sending it. Signing for it meant that she had accepted the

Runic Wheel painted on a wooden board by Nigel Pennick, 1990.

curse—it had been served upon her, just as a legal writ must be served personally upon the individual to whom it applies. It was apparent that, for whatever reason, she had a serious enemy.

Sonny asked me what she could do, so I told her to conduct a ritual disempowering the curse. The bowl was to be smashed, and the fragments cast into the running water of a river. Materially, it was worth hundreds of pounds—but spiritually, it was a lethal artefact. But she could not bring herself to break it up, or even to let me smash it myself. She was taken by the glamour of the object. Finally, she decided that she would keep it inverted on the window ledge. My protests that this would have no effect were ignored.

The last time I went there before her death, the bowl was still there, inverted among the potted plants. Not long afterwards, she died.

Some years later Paul Smith told me he had known Sonny Howe and was left a macabre legacy by her. Paul, who died in 2021, was a staunch supporter of our May Day events and Scot-Ales. Spiritually, he was a Druid; musically, a bodhrán player and singer of traditional songs; and his profession as a butcher paralleled his role as The Butcher in our "Old Tup" (Derby Ram) mummer's play. In her Will, Sonny Howe left him her right forearm. She intended that it should be preserved so that Paul could use it in rituals. It was not permitted, and so her arm did not outlast her body.

What happened to the crystal bowl, I never found out.

No Door Is Ever Closed to a Toadman

The first I ever heard of Toadmanry was from John Thorn at the Granville. Since I was a boy, I had wondered what magic the farmworkers in my grandmother's story had used to stop the horse on the railway crossing and kill the farmer. John told me it was "by the bone." He never showed me any bone, but I had the impression that he knew a lot more than this cryptic allusion suggested. In my *Cambridge Voice* days, I had asked Enid Porter, curator of the Folk Museum, about the toad bone. Apparently, different farm labourers carried more than one of these powerful magical implements, and there was even a secretive rural fraternity known as the Bonesmen who had a system of signals and signs of recognition. The Black Cat Bone of American Hoodoo that I learned about from a blues song by Lightnin' Hopkins was clearly related to this tradition. And John Lee Hooker's "Ground Hog Blues" (1949) talked of "toad-frogs' hips" as the *materia magica* used to "kill that dirty groundhog."[5] The toad bone is a hook-shaped "hipbone."

But to me, Toadmanry seemed to contain a deeper mystery, in the medieval sense of the word. I found several folklore books

---

5. The 1960s British blues-rock band the Groundhogs, led by Tony McPhee, took their name from "Ground Hog Blues," and McPhee recorded several extended virtuoso versions of this song.

Cunning Man. Unused illustration for *In Field and Fen* by Nigel Pennick, 2009.

that described the rituals for gaining the bone, which the authors had recorded from actual named practitioners. I also discovered other oral accounts of the tradition, and found it mentioned in literature as far back as the ancient Roman author Pliny. This research was collected in my book *The Toadman*, published in a limited toadskin-bound edition in 2010 by the Society of Esoteric Endeavour.

Long before *The Toadman* was published, I had gained the bone by chance. In the road outside my house, I saw an injured toad that appeared to have been run over by a vehicle. I put it in my back garden in the hope that it would recover, but by the next morning it was dead. This was a sign that I must perform the toad-bone ritual! The Fenland tradition is to put the toad in an anthill until it is defleshed, and I had a compost bin that was host to a colony of ants. So I put the toad in the bin and left it. Some months later, I removed the skeleton, partly disarticulated. At the proper time, I took it to a nearby stream which flows north–south. I threw the bones into the water and watched as two tarried while the others tumbled away in the current. These two were the famous "toad bones." I pulled them from the water, and hence I became a toadman.

Contemporary with me were the "speculative" toadmen (i.e., those not connected with farm labour) Andrew Chumbley (1967–2004) and Michael Clarke (died 2022). Both had connexions with rural magic—Chumbley in Essex and Clarke in Norfolk—but they also practised other magical traditions as well as Toadmanry. Chumbley's main work on his version of Toadmanry from the viewpoint of the Cultus Sabbatai was *The Grimoire of the Golden Toad* (Xoanon, 2000). I knew Michael from our common participation in a Pagan group in Norwich. He had a collection of "esoteric artefacts" including a magic horn, probably from the nineteenth century, bearing the name Baal in Theban characters, which I photographed and published in two of my books. My own connexions were mainly with other folk practitioners in East Anglia, but as far as Toadmanry is concerned, it was always a personal thing and not part of collective practice, or even overt magical doctrine or theory. The Nameless Art is not categorizable in modern taxonomic terms, nor can it be encapulated in a loaded word like "witchcraft" or "magic." As a cultural transposition of tradition, it represents something more.

In the 1990s I attended Pagan gatherings in Norwich, where they were often held in the Coach and Horses pub in Bethel Street. This was an unusual place, for it failed to observe the hated "licensing hours" for drinking, which had been imposed by the government during World War I as a temporary measure and never rescinded. Because the pub was close to the police station and the city's main theatre, it was a drinking place for police officers and actors. It was surmised that the police wanted somewhere to get a drink and so allowed the licensee to break the licensing laws. This situation made for some strange bedfellows; in addition to the police, the pub was also favoured by the local punks and it became the location for many Pagan Moots.

One evening in Norwich, an event of mine was staged by

the local Pagans. My talk was about the runes and had attracted a good audience, which was too large for the pub. So instead it was arranged that we would convene in a room at a nearby New Age centre. People assembled outside and we were let in by a janitor.

We scrambled up two or three flights of stairs to the upper room, where the organiser put the key in the locked door. It would not budge. Then someone else tried, but was dissuaded from causing damage. I asked to try and was given the key, which again jammed in the lock. Saying "No door is ever closed to a toadman!" I punched the door by the keyhole and it swung open. Some standing close were visibly shocked, but we all trooped in, and as it was already dark, switched on the lights, and distributed chairs from a stack. Finally, I was able to give my talk. After about twenty minutes, I was discoursing on the meaning of the rune *Laguz* (ᛚ)[6] and had just begun to intone "*Laguz, laguz, . . .*" when we heard rain beating upon the roof. It was a heavy storm and the roof began to leak. Rain ran down a cable from which one of the lights was hanging, and began to drip on the floor. I made a comment about the confluence of my *galdr* (runic chanting) and the rain, when the lights fused. We were plunged into darkness and had to find our way out of the room. Fortunately, the lights were still on in the rest of the building, but that was the end of my unintended practical demonstration. It reminded me of my rapid exit from the summit of Glastonbury Tor after inscribing the rune *Thurisaz* many years earlier, on my geomantic pilgrimage in 1968.

A strange coda to the subject of Toadmanry came to light in June of 2022 when the Museum of London Archaeology team announced the discovery of around 8,000 toad and frog bones in a forty-foot-long ditch on a site a quarter of a mile from where I wrote *The Toadman*. This site included a roundhouse used during the middle and late Iron Age (ca. 400 BCE–43 CE) and the bones were contemporary with those structures. Why they were preserved in the ditch was a puzzle to the archaeologists, but whatever the reason, the confluence is striking.

6. The Proto-Germanic rune-name *Laguz* means "lake" or "water."

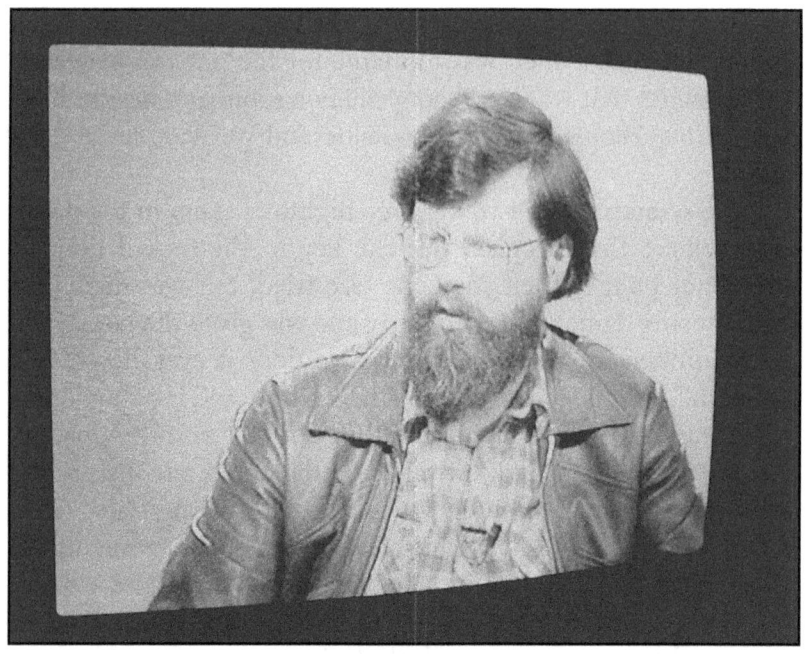

Nigel Pennick interviewed on television, 1984.

BBC and the Media

The British Broadcasting Corporation (BBC) is a strange institution. Begun in 1922, coterminous with Benito Mussolini's institution of the corporate state in Italy, it is a corporation with a Royal Charter. Funded by a so-called "licence fee," which everyone with a television has to pay whether or not they watch the BBC, this organisation claims to be impartial in all its doings. My dealings with the BBC have been equivocal. I have appeared a number of times on BBC radio, but never on BBC television. My first appearance on the BBC was a setup. I was asked by a religious affairs program on the local BBC radio station to be interviewed about Paganism. I turned up at the appointed time and was ushered into a studio where the presenter sat with another man.

Nobody had told me that this was to be a confrontation and I was not prepared for undisguised disrespect from anyone—but I got it, and in full measure. The other "guest" was a Christian fanatic of some stripe and he tore into me immediately. There was no dialogue, as the presenter clearly favoured my assailant. I was interrupted continuously and had no chance to say what I had intended. I pointed out that they would not have set up a Jew, Hindu, or Muslim in this way, but my analogy was ignored, either through indifference, ignorance, or malice. Instead of the philosophical words I had intended to say, I was forced to uphold religious freedom and the right not to be attacked.

Afterwards, friends asked me why I did not just walk out, but that is not what someone of the Northern Tradition does. One stands one's ground, no matter what. I contacted the BBC complaints department and they told me they would "look into it." After about a month, I received an "adjudication" that their conduct was above criticism, and my complaint was rejected. No respect from the complaints department. Nothing new there, either.

I have appeared on several television programs, although these were never live broadcasts nor were they made by the BBC. I was filmed briefly for an Austrian TV news item when I was in Salzburg conducting a runic workshop. A Norwegian crew filmed me in Cambridge, where at lunchtime they were about to leave a video camera (which cost £44,000) on the back seat of their parked car. I warned them that in Cambridge it was not a good idea if they wanted to use it again that afternoon. So they re-opened the car and took it to the restaurant with them. I went with them to Borley, where I had been before with the Borderline Science Investigation Group's all-night ghost-watch. Videoing me in front of the exterior of Borley Church, a church warden came out and began to berate us. Presumably he had heard the crew speaking Norwegian, and hence they must have been up to no good. I told him I was a member of the Church of England and he went inside again, seemingly satisfied. It was true—the Church of England has never excommunicated me, as any self-respecting religion maintaining tradition would have!

Another video that I appeared in was shot at a London studio better known for making pornographic movies. This was a performance of Aleister Crowley's *Gnostic Mass* in which I, along with Freya Aswynn, Prudence Jones, and many luminaries of the London occult scene, took part as the congregation.

Christian Protests

"Over the Rainbow '89" was a "celebration of spirit, mind, and body" held at the Athenaeum in Bury St Edmunds, Suffolk, on August 11 and 12, 1989. Staged by an organisation called Unlimited Futures, it presented a series of eclectic and diverse lectures and workshops on spiritual matters. These included the healing vibrations of food by Peta Gulliver, "The Use and Abuse of Astrology" by Brian Hewitt, a talk on the spiritual path of homeopathy by Catherine Eccles, and Stella Armstrong spoke on "Our Spiritual Nature." My lecture title was "The Runes," described as an "introduction to the northern European ancient symbolic alphabet, an understanding of the skills and wisdoms of the past, their significance today." Lauren Parsons spoke on "Healing the Earth" and there were other talks on iridology, crystal healing, psychometry, and hypnotherapy, as well as a Buddhist meditation workshop, Shiatsu healing, a circle dance and other sacred dances, a Medicine Wheel, and a "Colour and Creativity" class. There were several other workshops, along with counselling and craft stalls selling esoteric items and clothing. The Goodfood Café provided bodily sustenance. It was a splendid event full of friendliness, goodwill, and openness.

Almost opposite the Athenaeum stands St Edmundsbury Cathedral, from which emanated spleen and hostility as "Over the Rainbow" suffered a fierce attack from the church authorities in the press and on the radio. They condemned the event as "Satanic" and held prayers attempting to get it banned. At the end of the first day, I left the venue to go to a local vegetarian restaurant with some Pagan and New Age friends. I was walking along a street with Jess Cormack (who was actually a Pagan holistic counsellor and creative writing teacher), when we were joined by some others from the Athenaeum. We approached a mean building that passed for an evangelical church when, suddenly, a disturbed man ran out and confronted us. Clearly, he knew where we were coming from, and we could see from the

Nigel Pennick with runic headband preparing a magical item, 1995.

"dog collar" he was wearing that he was some sort of clergyman, a zealot of the "thou-shalt-not" persuasion. Quoting passages from the Old Testament book of Deuteronomy, this American pastor accused us of being instruments of Satan and uttered other tropes from the playbook of the Witchfinder General. He continued to berate us in a rant sprinkled with biblical quotations. Both Jess and I had been indoctrinated at Sunday school, so we knew the Bible as well as he did. So did my young biker friend, who had lost a leg and been rendered a eunuch in a terrible motorcycling accident. Immediately he quoted Deuteronomy 23:1 back at the pastor: "'He who is cut off in his privy member, or wounded in the stones, shall not be admitted unto the congregation of the Lord.'—*How cruel was that?*" he asked. The pastor did not reply, going off on another tangential rant about witchcraft and Satan.

We argued as good as we got. Of course, it was a waste of effort, but we were fired up and determined not to be "druv." Then there was a shower of rain, yet the fanatic persisted in shouting at us. On the long August evening the sun was still shining and, refracted through the rain, a full double rainbow appeared in all its splendour. It was an *ostentum*—a sign that appears unexpectedly and is perceived as having a meaning, either as a portent or a confirmation. We pointed to it with glee, but the pastor asserted that the rainbow was a symbol of evil. No, on the contrary, we told him, according to *his* holy book it was God's sign at the end of Noah's Flood. Clearly realising that he had made a faux pas and we were right, looking dejected he suddenly stuttered, turned round, and slunk back inside his church. We were delighted, but he had wasted twenty minutes of our precious time. And we were hungry.

In 1989 I was also invited to speak at the Pagan Federation's first national conference. It was to be held in a hall at the University of Leicester. Prudence Jones, then a main driving force in the Federation, took me from Cambridge in her car. We arrived at the venue, and people were standing around though the hall should have been open. We were shocked when we found out the reason: the gathering had been cancelled. It appeared that someone saying they were from a Christian fundamentalist organisation had telephoned the University authorities and told them that there might be violence if the event went ahead, a not-so-veiled threat that fundamentalist activists would come to disrupt the proceedings. Instead of engaging security guards or police officers to protect our free speech, the craven university authorities closed down the conference.

Several years earlier, in 1986, Prudence Jones and I had founded the Pagan Anti-Defamation League precisely to counter this sort of faith-based persecution. We had defended others who were suffering similar harassment by Christian fanatics, and now it had happened to us. We were outraged, drove into the city past a mosque, a Hindu temple, several churches, and a gurdwara (a Sikh hall for assembly and worship), and went to the office of the local newspaper, *The Leicester Mercury*. After explaining what had happened to members of the staff, the editor was summoned. Then we had a stand-up row with him. He could not—or would not—understand that for fanatics to threaten violence and so close down a legitimate meeting of a religious group was a flagrant violation of the principle of free speech and freedom of religion. We pointed out that Leicester was a multicultural city,

LET THE FUN BEGIN: Nigel Pennick, Anna Franklin and Nick Tolladay blowing horns to mark the opening of the May fair

Leicester Mercury clipping, 2006.

and that Pagans had the same rights as the other religions whose places of worship we had just passed. But he refused categorically to allow us to tell our story in his newspaper. It was appalling for a journalist to behave in that way, and after arguing with him for an hour or so, we gave up. One of the other journalists (who clearly sympathised with our plight) suggested we go to the local radio station, so we did. We were received with interest and courtesy, and within half an hour, broadcast live on radio what had happened. Seventeen years later, accompanied by local Pagans, I was invited to open the Leicester May Fair. Dressed in my ceremonial tatters, I gave the customary May Day speech, and then, along with Anna Franklin and Nick Tolladay, we blew the May Horns. *The Leicester Mercury* was there and printed a photograph of us three winding our horns. It was a sign of how, by then, things had changed for the better!

Pagan Federation conferences grew in size each year. Like the other moots and symposia, they included talks, workshops, discussions, ritual, and musical performances. At the Pagan Federation Conference held on November 25, 1995, at the Conway Hall in Central London, I gave a talk titled "The Nature of Sacred Places and Temples in the European Pagan Tradition," Prudence Jones spoke on "The Goddess and the Grail: Pagan Spiritual Development," Rae Beth talked on the path of the hedge witch, Jackie Huxter-Freer presented a slide show on Druidic star-lore, and Freya Aswynn ran a Northern Tradition workshop on rune magic. In other rooms of the Conway Hall there was an open session by the Dragon Environmental Group, and a discussion led by Naomi Ozaniec on how Pagans could fare in the "Third Millennium."

Around that time, Prudence Jones gave a series of adult education evening classes in Witchcraft and Astrology. One place she taught was the Manor School in Arbury, Cambridge. For some reason, one week she could not get to the class, and, as that week's subject was geomantic in theme, she asked me to teach it in her place. Just before we were about to begin, we heard an awful din outside. It was people shouting and chanting. As we were nowhere near a football ground, it could not be football hooligans, so I went out to look. It was neither football hooligans nor skinheads, but Christians. I looked over the fence at a group of people standing there who, when they saw me, abused me and shouted: "Witches go to Hell!" Whether this was a statement of their belief or an instruction, I was not sure. The people in the group looked threatening and I was apprehensive that things would turn violent as they began to chant "Witches go to Hell!" once more.

This was yet another tiresome attack by Christian fanatics who did not believe in tolerating difference, so I went back inside. Meanwhile, the Principal had telephoned the police, who arrived with commendable swiftness. A policeman had a word with them, and they dispersed. So I was able to teach the class at last, as were the teachers of the other classes. The next day I found out that these troublemakers were from the congregation of the local church, whose vicar later became the Archbishop of Canterbury.

Strange Events

Being a veteran of hundreds—if not thousands—of events ranging from small pub moots to crowded lecture-hall talks, I have experienced some strange scenes. In 1998 I was invited to speak at a Pagan event in Preston in the northwest of England. After a two-hundred-mile drive, I arrived at the house but there was nowhere to park in a Victorian street full of cars. I found a parking place a few hundred yards away. I walked back to the house and saw that the front garden had been concreted. The house had spotlights attached and a CCTV camera, which the couple who had organised the meeting told me were for their protection. There was another set of lights and a camera covering the back garden. Apparently, my hosts had announced in the media that they were witches and had received a barrage of abuse: objects thrown at their house, and their car vandalised repeatedly. So they made their residence into a fortress. Why they had deemed it necessary to publicise their witchcraft so widely, they did not tell me. I was glad I had not parked my car on their driveway, only to become a target for local rowdies.

The next morning was the day of the event. While my hosts were out, I had a cup of tea with the mother of one of them, who told me she had been a guest-house landlady in Blackpool, twenty miles west of Preston. We had a chat about the fun of Blackpool—the pier shows and seagulls, Blackpool Tower and its circus, the seafront trams, and the good times of the holidaymakers. It was a relief from the earnest witchcraft talk I had endured the previous evening. Then the car returned and I was taken to the venue, which was the Preston Rugby Club. As usual, the event featured a series of speakers in a hall with stalls selling robes, incense, pentagrams, jewellery, and Wiccan paraphernalia. Many of the people there appeared introverted, preoccupied with something, and quite unfriendly. There was the usual smattering of poseurs in costumes that now would be called cosplay, acting out their fantasies. In my normal street clothes,

Woden by Nigel Pennick, 1993.

I looked out of place amongst this finery of reenactment and renaissance fayrey. Still, I know who I am, and in my tradition we do not do this sort of thing. I am not impressed by dog collars or ecclesiastical habits—and the same goes for "Gandalf" robes, antlers on hats, or leather trousers with false phalli. I have seen them all at Pagan gatherings.

There was a lunch break, and then eventually I gave my talk. It was about the historic temples of northern Europe, including the halls of the *goðar* of Iceland;[7] the great temple of the gods at Uppsala; the temples on the holy island of Rügen; the shrines of the Wends; and temples in Lithuania, Poland, and Kievan Rus. I was the final speaker, and, surprisingly, no one asked any questions. I stood around as the merchandise was packed away and the stalls demounted. No one spoke to me. Gradually, the hall emptied and I was left there alone. My hosts had driven off with a full car and would return soon to pick me up.

Then in walked a young man, a rugby player. He talked with me about playing rugby and the proud traditions of his club. Here was someone *authentic*, at last, after a tedious time with the others. At the back of the hall was a large glass case in which were the relics and trophies of the club. Proudly he told me how the club had been founded in the nineteenth century by rugby players from Cheltenham College, an expensive Public School in southwest England. One of their original shirts was in the case. Then he pointed out the shirt of a club member who had played for England, as well as trophies and ancient rugby balls from the nineteenth century. His friendliness, enthusiasm for the game, and loyalty to his club were admirable. Some of his teammates began to turn up and he wished me well and went off to train with them outside. It was salutary to me to understand that I had more in common with this rugby player than I had with all the Pagans at the event. Eventually, I was picked up and went to the besieged house for a meal. I stayed the night and left very early before breakfast on my southbound journey home.

After speaking at events, people often come forward from the audience to talk with me. One time a man came up and shook

---

7. The plural term *goðar* (sg. *goði*) refers to the male local leaders in medieval Iceland who in pre-Christian times had a religious function. The corresponding term for a female practitioner is *gyðja*.

my hand. He thanked me profusely. He had been contemplating suicide, he told me, when someone gave him a copy of one of my books. He read it, and it gave him a reason to live. After a runic lecture, another man came up to me and told me he wanted to become a warrior. Probably he thought I would put him in contact with a Viking reenactment group, but I told him to join the Royal Marines. He seemed puzzled, but I hope that later he understood the difference between being a show-warrior and actually fighting in real, life-and-death combat. Authenticity is what we should all strive for.

Pagan Books of the Nineties and Noughties

In 1995 the scholarly press Routledge published *A History of Pagan Europe* by Prudence Jones and myself. It was a subject that no one before us had attempted—an overview from antiquity to the present showing the continuity of the Pagan tradition. Launched at a hotel near the British Museum, where we raised our glasses to the memory of King Penda,[8] it was well received in English and has been issued in several translated editions.

In 1995 a new imprint also appeared, ostensibly a community publisher of Pagan books. Called Capall Bann (after the white horse of Uffington), its beginnings were auspicious. Yvonne Aburrow was a regular at my Pagan Moot and hers was one of the first books released. The launch party for *The Sacred Grove* was held at the Dew Drop Inn on Gwydir Street, Cambridge, a pub with an eccentric landlord known for his after-hours "lock-ins."[9] He later ran the Waggon and Horses at Milton, where he promoted the spoof political party, the Monster Raving Loony Party, founded by horror-rock maestro Screaming Lord Sutch, who by then had committed suicide. Capall Bann went on to

---

8. King Penda was the fourth king of Mercia (The Kingdom of Mercia, central England, existed from 582–829 CE). Penda was the last Pagan king, known for his devotion to the Elder Faith. Having reigned thirty years (ca. 626–655), he died on the battlefield.

9. A practice in Britain and Ireland in which a pub locks its doors at the legal closing time, but the customers inside (usually trusted regulars) are allowed to continue drinking after hours.

Nigel Pennick's workroom, 1990. Several of his paintings hang on the wall: (L to R) *Sacred Geometry*, *Madonna and Child*, and *Magna Mater, the Great Goddess*. Photo by Nigel Pennick.

publish several of my titles. The scope of Capall Bann in its early days can be seen from the following: Yvonne Aburrow's *Auguries and Omens*; Pete Jennings and Pete Sawyer's *Pathworking*;

Futhark-hearth with Chimney Sprite, ink drawing by Helen Field, 2002.

Ronald Hutton's *The Shamans of Siberia*; *Angels and Goddesses: Celtic Christianity and Paganism in Ancient Britain* by Michael Howard, editor of the Wiccan magazine *The Cauldron*; and *Crystal Clear: A Guide to Quartz Crystals* by Jennifer Dent. My books included *Secret Signs, Symbols and Sigils*; *The Inner Mysteries of the Goths*; *Beginnings*; *Ogham and Coelbren*; and four books I wrote for which Helen Field provided most of the illustrations.

Helen had lived two miles away from me in the early 1990s, but I never met her. By the time we made contact, she lived on Jersey in the Channel Islands. My daughter Lindsey subscribed to a magazine called *Strix*, published by Sue Phillips in Hinckley, Leicestershire. Helen's drawings were prominent in *Strix*, and it emerged in correspondence that she would like to illustrate my books. So we were put in contact and collaborated on *The God Year*, *The Goddess Year*, *Muses and Fates*, and *The Book of Beasts*. All of our work was done over the telephone, as she consulted me on the proper attributes of deities, or what sigils should be used in the artwork. Several of her goddess images were self-portraits. Anna Franklin, editor of *Silver Wheel*, made extensive use of Helen's illustrations in *The Illustrated Encyclopedia of Fairies* (2005). After all these works were completed, we heard from Helen Field no more. All attempts by myself and Anna to communicate with her or locate her online were unsuccessful. She disappeared, and we presumed she was dead. Anna Franklin's publisher wanted to produce a new edition of the *Encyclopedia of Fairies*, but as Helen could not be found, it could not go ahead.

After about 2007, Capall Bann ceased to send out accounts, but still paid royalties sporadically. Then, the royalties dried up altogether. Other authors published by Capall Bann told me that they, too, could get no account statements, neither money nor their copyrights back. Numerous communications remained unanswered. Towards the end of Capall Bann's existence, Pete Jennings took legal action to regain the rights to his books, and he succeeded. Finally, in January 2021, Capall Bann was legally dissolved.

The May Garland

There is a widespread tradition in England and Wales of carrying specially made May Garlands on the first of May to keep up the day. It is known as Garland Day in Cambridge and other places in eastern England. An engraving of a May Garland of 1828 in Northampton is one of the oldest pictures of this type of May Garland. The traditional May Garlands of this part of England are circular, bedecked with green vegetation, Rowan and Hawthorn blossom and other flowers, with a white-dressed doll at the centre. In Cambridge and Huntingdonshire, she is called Madame Flora, the personification of the flowers of springtime

An illustration of the May Garland from Northampton, 1828.

and early summer.

In 2009 we decided to restore the tradition, and I obtained a doll and made the garland with a sprig of white May tree blossom at the top. The parade began at the upper end of Honey Hill in Cambridge, in the oldest part of the city that originates in Roman times. I was the garland-bearer. As we processed to the music of fiddle and accordion, we stopped at the Folk Museum, where they reacted with surprise, but warmly greeted us. Then we crossed the bridge over the River Cam and proceeded along Bridge Street to the Round Church and paraded through the city centre.

At key points along the route, we stopped and I made the May Call:

May Day at the Eagle Inn, Cambridge, 2012. L to R: Michael Czarnobaj, "Les," Nigel Pennick, and Swami Anahata (melodeon).

Today it is the First of May.
Come greet the summer sun.
Cast your clouts,
For May is out,
And summer is begun!

This was followed by summer singing of the May Garland Song, whose words were first written down in 1904 at the Peterborough May Day celebrations.

We sang the May Garland song outside the Round Church and then progressed along Trinity Street and St John's Street, where we were tailed by a police car. We stopped outside Trinity College, where a bowler-hatted porter came out and threatened us for trespassing—although we were not, for we stood on the public pavement. Onwards to the church of Great St Mary, which is the official centre-point of Cambridge, where music was played and the call made. Then to the Eagle Inn in Bene't Street and back via Peas Hill and the Guildhall (City Hall) to the west end of Petty Cury. At the Eagle, the Guildhall and the

west end of Petty Cury, the May song was sung and the call was made. Then along Petty Cury to the other end for the call again. This was the customary dancing-place of the Molly Dancers each Plough Monday. Towards the end of the route, we entered the Community Café in Jesus Lane, where we played and sang. The parade finished, appropriately, at the Maypole public house.

Our May Garland was the first to be carried through the streets in fifty years. The tradition of carrying the May Garlands in Cambridge had been summarily terminated by the police in 1959 when the Chief Constable decided that girls carrying garlands were begging and an order went out to the constables to arrest them. It was customary for passersby to give the garland-bearers coins or sweets in exchange for a view of the doll—Madame Flora—they concealed beneath cloths at the centre of their garlands. Of course, after the police announcement, no one dared to go out on the streets that year, so a charming custom was brought to a sudden end.

In restoring this ancient custom and keeping up May Day, Northstow Mummers collected no money, because we did it *to keep up the day*: for love and not for money. We continued to carry the May Garland for several more years, before illness intervened. Nevertheless, it is important that traditions such as this regain their true vigour and their place in the community—despite mindless opposition from officialdom.

VI
CROSSING THE BORDERLINES

Little Devil Doubt: "How came you to be a doctor?"
Doctor: "By my travelling."

—Old Yorkshire Mummer's Play

Nigel Pennick on the meridian of Prague, 1991. A meridian marker in this spot had been used for telling local time from 1652 to 1918. Photo by Rosemarie Kirschmann.

Geomancy Returns to Germany

In May 1985 I went to Warburg in West Germany at the invitation of Professor Waltraud Wagner. In the previous year, she had published *Maßsysteme der Tempel* (Measuring Systems of the Temple) by herself and John Michell. It dealt with the sacred geometry, numerology, and dimensions of ancient structures. My work on geomancy was known in West Germany already through the German translation of my 1973 Cokaygne publication *Geomancy*, pirated as part of Werner Pieper's Grüner Zweig series. Apparently, this had circulated widely. Laughably, another German magazine at the time unwittingly published a translation *back* into German from English of one of Josef Heinsch's most celebrated papers! So, from Heinsch's original German, it went through Michael Behrend's English translation, and then back into German. I never compared the texts. By then my 1979 book *The Ancient Science of Geomancy* had been translated into German by the Dianus-Trikont publishers in Munich.

This company Trikont, whose name was inspired by the "Tricontinental" revolutionary movement, produced an eclectic series of books.[1] In 1983 these ranged from Che Guevara's diaries and Stephen Skinner's book on Chinese Geomancy, to works on the Dalai Lama, the last tribe of the Algonquin, a history of the Bantu by Vusamazulu Credo Mutwa (described

---

1. The Tricontinental conference took place in Cuba in 1966 to foster solidarity between anti-colonialist revolutionary movements from Africa, Asia, and Latin America. The German publishing company Trikont originally had a radical political focus; over time its purview became wider ranging and less polemical, and the name of the imprint was revised to Dianus-Trikont.

as a Johannesburg "witch-doctor"), Barbara Meyerhoff's *Der Peyote Kult*, and other books on spiritual currents, re-enchanting the world, and traditions of resistance. Their approach was both radical and perceptive. The entry for Martha Sills-Fuchs's book *Wiederkehr der Kelten* (Return of the Celts) described the Celts as "*die 'Indianer' Europas*" (the "Indians" of Europe)—that is, the Celts were seen as the downtrodden indigenous people of Europe. Into this mix—which was like a German version of Cokaygne Press, but on a larger scale—my book fitted perfectly.

In Warburg, I took part in a weekend geomantic event where I met some people who invited me to speak to them on matters of the Northern Tradition. They were followers of Herman Wirth and the runemaster Friedrich Bernhard Marby. Some of them had known one or the other of these masters, or both, and had been taught by them. Marby had died in 1966 and Wirth in 1982. I practised some of Marby's *Runengymnastik* or "runic yoga" exercises with them. I was taken to the Externsteine and participated in a Walpurgisnacht (May Eve) ceremony in Warburg, where we all leapt through a giant bonfire. I also visited several other notable places that Wilhelm Teudt had written about in his geomantic books nearly fifty years earlier, and walked along some of his alignments.

There was a bizarre incident when I visited the round chapel at Drüggelte near the Möhnesee in North Rhine-Westphalia. I wanted to see for myself the orientations described in Brachvogel's 1942 paper in *Mannus* that the IGR had published. I had just arrived at the chapel and was walking around it when a motor coach pulled up. About forty dowsers, rods in hand, rushed from the bus and ran towards the chapel. With rods twitching, they shouted to one another and crowded inside. It resembled a mass attack by demented fanatics. The chapel was too small for all of them at once, so they came and went in waves. The dowsers outside ran about with their rods, seemingly willy-nilly. I stood back, astonished. After about only ten minutes, someone shouted and they all crowded back on to the coach, which drove off. Peace was restored to the holy place again. Then I was able to see the round chapel of Drüggelte.

Nigel Pennick with a geomantic compass and mete-rod at the Externsteine in the Teutoburg Forest, North-Rhine Westfalia, Germany, 1985. Photo by Waltraud Wagner.

In a village close by, I met a man who, as a boy, had survived the flood caused when the Möhne dam, which held back the Möhnesee, was bombed by the Royal Air Force in "Operation Chastise" on the night of May 16–17, 1943. Over 1,500 people were drowned, he told me, including his mother. The crews of the British bombers, many of whom were shot down and killed, also destroyed another dam and missed a third. Later, they were mythologised as the Dam Busters. A movie of the same name was made in the 1950s, and the music written for it—a stirring march—is still played occasionally by military bands.

In 1986 I returned to Warburg for another geomantic weekend. One of my practical teachings was laying out a foursquare ground-plot by observation of the sun in the morning and the

WYRD TIMES

Pavement labyrinth designed by Nigel Pennick, Baltmannsweiler, Germany, 1993. Photo by Nigel Pennick.

afternoon. I had done this demonstration in England before, and later in Germany I taught the construction of sundials, which is part of the same technique. I went to Waldeck-Dehringhousen to stay with the publishers of Felicitas Hübner Verlag. There were occasional visits from bikers, some of them members of the Black Angels of Bavaria, riding their high-powered BMWs and Moto Guzzis. Beer flowed freely, and talk alternated between the martial arts, white-knuckle rides from Kassel to Hamburg at unbelievable speeds, and how Harley-Davidsons were useless, outdated machines. Between partying with the bikers, I was able to sign a contract for a geomantic book which came out in 1988 as *Einst war uns die Erde heilig* (At One Time the Earth Was Holy to Us). It has never appeared in English.

I was due to be picked up by Waltraud Wagner to do another event in Bochum, where she was a professor at the university. We were watching television, when a newsflash told us that abnormal levels of radiation had been detected near the East German border. Updates told of rumours that a nuclear power station had blown up in the USSR. It was suggested that we watch East German television to find out about it. The DDR broadcasts could be picked up there, and we saw a news item, which was dreary Communist propaganda about factory production and the success of some DDR sports team. No mention of radiation, nor where it came from: Chernobyl.

Waltraud Wagner picked me up, and we drove to Bochum, where she borrowed two Geiger counters from the university physics department. We went outside, and the meters registered levels many times higher than normal—"normal," of course, meaning post-1944 levels, after which radiation had entered the atmosphere increasingly from the first atomic bomb test, through Hiroshima and Nagasaki, to the tests rolling on periodically until the 1970s—not to mention leaks from nuclear facilities including Calder Hall in England. (This notorious place was subsequently renamed Windscale and then renamed a second time, Sellafield. Changing names serves to erase memory.) Then it began to rain. The radiation levels in the air dropped, but when we pointed the Geiger counters into the street gutters, they almost went off the end of the scale. We were outside in all this, but inside there was no escape, either.

Back at Warburg, we performed experiments with an ultrasound machine. We floated aluminium powder on a metal tray filled with water. Then, when the machine was turned on, Chladni patterns formed on the surface of the water as the powder assumed geometric forms that depended on the frequency of the sound. The images reminded me of the gyrotaxis experiments I had conducted with Professor John Kessler at CCAP in 1983. We had worked there on the self-ordering systems of large numbers of motile algae in a water current, or over a flat surface, and we had published a paper on the mathematics of the fluid mechanics of those systems. There was a practical application of gyrotaxis, but my scientific career had ended, and I never found out whether anything was done with it. The experiments I conducted with the German professor were never published.

Subsequently, I was invited to talk at many events and give one-off lectures in West Germany, Switzerland, and Austria. Before I was at Warburg, I had given talks, slide shows, workshops, and labyrinth-creating teachings in 1983–1984 at

Eindhoven University in the Netherlands, and at Interlaken and Zürich in Switzerland. A lecture in the latter city was held at Hürlimann brewery, where the owner told me they had water from a borehole located by a dowser—a proper water diviner, that is, not an "energy dowser" of the Bakewell and Drüggelte school.

One time in Zürich, the organiser of an event I was involved with took everyone to the Uetliberg, the holy mountain of Zürich where sacred yew trees once grew. In a wooded area, we all sat on the ground in a circle, eyes closed, while he conducted a path-working. As my understanding of Swiss German was poor at that time, I could not follow what he was saying, so I opened my eyes. A strange brown animal emerged from the woodland. It resembled an American groundhog (also known as a woodchuck), but I had never heard of a European one. After the meditation ended, I told the organiser what I had seen. He told me it was a *Murmeltier* (or marmot, in English). It was a rare animal, and I was fortunate to see one—but why hadn't I alerted him and the others to this rare appearance? Of course, I was not going to interrupt a path-working in the middle just because I saw a strange animal! The meaning of this *ostentum* was clear.

I was a workshop leader at a vast New Age event in Interlaken which was opened by the Dalai Lama, who was surrounded by bodyguards resembling Sumo wrestlers. All sorts of traditions were represented. Yet there, in the centre of Europe, I was the only one upholding European traditional spirituality. There were shamans (only a few of whom seemed authentic to me), Buddhists, Native Americans (none of whom was teaching much that was traditional), and various other New Age practitioners of a psychological tendency. A splendid time was had by all. I was paid well, stayed in a good hotel with fine food and wine, and had good company.

My role was to impart something of the eldritch world as manifested in stone circles, Celtic sacred landscapes, the runes, and Ogham. With a crowded schedule and so many different cultural practitioners, each promoting their own worldview, the chances for actual dialogue were few. In a bar one night, relaxing after "workshopping" for many hours, I was sitting with three other participants. Two were Native American, and one a Shona ritual specialist from Zimbabwe. After some beers, one of the Native Americans began boasting about how much money he was making from his gullible European followers. Talking to the Shona, however, I felt an immediate rapport. His practices in the landscape would have been recognizable in the East Anglian tradition. The Native Americans were not interested in our "shop talk" of divination, magic, and witchcraft, and began to chat with each other about the Superbowl. If they had been discussing soccer or cricket, I would have joined in. Years later, at the Strawberry Fair in Cambridge, I met some authentic Siberian shamans and they, too, were surprised at how close our local East Anglian tradition was with theirs. Taking away the cultural differences, the same principles can be seen to operate.

A few years later, one of these Native Americans was condemned as a charlatan by the elders of the tribe to which he claimed to belong—he was a *Métis* (of mixed indigenous and European background), attached to no tribe, and his teachings bore little resemblance to any authentic tribal tradition. In ancient Scotland such people, who were not members of any clan, were called "broken men." He espoused the Apocalypse of St John and held paramilitary training camps in Switzerland for his devotees, who were to be among the elect who would survive Armageddon. This belief had appeared in Wovoka's Ghost Shirt movement that had ended in 1890 with the devotees massacred at Wounded Knee. In this sense, he was a *mumpsimus*.

Border Transgressor

All this travelling necessitated having to cross and re-cross borders. Sometimes I would encounter an overzealous border guard who searched everything I had, and, on the next occasion, I was "waved through" the same border. As with all authority, it was arbitrary. On a hillside near Salzburg, I noticed a line of posts about thirty feet apart. There was a small road running up the hillside, and this had a red-and-white painted bar pivoted on a post so that it could be brought down to close off the road. I found out that this was the line dividing Austria and Germany. It was possible for cows and humans to wander on the grass between the posts and cross the border. I was there two days after border guards on a train from Munich had searched my bags and scrutinised my passport long and hard. This was before the Schengen Agreement, when all border checks were removed in the European Union (except for the UK, which finally left the EU in 2020). Sometimes, with others on a long journey from Germany to Italy, we took turns driving through Switzerland. We were always in a German car. Years later, I discovered that every time I drove in Switzerland it was illegal, as I was lacking certain documentation that I knew nothing about. If I had been stopped—and I never was—I would have ended up in a Swiss courthouse.

One particular visit demonstrated the absurdity of these border controls. I travelled from London on the last flight of the day to Stuttgart. As I only had hand luggage, I was first through the border check. But there was no one there and I walked through. The next day, I did my teaching in Stuttgart and had to go on to Salzburg for another event. Someone took me by car, and we were waved across the Austrian border without stopping. The same thing happened on the way back after the event: straight through, with the wave of a hand. That evening we were talking and I mentioned the name Nideck, which I had used for some of my publishing ventures. It had come from an old engraving cut up for the montage on the cover of *Cambridge Voice* no. 10. I was told that Nideck was a castle in Alsace, France, and would I like to go there? Always up for visiting interesting places, I agreed, and the next day we set out for Alsace. We drove to the shortest route, which was via a small car ferry across the Rhine. There was a customs checkpoint before the ferry, but this was unmanned.

Across the mighty river the ferry took us, but on the French side the checkpoint was also unmanned. We drove to Nideck, walked up through the forest, and ascended the remaining tower. According to legend, this was the last place giants lived on earth. It was strange to be in Nideck—a name I had used without

Nigel Pennick at Nideck, Alsace, France, 1980s.

knowing anything about it. Yet it signified the last outpost of an older order, something my colleagues and I had always considered ourselves. Nideck was another example of an unexpected place-connexion which appeared unintentionally. Driving back via the city of Strasbourg, we passed a signboard reading Café Château de Nideck, then across the border to Kiehl into Germany with no check. I was a foreigner who had crossed five borders in a few days, unhindered. Only when I was at Stuttgart airport on the way back to England was I stopped. The border guard scrutinised my passport with great concentration. She fiddled with a corner where the lamination had slightly lifted as though she were about to detect a counterfeit. Then, finally, she let me through. If only she had known where I had been in the last few days.

Herman Haindl and the Runes

In 1988 I was invited to Salzburg to give a teaching on the runes to a local esoteric group. Afterwards, in a city street, I was introduced to the artist Hermann Haindl, who had come from Hofheim in West Germany. He was making a series of runic paintings which would be photographed and produced as divination cards, and he wanted me to write the accompanying book. Berlin-born Haindl, who had fought as a seventeen-year-old in the last months of World War II against the overwhelmingly superior Red Army, had been taken to the Soviet Union as a prisoner in 1945. He had remained there, as all German prisoners-of-war did, until 1948 when the two new German states were set up as legal entities. German prisoners in Britain, as well as in Russia, had been used as slave labourers after the war. It was argued that they had no legal status because their country did not exist and so the Geneva Convention did not apply to them. Clearly, he had been scarred by his experience of defeat and captivity.

I visited him at Hofheim and he showed me rune paintings he had already completed. They were Armanen in spirit, painted on hexagonal canvases. It was his intention to make a divination system with a mosaic of hexagonal cards that would be fitted together. He showed me some of his other paintings, which to me appeared surrealist, echoing Max Ernst's landscape of *Europe after the Rain* of 1942. Haindl's paintings *Baumkreuz* (Tree Cross, 1983), *Vulkanlandschaft mit Regenbogen und Feder* (Volcanic Landscape with Rainbow and Feather, 1984), *Wandlung* (Transformation, 1985), and *Hexensabbat* (Witches' Sabbat, 1986) have elements that appeared in the runic images. To me, the sphere in *Vulkanlandschaft* recalled the mystic globes in the symbolist painting series *The Days of Creation* by Edward Burne-Jones and George Frederic Watts's painting *The All-Pervading*, which is the enigmatic non-Christian altarpiece of the Watts Chapel at Compton, Surrey.

Previously, Hermann had made seventy-eight paintings for a tarot card deck, which he told me had nearly killed him. His cards bore the Hebrew letters which had been ascribed to the trumps of the medieval tarot by the Hermetic Order of the Golden Dawn in England around 1895. Now, he wanted a runic deck. He had already painted cards 0/25, 3, 5, 9, 10, 16, and 23 before I started to write the book that was to accompany his deck. These runes were titled *Yr, Dorn, Hagal* (which had a six-branched form), *Rit, Not, Sig,* and *Odal.* The other runes were painted after our discussions. There were twenty-five cards in all, essentially the row of Elder Futhark runes plus one. Rune number 25, *Yr,* which was also zero, had echoes of the "blank rune" that some modern writers had invented as a parallel to the Joker in playing-card decks. We had a disagreement over his painting of *Gebo,* which depicted the sun emerging from behind a rock pillar, emanating four rays in the form of an "X." It was supposed to represent this, but in Haindl's painting, the sun was on the left of the pillar. This meant that the sun, travelling clockwise from left to right, was not emerging, but about to disappear. The runes are a northern hemisphere system, and a southern hemisphere sun would be inappropriate. He refused to change it, nor would he agree to have the photographic artwork flipped left–right. So it remains anomalously antipodean. Almost every work that actually comes to fruition is a compromise.

The cards were designed as hexagons, intended to form a mosaic spread in "three dimensions," but the publisher decided it was too expensive to cut hexagonal cards and make a hexagonal box for them, so they were issued as normal rectangular cards. This meant that the painted hexagonal area was surrounded by a light background on which the rune, its name, number, and phonetic equivalent were printed in an uncial Celtic typeface. The rune-names were a somewhat chaotic mixture that emanated from the work he did before me and some of my Anglo-Saxon usages. In the book, however, I gave the rune-names in their Germanic, Gothic, Old English, and—where appropriate— Old Norse forms. *Das Runenorakel* (The Rune Oracle), with 25 cards by Hermann Haindl, finally emerged with myself as the author; there was also a foreword by Rachel Pollack. Soon after, an Italian edition appeared, and in 1998 U. S. Games Systems issued the book in English without the cards as the *Haindl Rune Oracle.* Rachel Pollack's foreword was removed from this edition.

Bright Lights, Big City

After meeting Haindl for the first time at Salzburg, a German participant at my event offered to take me to Stuttgart to visit

A street view of the Strassenbahn on the route to Vogelsang and Botnang, Stuttgart, 1989. Photo by Nigel Pennick.

people who were interested in putting on other engagements for me. We left in the morning and drove across the border into West Germany. We stopped for lunch at Kaufbeuren in Bavaria, once the site of a famous turf maze. It was twilight when we approached the city and we had the radio on, playing rock music. As we came over the brow of the hill at Degerloch, we could see the lights of the metropolis laid out before us. At that moment, the Jimmy Reed blues track "Bright Lights, Big City" came from the radio. It was an *ostentum* of sorts. Every time I hear that song now, I can see a vision of Stuttgart laid out in twinkling lights before me. This was the beginning of many visits to Stuttgart, a city I now know better than many British ones.

I put on several geomantic events with Karl Aldinger at his house near Killesberg Park in Stuttgart. Like many houses which had survived the massive destruction of World War II, it still had its heavy gas-proof steel door guarding the cellar. Aldinger made re-enactment weapons, especially swords, but he used manufactured spring steel, readily available in industrial Stuttgart, for the blades. He sold woven carpets with Armanen runes and other *historische Gegenstände* (historical objects). He was proud of his Alemannic heritage and ran an Alemannic re-enactment group, who performed demonstration fights with sword and shield in costume. They were very impressive. Spring steel was probably all right for theatrical performances. But more serious knifesmiths existed in Germany. At a medieval fair some time later, I met a smith named Axon who showed me the best damascened blade I had ever seen. He told me that he had learnt from one of the smiths who, in the 1930s, had recreated handmade pattern-welding at Solingen and made the now-lost *Reichsschwert* (Imperial Sword) that had been presented to Adolf Hitler and exhibited at Aachen where Charlemagne had his royal palace. I would have bought Axon's masterpiece, but it was too expensive!

The centre of Stuttgart was all modern buildings, except for the nineteenth-century classical Königsbau, the Schloss, a medieval church, and Paul Bonatz's famous Hauptbahnhof railway terminus. Only these had been restored from their wrecked condition after the war. The city centre had been almost razed to the ground by Bomber Command of the Royal Air Force in 1944. Travelling through the city on a tram, one reached the place where old buildings began. Here, at least, the bombs had not destroyed everything. Stuttgart is a hilly city, and on one high point, Pragsattel, stood a massive concrete tower covered with advertisement lettering for Mercedes-Benz and other Stuttgart businesses. On closer inspection, this proved to be an octagonal *Flakturm*, built towards the end of the war as a gunnery platform for anti-aircraft artillery. Similar structures were built in other cities, and one in Hamburg was reputed to have survived a direct hit by a 500-pound bomb. The massive walls, several metres thick, were impregnable, and demolishing this modern castle was deemed too expensive. Indeed, this was the legendary "indestructible castle" in physical form!

On one occasion, the man I was staying with had to take his dog for a walk in the nearby park. It was a very small park, not one of the extensive parks that grace the city. As we approached an empty space by a wall, I was told that it had been the site of a

National Socialist memorial, blown up by the French occupation army in 1945. Until that moment, I had no idea what had been there. It was an empty space in a park I had never seen before. Suddenly, I knew, and the memorial, though long since blasted away, reappeared in the form of knowledge and memory. These are the mythic shadows that overhang our lives. It is not so easy to destroy a monument.

The escalators to the street from the subway station under the Hauptbahnhof had a particular synthetic rubber smell unlike any other. Coming up another escalator from the S-Bahn station at Stadtmitte sometime after Germany was reunified, I heard a virtuoso musician playing Bach on a full-sized button accordion of a kind favoured by Eastern European musicians. I stopped to listen, dropped a couple of deutschmarks in his box, and talked to him. He was Russian, and spoke English. He told me he had once been a classical musician in a Soviet symphony orchestra that was closed down suddenly under perestroika. At a stroke, the musicians all lost their employment. His story resonated with my experience as a scientist. Unemployed, he made his way to Stuttgart and eked out a living as a busker playing classical music on the street.

Geomancy in Germania

Rosemarie Kirschmann, who had been in the International Labyrinth Team on my Ireland tour, was a leading light in Arkuna, the Stuttgart women's centre. Over a twelve-year period, she, Maria Diehl, and others organised many events for me in Stuttgart on themes that included Paganism, the runes, geomancy, labyrinths, and Celtic spirituality. I also did several events in Wiesbaden, Karlsruhe, Salzburg, and Baden-bei-Wien, the latter two being in Austria. Rosemarie's brother, Hans-Martin Kirschmann, was a biological architect who worked on ecologically sound buildings. A small apartment block he designed has a foundation-stone I laid beneath it according to traditional ritual. He also commissioned me to do a painting of an alchemical goddess for his office.

Often, my Stuttgart events ended in the Café Sommer,

Women's dance at ritual labyrinth laid out by
Nigel Pennick, Cologne, Germany, 2003.

which had a fine interior combining modernism with Swabian traditional architecture. It was a unique artistic style which appeared to have lasted three or four years in the mid-1950s before being overwhelmed by banal, unornamented modernism. I always used to like to end my city centre events with coffee and cakes there. Its elegant atmosphere was unique, and it was a tragedy when it was torn down.

My events outside the city included geomantic walks at notable places in the landscape. A favoured spot was the Teck, a holy hill with a mysterious cave, the Sybillenloch (Sybil's Cave). Womens' groups would go there to perform rituals and commune with nature. I devised a geomantic walk that involved the legend of the Sybil, and how she was driven out in a fiery wagon that left its mark as a straight track across the valley below. There was indeed a straight line that went through a smaller hill topped with a dense clump of pine trees, identical with a mark-point on Alfred Watkins's leys. It was believed to be an ancient Roman defensive rampart. The Teck also had a very good café in a building near the summit, which made it an ideal place to finish a geomantic event.

Occasionally, I did geomantic walks without preparation, as in a town where I gave a talk and decided to go out afterwards with the participants and show them geomantic features which I knew I would find. Mostly, I prepared with an advance visit. On one occasion, I went to a place with rocks and water, and on one flat rock surface I discerned natural cracks that could be interpreted as runes. They were plain to see. When I conducted the geomantic walk a few days later, I reached the rock and it looked the same. It had not been cleaned or damaged in any way. But the runes were no longer visible. I wonder how many events I did when the runes or Oghams *were not* visible when I tried to show them to my students? Having experienced similar things in my walks before, I never raised expectations only for them to be dashed.

On May Day in 1993, I was taken to Belsen in Mössingen, Baden-Württemberg (not to be confused with the concentration camp site in Lower Saxony), where there was an ancient chapel with carvings of the god Béel and the heads of cattle and pigs on stone blocks inserted into the gable. Above them was a Christian cross, clearly installed at a later date than the ancient Pagan deity on whose sacral day we were there. We performed a ritual at an ancient oak nearby and walked in the forest during a shower of rain. After the storm broke, we came upon a tree with gleaming droplets refracting the sun: green, red, and golden. It was otherworldly. This was the Jewel-Bearing Tree I had read about in the works of the Spiritual Arts and Crafts master, William Richard Lethaby. It was an *ostentum* on a special day at a special place. We stood, entranced, until the sun went in again and the downpour resumed.

Once I was back in England, I commissioned the London silversmith Jungleyes Love to make me a runic ring in commemoration of the May Day *ostentum* that had manifested in Germany. Jungleyes—or Jungle, as he was called by his friends—had first learned about the runes from me, but he said he gained the ability to really "work them" after he went to West Africa and a "wise man" there taught him the means of empowerment.

Runic bracteate made by Jungleyes Love. Photo by Nigel Pennick.

Magical techniques often work across systems. Jungle was one of the few artisans who produced pieces using Northumbrian runes. Besides the runic ring, I also have a bracteate with Elder Futhark runes made by him—he hammered the runes into it accompanied by *galdr* (ritual chanting of the rune names) during a full moon.[2]

In 1997 I delivered the manuscript of my *Complete Illustrated Guide to Runes* to the publisher, Element Books, and was working with the art co-ordinator. I had already, in London, in a restaurant

---

2. Sadly, Jungle died twenty years later, in 2013, at the age of 56. He received a colourful obituary in the *Daily Telegraph*, which among other things described him as an "old Harrovian hippie who traded in runic jewellery, dinosaur eggs and fossilised animal excrement, which he sold from his shop on the tourist trail to Kew Gardens. He learnt the tradition of rune–lore in the 1980s. . . . a rune being a Norse hieroglyph which, when scribed (or struck) on to an object or metal and its name chanted phonetically, reputedly invests the wearer with power. His runic jewellery was much sought after by customers at his tiny shop, called World Tree Mend Us."

near King's Cross that was once a horse-bus stable, decided on all the archival illustrations. I was in Stuttgart when they did the photo shoot for images that would demonstrate the runic yoga. I received a call on my mobile phone to ask some questions about the positions. At that moment I was in the Celtic department of the Baden-Württemberg Landesmuseum (regional history museum), arranging a guided talk for the weekend. So, by the magnificent trappings of the Hochdorf burial of circa 500 BCE, including the birch-bark hat of the buried lord, I assisted the photographer in posing her model in a town on the south coast of England. As I described the runic postures, I reflected on this incongruous integration of the eldritch with modern technology.

The Celtic Mysteries event in the museum was a great success, and would be repeated at a later date. I always found that in mainland Europe I was received as an equal, and honoured as a man of knowledge and expertise. I lectured in universities, museums, and churches without any problem. In Britain, on the contrary, such openness did not exist. Class attitudes, professional guardedness, and a fear of doing "something wrong" amongst the staff meant that I could never hold such an event in a British museum. Although no door is ever closed to a toadman, these British doors admitted me only as a spectator.

Beware the Consequences

While travelling in Germany and on a visit to Munich in 1999, I walked into Marienplatz to view the famous dragon and labyrinth. There I was confronted not with a serene and noble urban space, but an unexpected scene of human hatred and potential violence. Two enraged mobs were being kept apart by a phalanx of policemen and policewomen with dogs. It seems that the mobs were supporters of two rival football teams who were clearly deadly enemies. It was a familiar scenario, though potentially far more violent than the encounters I had experienced as a dedicated Arsenal fan almost forty years earlier. It was a clear instance of the "We are the people—they are the cunts" mentality.

In Marienplatz, however, the animal-like screams of abuse

that rang through the venerable place reminded me at once of the almost subhuman noises one hears when listening to broadcasts of the British House of Commons. In this institution, the members of Parliament, who are supposed to be educated people (and are certainly highly paid), make cat-calls of abuse to one another, shouting insults at their opponents just like football hooligans do. Clearly, there is little cooperation and much conflict in this place where such important decisions are made. The bitter and vocal opponents who abuse each other are said to be "on opposite sides of the house": "Government" and "Opposition." They are members of rival gangs who attempt to rubbish everything that the others propose when "in opposition" or, conversely, when their rivals are "in government."

But how did this destructive factionalism come about? Surely it is not the only way to run a representative democracy. Unexpectedly, this adversarial system is an instance of an inappropriate geomantic leftover. In Christian monasticism, the chancels of abbeys are arranged with benches along the sides of the north and south walls, facing one another. The House of Commons is an unconscious recreation of this.

The Parliament of England once held its meetings in Westminster Abbey, a Christian sacred place built on the former holy island of Thorney, which in the days of Saxon paganism was sacred to the thunder-god Thunor. The Commons met in the eight-sided Chapter House. This octagon, which still exists, is one of several such polygonal structures in English cathedrals and abbeys. Fine examples can be found at Lincoln (1230), Westminster (1246), Lichfield (1249), Salisbury (1263), and Wells (pre-1306). They are all masterly examples of sacred geometry; stone constructions with a central pillar from which radiates an umbrella-like vault that roofs the polygon. Seats are arranged around the walls, where the monks sat when they assembled there for discussions and deliberations.

This central pillar symbolises the Holy Spirit descending from heaven to earth. The chapter houses were a reenactment in stone of the story of Pentecost when the Holy Spirit poured down from above upon Jesus's apostles. Abbot Richard de Ware of Westminster (1258–1283), described the chapter house as the "workshop of the Holy Spirit where the sons of God assemble." Those who met in such places were constantly reminded of the divine spiritual wisdom that is accessible to those in the proper frame of mind. So it was that the early English Parliaments met in a spiritual place to be reminded of their duty of true thought and speech that they owed to God and their fellow human beings.

Perhaps British politics would have gone a different way if the Chapter House had remained the place of Parliament. However, in an attempt to rival the new Sainte-Chapelle in Paris, the marvel of the age, the English king, Edward I, built a similar chapel, St Stephen's. In 1348, King Edward III converted the royal chapel into a religious college served by a Dean and twelve Canons.

To accommodate the college, St Stephen's Chapel was reconstructed with an interior arranged with opposing choir stalls. During services, college members sat on one one side or the other—the Dean's Side, or the Precentor's Side. It was then that these facing stalls, places for divine worship (not conflict!) finally led to the political system of a rival "Government" and its "Opposition."

When the Catholic religion was suppressed in England, the college was disbanded, and the Commons took over the chapel for their Parliamentary affairs. A whole set of customs and usages gradually came into being, centred around this particular space. So it was, when the old Palace of Westminster was destroyed by fire in 1834, that a new Houses of Parliament was designed in medieval style. The layout of the new nineteenth-century House of Commons reproduced the form of the medieval chapel. The benches of the "Government" and "Opposition" were arranged facing one another, like the old collegiate choir stalls. To minimise physical violence, it was arranged so that the space between the two sides was two sword-lengths.

It seems to be a human trait that things which started out as sacred become profane. Theatre began as the ritual enactment of sacred themes; it gradually transformed into entertainment.

Wine-drinking began as part of the sacred rites of Dionysos, but later deteriorated into a regular pastime. Tobacco-smoking, too, started as a sacrament among the Native Americans, just as surfing was a religious rite performed as part of the inauguration of the Kings of Hawaii. Now these are all mere recreations, their origins unsuspected by most who enjoy them.

My experience in Munich made me recall the hostile animal noises of the British Parliament, but of course such violent divisions over football are not restricted to Germany. I have witnessed similar examples of brutal football sectarianism in London, Sheffield, Glasgow, and Brussels. In some of these places, certain teams are associated with local, religious, or other divisions, which fuel the hatred. It seems that if human beings are given the opportunity to identify with one "side" or other, then they will vent their aggression on others they identify as belonging to the other "side."

This seemingly bizarre origin of the adversarial political and legal system in Anglo-Saxon countries is a warning from history. We should be aware that anything we make can unwittingly create artificial oppositions that force people to belong to one "side" or another, as the architect of St Stephen's Chapel unintentionally forced the English Parliament to do so long ago.

Folkways on the Continent

Staying in Bavaria after an event, I was taken to a theatrical performance of the *Rauhnacht*[3] despite a driving snowstorm. In England, I would have not ventured out of doors in such conditions. But I was assured it would be all right, and it was. We travelled on the autobahn through conditions which would have brought a British motorway to a halt in seconds. A snowplough and gritter every few minutes in each direction kept the road free and the traffic flowing. Snow was several feet deep on either side of the road. It was an instance of German organization at its best.

---

3. *Rauhnacht* ("Smoke Night") covered more than one night—the nights between the winter solstice and Twelfth Night (Jan. 6). Houses were fumigated with incense to drive away the harmful spirits abroad on these nights.

WYRD TIMES

We arrived at the village hall where the *Rauhnacht* performance was to be held by the *Perchten* group Charivari.[4] Narrated in the strong *Boarisch* accent of that part of Bavaria, performers personating *Perchten* acted out the myth to folk-rock music. The show ended when the lights went out and we experienced the Wild Hunt riding over us courtesy of the excellent surround-sound system. It was a notable performance!

A year later, at New Year in Sankt Johann im Pongau, Austria, I experienced the real *Perchtenlauf*, or "*Perchten* procession," in the darkened icy streets, and felt their cut-off horse-tails as they ran past, bashing me below the knees. I avoided the guisers with bundles of birches who also chastised onlookers. Over the years I visited and participated (where possible) in various traditional festivals in Germany and Austria such as *Fastnacht*, *Fasching*, or *Karneval*. This was always a time of misrule. One *Gründonnerstag* (Maundy Thursday) I was riding on a tram in Bad Cannstat (across the River Neckar from Stuttgart) when a group of wild women got on. They were carrying scissors and cut off the ties of all the men who were wearing them. As I have always worn neckerchiefs, I was spared. *Fastnacht* (Shrove Tuesday, Mardi Gras) in Bad Cannstatt was always a case of "*der Bär ist los*" misrule, with people in fantastic costumes carousing and revelling long into the night.

One year at Wilflingen in the Black Forest region I saw the Straw Bear. I had played in the band accompanying the Straw Bear's perambulation at Whittlesey in Cambridgeshire, so it was an interesting comparison. The village next to Wilflingen had traces that a Straw Bear had been there, also. Although these events were catalogued, that particular village was never mentioned, so I suspected that there were traditions that even the "folk experts" did not know about. I also went at *Fastnacht* to Rottweil-am-Neckar to see the costumed guisers' parade. On the

---

4. The *Perchten* are the entourage of the Germanic goddess Percht (aka "Frau Percht"). There are two varieties of *Perchten*: the *Schönperchten*, who are beautiful and sometimes bejewelled; and the *Schiachperchten*, who are dressed in pelts and wear demon masks with boars' tusks and animal horns, and carrying bundles of birch or horses' tails with which they assail bystanders.

Straw Bear and keepers, Wilflingen, Black Forest, Germany, 1999. Photo by Nigel Pennick.

snow-covered main streets, men and women in wooden masks with boars' tusks, clad in red costumes with feathers attached, leapt into the air. They carried a staff with a metal spike at the end. Running, the spike was thrust into the ground, and the guiser went forward, pivoting on it, legs horizontally in front, effectively off the ground, flying. Also at Rottweil were the *Brieler Rössle*, hobby horses to which were attached by ropes three masked performers carrying whips. The hobby-horse guiser had to keep the ropes taut to avoid being hit.

Schiebenschlagen (disk-flinging) is another ceremony in which I participated. It is an ancient traditional rite performed in a subalpine landscape at twilight around Twelfth Night on a low mountain overlooking the snowy forest below. Each disk, called a *Schiebe*, is made of chamfered pine, nine centimetres square, flat and smoothly finished by a craftsman, with a hole drilled through the centre. Stacks of them are prepared beforehand, and one buys them from the maker. They are pushed on to the end of a flexible rod about five feet in length and the *Schiebe* is held in a bonfire to light it. Repeating the dialect formula "*Schiebi, schiebo, wem so' da scheba go?*"[5] and saying the name of a person you are sending it for, the burning *Schiebe* is hit against a board mounted by the side of the steep drop towards the forest. It spins off the end of the rod as a flaming wheel that flies down into the valley far below, eventually hitting a tree in a flurry of sparks or disappearing from sight. To perform *Schiebenschlagen* is an indescribable experience.

The last time I ever had a birthday party was in Germany on my fiftieth in 1996. My health was deteriorating, I had been put on various medications, and so I found travelling more and more harrowing. During the First Gulf War to liberate Kuwait, I had flown to and from Stuttgart Airport amid heavy security. On one wide-bodied Airbus plane, I was one of only twenty-eight passengers. It seems people were terrified that their flight would be hijacked, blown up, or shot down, and so were not travelling. At least we few who did fly got first-class service! I continued to travel and do events, but my health took a turn for the worse and each journey became more of an ordeal. Sometimes, I became heavily fatigued almost to the point of collapse. But "the show must go on" as they say, and I continued.

The end came in 2001. I had been in Rome and was travelling back to Stuttgart, which involved a change of aircraft at Charles De Gaulle Airport in Paris. It was the tenth of September and there was heightened security at Rome airport. Guards with assault rifles stood around and sniffer dogs were checking passengers' luggage. I suffered additional bureaucracy at passport control, and we were delayed in boarding. Arriving at Paris, security again was tight. I was searched and all my medication examined with heightened suspicion. After a walk under oppressive concrete shell-shaped roofs for what seemed to be a mile, I arrived at the departure gates, where I was subjected to another search and more bureaucratic document-scrutiny. Finally, I was on the plane to Stuttgart, where I got through normally.

I stayed the night at Stuttgart and returned to London by

---

5. "*Schebee, schebo*, for whom should the disk fly?"

air the next day. Security at the airports was around the normal level, and I arrived at Heathrow, totally fatigued. There was still a coach trip ahead lasting two or more hours, then a bus home. At the coach stop, I heard someone say something about New York and a disaster. Only when I reached home, after sleeping on the coach, did I discover I had been airborne during what became known as 9/11. The Rome and Paris security alert now made sense. But American security had failed spectacularly, with the death of thousands as the result. In the days afterwards, the media uncritically reported stories of zealous security guards confiscating ladies' antique brooches in case they used the pins to hijack aircrafts and other absurd overreactions. After my run-in with a French guard about my medication, which included needles, I decided I could no longer risk travelling by air and having my life-sustaining medicine confiscated in a faraway country.

I gave up being a "frequent flier" after 214 individual flights. My last two flights were to and from Maastricht, Holland, in 2003, from where I then travelled to do my last event across the border in Germany. While there I also visited the shrines of two Black Madonnas, one in Ludwigshafen and one in Cologne;[6] made a labyrinth; and saw the oldest piece of stained glass in the world in the museum in Darmstadt. But my connection with Germany was not completely severed, as for several years I wrote a regular column for each issue of the geomantic journal *Hagia Chora*, edited by Lara Mallien and Johannes Heimrath. *Feng-Shui Aktuell*, edited by Marianne Rattay, also carried my material in 2007. Some of my *Hagia Chora* work later emerged in two books, *Was ist Geomantie?* (2008) and *Genius Loci* (2009).

Barrier Crossing at Home

In 2002, I made a journey from Cambridge to Croydon in south London. At Cambridge railway station I purchased a ticket which enabled me to go to London and back and also to travel

---

6. The shrine of the black Madonna in St. Maria in der Kupfergasse in Cologne had the most powerful numinous energy I have ever encountered in a church.

on the buses, trams, and the Underground in London. In those days, there were no automatic barriers at Cambridge Station, so I walked on and boarded my train which was bound for London. There was no ticket inspection on the train. When we arrived at Finsbury Park, the last stop before the terminal King's Cross, I decided to get off and use the Underground from there. Staying on the station without my ticket being checked, I walked down the stairs to the Victoria Line, which I rode to Victoria, where I changed (with no ticket check) to the District Line. From there, I rode to Wimbledon station, where I walked along the platform and boarded a tram. There was no ticket check on the tram, which ran several stops on its own right-of-way and then onto the streets of Croydon. I got off in the street, having arrived without a single inspection of my ticket: I could have made the entire journey without one. Subsequently, barriers were installed throughout the rail system, and inspections made on the trams. But no door is ever closed to a toadman.

VII
SPIRITUAL ARTS AND CRAFTS, MUSIC AND MUMMING

Man requires many instruments for his external works; much preparation is needed before he can bring them forth as he has imagined them.

—Meister Eckhart

Nigel Pennick at his "Visionary Steeples" one-man art show, Cambridge, 2011.
Photo by Linda Kelsey-Jones.

Art

Art was a "subject" in school, though not until I was about twelve did I get any instruction in drawing. My grammar school included technical drawing in its curriculum, so I was taught about correct techniques for sketching things such as boxes or wheels. I learnt the use of instruments such as the pantograph for enlarging or diminishing scale images. In carpentry class, we had to draw the things we were going to make. In mathematics classes, we were also taught classical Euclidean geometry (which was easier for me than the rest of the subject). Art involved tuition in proportion and perspective. All of this, of course, was pencil on paper, for lines on electronic screens had yet to be invented.

School art also involved essentially playing around with paint and coloured pencils, with little tuition on colour theory, light and shadow. But I was able to look around me wherever I went and—as I always carried a notebook, ballpoint pens, and a pencil—I sketched things that were of interest. I was fascinated by the various forms of lettering, such as I saw every day on diverse shop fascias, advertising posters, and the 1906 signs and station names in the Piccadilly and Bakerloo lines of the London Underground. I also sketched the shapes of leaves on trees, notable stones and fossils I possessed, and other random things that took my fancy. Ornament on ancient buildings, the silhouettes of skylines, and notable cupolas, turrets, and weathercocks on old buildings also attracted me. In libraries I found books about these shapes, and learnt the technical names for leaves, fonts, and architectural features.

Reading books on art and architecture led me to visit famous buildings when I could, and seek out the originals of certain artworks in public galleries. I took to visiting the Tate Gallery frequently, as I admired many of the modernist artworks I saw there, especially op art and kinetic art. The "mobiles" of Alexander Calder were well known, having been first exhibited in Paris in 1932. I often saw pastiche versions of them in the houses of my friends' parents. (I am sure there were no original Calders there!) I visited a retrospective exhibition at the Tate in 1962 and saw many of his "stabiles" and "constellations" as well as the celebrated "mobiles." I also saw the early op-art works of Bridget Riley at the Tate. If one stared at them long enough (which I did), Riley's designs could cause something like hallucinations. I attempted to make Indian ink drawings that would produce the same effect, but I had no technical drawing pens at the time, and a brush was too inaccurate to engender optical effects.

In my late teens, I obtained a dip pen and began to make ink drawings of my pencil sketches. From this came all my later work, though I had obtained "rapidograph"-type pens by the time I went to the Tech. My drawings of Cambridge buildings at the time were done with these. I continued to make pencil drawings of plants, bones, whole animals, and fossils from my various geological and biological studies. Having no photographic equipment, everything seen under the microscope had to be drawn. So I learnt to observe the salient features of organisms and to make accurate drawings of them. It was an essential part of passing the examinations, but it also stood me in good stead for my later works in magazine and book illustration, and artwork in general.

Celtic Art

I bear a Celtic surname derived from the Cornish *Pen Knegh*, meaning head or summit of a rock or hill, specifically the hill now called Penknight at Lostwithiel, the former capital of Cornwall, where the Stannary, or tin-miners' parliament, met. The earliest record of this surname is from Penzance in 1415.

Ethnically Anglo-Celtic, I have an ancestral connexion with traditional Celtic culture, especially the symbolic art

Celtic art by Nigel Pennick, 2002.

form generally called Celtic Art. Based upon geometry and mathematically complex interlacing patterns, this art form has links with similar knotwork in Anglo-Saxon and Viking metalwork, manuscripts, and stone carving. The eighth-century Irish *Book of Kells* and the seventh-century Anglo-Saxon *Lindisfarne Gospels* are the most magnificent examples from this era. When I was young I saw the latter volume in the British Museum, and was enthralled by the fineness and complexity of the ancient scribe's work.

In Ireland in the early 1960s I saw several Celtic crosses on their original sites, and in Dublin I saw magnificent ancient Irish metalwork and found a second-hand copy of John G. Merne's book *A Handbook of Celtic Ornament*. Merne described the principles of Celtic interlace, and I began to experiment with it. Subsequently, I applied Celtic knotwork to many of the ink drawings used as illustrations in my books, including *Celtic Sacred Landscapes* (1996). In 1998 I contributed to the book *New Visions in Celtic Art: The Modern Tradition*, edited by David James and Stuart Booth. Subsequently, in 2002, some of my Celtic artwork was exhibited in the Central Library in Birmingham, and a decade later in an international Celtic Art exhibit in San Marcos, Texas. I continue to use the principles of Celtic Art in my drawings.

My Underground Lettering

From my earliest days I saw many styles of lettering, and it was the variants of creative and ornamental forms that I liked the most. Russell Square underground station had an elegant formal type on its facade that dated from 1906, and below, in the tunnels, were freer variant forms in directional signs and the original station names on the tiled walls. The London Transport roundels, however, displayed the sparse modernist typeface designed by Edward Johnston in 1917. There were fine examples of ornamental lettering on the two major hotels close by, both constructed around the turn of the century, the Russell and the Imperial. Clad in carved stone and terracotta, these fine hotels bore art nouveau and gothic elements with various fine signage in non-modernist characters. The Passmore Edwards Settlement, proudly bearing cosmic eggs and the Tree of Life, had Arts-and-Crafts lettering over its main entrance. In addition, many local shops still had their original sign-painted fascias or gilded Victorian lettering behind glass.

When I was old enough to travel alone on the underground, I used to copy the original lettering that still survived then in many stations. I liked best the Arts and Crafts–derived lettering on the three Yerkes tube lines: Bakerloo, Piccadilly, and the Hampstead branch of the Northern Line.[1] These stations had been designed by Leslie W. Green, who died tragically young shortly after they were finished in 1907. Only in the twenty-first century was he recognized as a remarkable architect. During the early 1960s, so many of these fine buildings and almost all of the lettering was destroyed as "old fashioned." Modernist fonts became the norm, and at that period it became fashionable to mix upper and lower case on posters and in magazines. When

---

1. American public transport entrepreneur Charles Tyson Yerkes financed these three London underground lines.

NIGEL PENNICK

Nigel Pennick at Mary Ward House, the former Passmore Edwards Settlement, May 2008. Photo by Linda Kelsey-Jones.

I visited Amsterdam first in 1967, I was dismayed to see the destination blinds of trams and buses in lower-case Helvetica or a similar bland font, without initial capitals—"centraal station" or "osdorp" looked weird and were hardly legible (the old route colours, dating from the days when many were illiterate, were still displayed next to the destinations). However, the unique lettering of the Amsterdamse School was visible all over the city on buildings built by the municipality between 1913 and 1930. In my travels in mainland Europe around that time, I also saw Hector Guimard's famous metro entrances in Paris with their fabulous lettering, and the signs of Victor Horta and others of the Art Nouveau era in Brussels.

In the latter half of the 1960s, the underground press was emerging, and hand-drawn lettering was coming into its own again. Back in England, I bought American underground newspapers from the rare outlets, and there was also an emergent renaissance in lettering. Much of it was inspired by

Issues of *Albion* magazine (1979 and 1980) with lettering and design by Nigel Pennick.

the work of Art Nouveau artists including Aubrey Beardsley and Alfons Mucha, as well as lesser-known figures from the Vienna Secession and German Jugendstil movements.

Around London, posters by Hapshash and the Coloured Coat and Michael McInneny with "far out" lettering advertised gigs by psychedelic bands such as Pink Floyd. Martin Sharp's lettering designs on posters, in *Oz* magazine, and on album sleeves for the supergroup *Cream* were in a different style, but also far from the *Radio Times* or a British Railways poster. Later, the work of San Francisco poster and album-sleeve artists reached England, the albums via the "West Coast, Underground" section of local record shops. I was particularly interested in the formal psychedelic lettering of Rick Griffin, as on the sleeve of *Aoxomoxoa* by the Grateful Dead.

Much of what existed outside the "art-poster" world was ephemeral and is lost. To the rightfully famous exponents of the psychedelic lettering style can be added many others, some derivative, and some original in other ways, whose work could be seen on walls, handbills, and in small magazines. *Sic transit gloria mundi*. I have continued to use hand-drawn lettering in my publications up to the present. It is almost a bygone art in these digital days. The mastheads of my old publications like *Armeswerk*, *Albion*, and others; my two different *Runestaff Crafts* logos; and various other illustrations in the present book provide examples of my diverse but connected lettering styles.

All Sorts of Printmaking

From the early 1960s I was printing things. My first prints were rough lino (linoleum) cuts done on scraps of paper. We were not taught this technique in school and, apart from a Dryad leaflet about the technique, I knew nothing. I had discovered a set of linocut tools in a drawer at home. The tools had belonged to my father when he was at teacher-training college after he left the Royal Air Force, but they had lain neglected ever since. When I first taught myself how to work with the medium, I was unaware of the adventurous linocuts done by the Dadaists and Expressionists, or the astonishing virtuosity of technique displayed in the Grosvenor School linocuts. These artworks were not exhibited in galleries and there were no books available depicting them. The modernist multicolour printing technique pioneered by Claude Flight and his pupils Sybil Andrews and Cyril Power was also unknown to me. Many years later, I saw Power's now-famous linocut "The Tube Staircase," which for me evoked an impression of the spiral emergency stairs at Russell Square Station that I knew so well. But I had given up linocuts by then, as linoleum was no longer readily available, having been superseded by vinyl flooring.

When I went to college and people asked me to design advertisements for events, I painted individual posters under the aegis of the Like It or Lump It Poster Company (the events took place on the college campus, so two or three originals were sufficient to promote an event). The Anglian Diggers' *postermanifestoster* and the foldout of King Street in *Cambridge Voice* no. 2/5 were printed using offset lithography; the Diggers' one was composed of collage and type; and the King Street one was based on my "bird's-eye-view" drawing. The latter poster was an advertisement for King Street Market, a shop whose fascia name-board I had painted as well. Another offset-litho poster designed by me in 1972 was for the opening of Cokaygne Bookshop, mainly lettering in an Amsterdamse School cartouche. One was posted on the window of the abandoned Cyril Lord carpet shop in the city centre. The shop remained empty long afterwards and the poster, partly overpasted with others and written on with pen graffiti (spray cans were not in use by vandals then), survived there for two years. Also in 1972 I designed a poster in opposition to the construction of an airport on Maplin Sands in the Thames Estuary. The main opponents of the airport, which would have destroyed a key sandbank visited by migratory birds and the marine environment around it, were the Defenders of Essex, but a more radical offshoot, the Desperate Society for a Change in Political Attitudes Towards the Environment, based in Southend-on-Sea, commissioned me to create the poster. Fortunately, the campaign (helped by the economic crisis then current) led to the scheme being cancelled.

In 1974 I drew the first poster advertising the new Strawberry Fair. I had been at the original meeting to set up the event. Official statements in later years said that it was inaugurated by a group of University students, but this was not the case, for in addition to grads, the meeting involved myself, members of the Town Anarchist group, various Townies with an interest in performance, and another Digger. I was commissioned to make the first poster, which was in hand-drawn lettering and concluded with a statement by the fictitious clerk of the fair, Hezekiah Bonkers. The fair continued annually on Midsummer Common well into the twenty-first century. Its name was a reference to the traditional folk song "Strawberry Fair" as well as the "revolutionary" 1970 film *The Strawberry Statement*.

I also owned a series of duplicating (or mimeograph) machines, made by the firms Roneo and Gestetner, from which I issued numerous publications over a twenty-year period. I even printed things for other people, including a number of issues of *The Wiccan* magazine for the Pagan Federation and a publication

Albion Series no. 1: polymer clay plaques with gold, silver, and copper leaf by Nigel Pennick, 2020.

about George Pickingill, a nineteenth-century Essex cunning man reputed to have founded several witch covens.[2] To make the publications more interesting, I developed a technique of line drawing on stencils with a sharp tool and other means of making textures with metal tools. One of the Dada magazines employed "typewriter art," where images were made by typing a series of different letters on the stencil to produce a textured effect. I also paid for scanned stencils to be made from drawings and photographs. Sometimes, I had access to a Roneo machine that belonged to a friend. It was in a house in Bateman Street reputed to have been Aleister Crowley's lodgings when an undergraduate at Cambridge. This machine had three interchangeable drums with different colours of ink. The drawback of multiple colours was that registration (aligning the different colour prints on a

---

2. The term "cunning man" described a man with magical knowledge and abilities. Often cunning men were resorted to for removing curses, countering malevolent witchcraft, identifying thieves, and recovering stolen property.

single page) was well nigh impossible.

I was commissioned by a man who called himself Sniknej to produce a "Wanted: God" poster in A4 size (the standard paper size in metricated Britain). It listed crimes, persecutions, wars, genocide, famines, and natural disasters as Acts of God and indicted God as responsible for them. Sniknej went round churches in Cambridge and pinned the posters on the notice boards when there was no one about. Visiting them later to see what happened, he noted that most were taken down quickly, but in one church it took five weeks before the offensive poster was removed.

Necessity is the mother of invention, and the absence of money to pay for lavish print jobs led to the development of new techniques. In Amsterdam, I was shown a silkscreening method which used sugar as a binding medium, producing a granulated effect. It was utilised on the covers of several issues of *Hapt*. In the late 1970s I built a silkscreen frame and silkscreened posters and T-shirts for the Institute of Geomantic Research using proprietary inks. In 1977, as a counterblast to the jamboree promised for Her Majesty the Queen's Silver Jubilee, I produced a two-colour silkscreen poster with the title "This Sceptered Isle." It depicted a derelict building, partly on fire, bedecked with Union flags, which pointed out the disconnect between the official rejoicing for the Queen's twenty-five glorious years on the throne, and the visible decline that her subjects were actually experiencing. This and similar posters at the time were produced by Bugram Hall ("bugger'em all"). Some were fly-posted on walls in Cambridge.

By the late 1970s I had given up making posters. In the hard times of the mid-1980s, I was earning money by writing books, and my frequent visits to speak at events in Switzerland, Austria, and West Germany put my printmaking at low priority. I only took up making prints again almost thirty years later. In 2008 the artist, photographer, and astrologer Linda Kelsey-Jones, curator of the Walkers' Gallery in San Marcos, Texas, taught me the new technique of acrylic transfer-printing. It involves printing out artwork with a computer. The artwork must be printed in reverse,

Cyril Papworth's Broom Dance in Cambridge,
acrylic transfer print by Nigel Pennick, 2011.

as the paper is covered with acrylic medium and placed face-downwards on prepared canvas. It is then allowed to dry before being moistened and carefully removed. This is a delicate task. When the paper is peeled back, the image is allowed to dry and is then varnished to protect it. I made over a hundred prints on canvas with this technique using scans of my original drawings of the towers of churches built after the Great Fire of London. Photographs of some of them appeared in my metaphysical book *The Ideal Tower*, published by the Society of Esoteric Endeavour in 2018. Linda Kelsey-Jones designed and curated an exhibit of this body of work, held in May 2011 at the Emmanuel United Reformed Church in Trumpington Street, Cambridge. The show was titled "Visionary Steeples."

Linda Kelsey-Jones also taught me printmaking using gel media, on which I made monoprints. The first were abstract, though some were based on the theme of the Cosmic Egg, and others used stencils I cut from card, including insects and Celtic knotwork. I developed a further two-stage variant of the gel-printing technique that involved using an additional intermediary plastic plate on which I could inscribe images, runes, or other artwork. During the Covid lockdown of 2020, I used this method to produce a large series of runic prints which ran to forty-two runes (Northumbrian plus medieval) as well as prints of Odin hanging on the windy tree, Yggrasil. I produced another series featuring the legendary ancient Celtic kings and queens of Britain, including Brutus, Gwendoline, and Bladud.

A Theophany of Light: Stained Glass

Always experimenting with art, and wishing to expand my possibilities, I attended classes in stained-glass making between 2001 and 2002. After completion of the course I received a certificate of proficiency. I then learnt traditional glass painting in the glass workshop in the triforium of the south transept of Ely Cathedral. In my stained-glass productions, I saw myself as a practitioner whose work was a spiritual continuation of all the light-smiths that went before me. My stained-glass work, which I sold as "Jewels of Light" (a phrase from William Blake), ranged from small sun-catchers and lampshades made with copperfoil technique,[3] to lanterns and larger windows which are glass-in-lead. I made them all with symbolic purpose, according to the principles of the Spiritual Arts and Crafts.

One element of my work was the technique of fragmentation. Spiritual tradition asserts that any sacred artefact damaged or taken out of use should never be destroyed or thrown away, because this would be a denial of its sanctity. In the case of weathered stone or wooden carvings, they must be buried in consecrated ground, just as a dead person would be. In the case of glass, it is taken from its lead surround and reassembled, paying particular attention to sacred images and symbols. This ensured the survival of much ancient church glass in more modern

---

3. Copperfoil is sometimes called "Tiffany technique," after the American glass and jewellery master Louis Comfort Tiffany (though Tiffany did not invent it!).

Stained-glass image of St George by Nigel Pennick, 2006.

A stained-glass panel by Nigel Pennick, installed above a doorway in a German house, 2008. Photograph by Rosemarie Kirschmann.

settings. Medieval windows assembled by fragmentation are the earliest examples of abstract art in the form of collage, predating by centuries the twentieth-century montages of the Cubists, Futurists, and Dadaists. In England, Scotland, and Wales, the technique was developed after the ravages of the Protestant Reformation, when Puritan fanatics roved the country, smashing every church window they could reach.

The most impressive examples of fragmentation can be seen in churches in England. St Mary's in Shrewsbury has many windows filled with medieval fragments from England, France, and Germany, reassembled in the nineteenth century. After World War II, when over 2,000 churches in Britain were damaged or destroyed in air raids, large quantities of damaged stained glass were rescued and reassembled in geometrical patterns by Stephen Dykes Bower, who collaged them in the windows of St John the Evangelist Church, Newbury. In fragmentation, the figurative and the abstract parallel one another through the constant reuse of old glass.

I made a number of large stained-glass panels, some of which

I sold. I sent these pieces to clients in the United States, Germany, and the Netherlands. Some were installed in windows. They had spiritual themes, including Sophia; the Cosmos; St Cecilia (patroness of musicians); the Welsh healing saint Dwynwen; and St George slaying the dragon, from a drawing I made of a window from the Commandery of the Teutonic Knights in Cologne, Germany. I also made a replica of the stained-glass window of Woden in Cardiff Castle. Some of my smaller pieces were printed using a technique I developed experimentally with clove oil. Like all my painted glass, they were fired in a kiln. Finally, I had to give up making large panels after a second heart attack and the unavailability of a workshop.

Spiritual Arts and Crafts

In 2005 I founded Spiritual Arts and Crafts Publishing to produce and sell my own books. I did all the work except the printing. Finally, there were four: *The Sacred Art of Geometry: Temples of the Phoenix*, *The Folk-Lore of East Anglia*, *Primal Signs*, and *The Spiritual Arts and Crafts*. My printer, Leighton Weymouth, was a meticulous craftsman who took great care to make everything perfect. He was the best printer I ever worked with. Sadly, he died in a mysterious fire at his office in 2020.

Sounds and Music, Signifying Something

The magic of sound and music has always been a source of joy and fascination to me, playing a central role in my life from my earliest days.

One Saturday morning in November 1958, the BBC broadcast its first "3-D sound" (or "solid sound") radio play, a Sherlock Holmes story. To hear the stereo effect, I had to stand a radio six feet from the television and tune them both in. One sound channel was broadcast on the TV and the other on the radio. I was able to hear stereo for the first time—Holmes playing the violin on one channel, while Dr Watson opened the door on the other. Although the sound balance was primitive with non-matched loudspeakers, horse-drawn vehicles panned across the space between the TV and radio, and a knife whistled across from one side to the other. (In a curious confluence, twenty-two years later I took part in a BBC "free-space" stereo recording in the Hellfire Caves at West Wycombe.)[4]

My father owned a reel-to-reel tape recorder, which he bought in 1955. He had worked on telecommunications and radar in the Royal Air Force during World War II, and, like many of his generation, was fascinated with electronics of all sorts. He had a television in 1950 when they were still relatively uncommon and programmes were only transmitted for a few hours a day. He also tinkered with radios and took me on expeditions to Lisle Street in Soho where there was a row of shops selling electronic components, many of them military surplus. I recorded music from the radio onto tapes, including Bill Haley and His Comets' "Rock Around the Clock," which was a sensation at the time. Having access to the tape recorder, which I was allowed to use freely, I began to experiment with sound. It is a pity that I could never use the very heavy tape recorder, dependent as it was on plugged-in mains electricity, to make "field recordings" of the sounds of the lifts at Russell Square station. However, over the next few years I recorded flushing toilets, doors slamming, birds outside the window, and dogs barking.

After I obtained a second tape recorder as a birthday present, I was able to overlay tracks and make loops of tape that ran around my bedroom on old cotton reels nailed to wood blocks. With my friend Austin Reeve, we wrote short plays and recorded them with sound effects mimicking shipwrecks, train crashes, and ghostly creaking doors, as well as music played on my harmonica and other improvised instruments: rubber bands on a cardboard shoebox, wire nailed to blockboard, and percussion on old cans and pieces of metal strip. There was a hardware store nearby that sold cheap off-cuts of blockboard and plywood for a few shillings apiece. I also made paintings on some of that plywood and later sold several of them at open art exhibitions in Cambridge. From these improvisations emerged a series of more sophisticated stringed instruments I made between 1965

---

4. See the section "Subterranean Worlds: The Physical Occult," pp. 200–206.

NIGEL PENNICK

Nigel Pennick's experimental psychedelic musical instruments, 1965–1969. Photo by Nigel Pennick.

and 1969. I gave these instruments generic names—the *zambo*, the *linn*, and the *dicros* being three of the more successful ones. In 1969 one of my instruments was almost featured on a record by the Cambridge group the Toby Jug & Washboard Band, but my train was cancelled and I did not get to the studio in time.

Some of my instruments were electric, amplified through the remains of a 1940s radio set I re-jigged as an amplifier. I had loudspeakers from scrapped radios, rigged up with recycled wires. The amp just sat on a table with no protective cover, literally "bare wires" and potentially lethal (but typical of the cavalier attitude we all had at that time to what is now termed "health and safety"). No one ever touched it while it was in use. None of these recordings survive. Later, around 1964, I got a battery-powered portable reel-to-reel tape recorder which enabled me to make "field recordings." I took it out and recorded traffic noise, steam locomotives, the sounds of riding on buses and tube trains, aircraft flying overhead, and the chants of football hooligans on their way to matches. The latter required the tape recorder to be concealed inside an oversize coat to avoid misunderstandings—or worse. Some of these recordings were later used by my band, Concrete Tapeworm.

In the late 1950s at grammar school I was taught to read music, play the double bass, and I appeared in the school orchestra. We performed various classical pieces, but as I did not have my own instrument at home to practice on, I never reached a competent level of playing and soon dropped out. On one occasion, during a rehearsal, my music teacher thought I was in a reverie and not paying attention, so he shouted "Pennick! Play me an E natural!" I did. He was surprised, as I am sure that he thought I was not interested. But he never hassled me again. One time, a pupil brought to him the sheet music of the rocked-up piano version of Tchaikovsky's *Nutcracker* called "Nut Rocker." He put it on the piano and proceeded to sight-read a fine performance of the rock 'n' roll bravado. His credibility among us was greatly enhanced.

At that time, music snobbery was still rife. My teacher was unusual in playing a piece of rock 'n' roll impromptu. The genteel commentariat on BBC radio and television used to sneer that musicians such as the Beatles and the Rolling Stones were upstarts who could not play their instruments. I had been playing the mouth organ since 1954 and I had taught myself how to play cross-harp blues, which was a world away from what was expected in school. Only the chromatic harmonica was deemed a proper instrument, as it was played by the likes of the consummate showman Larry Adler (who had become famous in Britain for his soundtrack to the 1954 film *Genevieve*). The diatonic harmonica, on the other hand, was associated in the genteel mind with repetitive and out-of-tune street buskers or drunken Irishmen in pubs on a Saturday night. Also known as a "blues harp," it was a key element of American blues, where some also referred to it as the "Mississippi saxophone" or—less kindly—the "misery whistle."[5] Yet it was precisely these more

5. The blues harp is a 10-hole harmonica such as the Hohner "Marine Band." The instrument can be played in Straight Harp, which is the designated key

Nigel Pennick playing a soldier's World War I trench fiddle, 2013. Photo by Jon Ward.

maligned musical instruments that attracted me, and I taught myself to play blues harp by listening to shortwave radio and vinyl records.

When I was at Cambridge Tech there was a common room for students taking degrees. Late in 1966 or early 1967 a fellow student called Mick would bring his acoustic guitar on a Friday and play in the common room after hours to anyone or no one. He was interested in the blues and we started to jam together, him on guitar and me on blues harp. At the time I only had a harmonica in the key of "C," so everything we played was in "G."

of the instrument, but blues is usually played in Cross Harp, which involves sucking and blowing. If a harmonica is in the Straight Harp key of C, it plays in the key of G in Cross Harp; a D harmonica plays in A; an E in B; and so on.

Our favourite songs were the Jesse "Lone Cat" Fuller number "San Francisco Bay Blues" and "Midnight Special" by Sonny Terry and Brownie McGhee. We tried to play "San Francisco Bay Blues" in the style of Fuller—not the prettified Peter, Paul and Mary version, which we abhorred. There was a lot of interest in the blues then. In 1968 Stefan Grossman played a small blues concert at the Tech one lunchtime almost unannounced, and afterwards gave a free lesson on bottleneck blues guitar technique.

Another song, "Gloria," written by Van Morrison, was a hit for the band Them, and, aided by prodigious amounts of alcohol, we sang it nonstop at a party at the Tech student house in Cherry Hinton Road. Our percussionist bashed empty beer bottles together, picking up another when one broke. He sat on the floor surrounded by broken glass, percussing away until he ran out of bottles. It was yet another instance of the pre–"health and safety" era. Unfortunately, I did not have my tape recorder with me at the time. At the Tech were several bands that played gigs, including Pontius Pilate and His Nail-Driving Seven, but I never performed with any of them.

Concrete Tapeworm began as a solo project in 1966. The name came from an asbestos pipe that stuck out from the side of a modernist building at the Tech. The reference was to experimental *musique concrète*, which I was able to find sometimes on my short-wave radio. As mentioned, for several years I had been recording ambient sounds such as running baths, WC flushings, creaking doors, noises on buses and steam trains, footsteps echoing, birdsong, and so forth. Once it was recorded on my primitive reel-to-reel tape equipment, I could splice and overlay sounds, and speed up, slow down, or even reverse the direction of the tape to play things backwards. Over this I played my improvised and home-made musical instruments. Again my amplification was primitive, using a radio as an amp. Lack of money and many other more pressing matters precluded my attempts to get a theremin and an ondes Martenot. (I finally got to play a theremin in 2013 at the Musical Instruments Museum in Oxford).

NIGEL PENNICK

In 1968 I played some of my tapes to musician friends and we tried to work out some way of performing together. We were very eclectic then. I was playing blues on harmonica and guitar, but we listened to a wide variety of music, including Praetorius, Buxtehude, Wagner, Vaughan Williams, Messiaen, Charlie Parker, John Coltrane, Stan Getz, the Grateful Dead, the Mothers of Invention, and the Groundhogs, as well as Martin Carthy and other folk luminaries of the time. A couple I knew had renaissance musical instruments—crumhorns and unusual recorders. Later they played with Karlheinz Stockhausen. But unfortunately, we never got an opportunity to perform in public, and all the tapes and written material are lost.

I was still making tapes as Concrete Tapeworm with occasional collaborators and had joined an experimental music ensemble set up at the Cambridge Arts Lab. Run by Dan Brodsky, the ensemble had a particular idea of what experimental music was supposed to sound like, so my unusual instruments and harmonica playing were not welcomed. Perhaps my string instruments looked something like the exotic *bandura* and other instruments on a then-current Incredible String Band album. (Not that I was a fan of that group—a girlfriend at the time played Incredible String Band records day and night, which was trying at times, to say the least.)

The only public performance of the ensemble was in St Michael's Hall, Trinity Street, at the national Arts Lab Conference held in Cambridge on January 25 and 26, 1969. I reported on the conference in *Cambridge Voice* no. 5:

> Day 2 ... started officially at 1 PM. I went to St Michael's Hall, at 12 o'clock as instructed, as I was "appearing" in the electronics and experimental music workshop, which was "accompanying" Bruce Birchall and company. At two or thereabouts, the Bruce Birchall ensemble had turned up, also Dan Brodsky, "leader" of the group. Ensuing noises/sounds/Birchall-isms/firecracker/piano bashing/whistles/feedback. Afterwards other things, Bruce Birchall's [play] *Exploits*. Brodsky had

brought a military-grade thunderflash with him and ended the performance by lighting it and throwing it inside the piano, blowing it up. The piano belonged to St Michael's Church. After Birchall's *Exploits*, whose political message can be seen from its title, the grand finale when the electric blues band The Blues Crusaders should have played was cancelled because their amplifiers had been banned (perhaps this was something to do with a thunderflash earlier?).

Unsurprisingly, there were no further Arts Lab performances in St Michael's Hall.

Later in 1969, the Arts Syndicate (not to be confused with the Arts Lab) was set up. It was a group of artists and designers associated with *Cambridge Voice*. An announcement in *Cambridge Voice* no. 10 stated:

> Arts Syndicate is planning in the near future an exhibition of members' works: paintings, sculpture, musical instruments, constructions, drawings, collage, etc. Arts Syndicate are [*sic*] contractors for many forms of artwork, including murals (interior and exterior), graphics, vision and design.

I painted a mural in the cellar of the YMCA under the aegis of the Arts Syndicate, but it was soon destroyed. The Arts Syndicate, like other activities connected with *Cambridge Voice*, received much hostility from the powers that be, and we could never secure venues for exhibitions or performances. Not surprisingly, the Arts Lab thunderflash had done irreparable damage to anything "alternative."

Travelling with My Harps

The advantage of the harmonica over other instruments is its small size: it can be carried in a pocket. That is why it was a favoured instrument of soldiers in the trenches of World War I and was employed as the "blues harp" by American bluesmen.

In my travels in Europe in the 1980s and 1990s, I always carried harmonicas with me and played when I could. After one visit to Stuttgart to give a geomantic lecture, I was going through security at the airport to fly back to the UK. The guard x-raying my bag pointed at what he thought were suspicious things. Actually, they were four harmonicas in different keys. So I opened the bag—"*Mundharmonikas!*"—and proceeded to play him Turlough O'Carolan's tune "Princess Royal" in its entirety, much to his annoyance. This was surely the only time that that tune was played at the Stuttgart airport on a harmonica.

Wherever I went, I visited ancient sacred places and, when possible, blew some harp there. I played in the crypt of a church at Rovere in the old Lucus Bormani on the Italian Riviera. The stone crypt, probably part of a Pagan temple of the Celto-Ligurian god Borvo or Bormanus, was a resonant place to improvise a "Blues for Bormanus." I played another subterranean tune in the Dictaean Cave on Crete, legendary birthplace of Zeus. Having been in a conducted tour, the guide switched off the lights (yes, electric light in a sacred cave, would you believe!), and I dodged back in to "get something" I said I had lost. Thus was I able to play a few bars there under the thunderbolt-like stalactites in honour of Zeus. Wherever I went, I visited old and interesting churches, and if there alone, or only with my local companions, I would play. I did not want to be intrusive to others who might take offence. Carrying an instrument at all times enables one to play when required—even to help out. On one occasion in 2008 at Hempstead in Essex, when the melodeon player did not turn up, I offered to play dance tunes on my harmonica for the Thaxted Morris dancers and held the fort until a hastily summoned accordion player eventually arrived to take over.

Melodeon, East Anglian Style

In 1996 I was driving to visit friends in Norfolk. In the village of Botesdale, I noticed a wide-fronted Victorian shop, situated at the end of a street that must once have been a marketplace. Interested, I parked my car and went to look. It was a melodeon shop. The next time I drove that road, I stopped off in Botesdale

Nigel Pennick plays melodeon in St Govan's cave-chapel, Wales, 1997. Photo by Rosemarie Kirschmann.

again and went inside. All kinds of melodeons hung on the wall, stood on the floor, or were on shelves behind the counter. The proprietor and a frail old man sat on a chair near the window talking. I made myself known, and asked questions about the instruments. Of course, I had encountered melodeon players when watching morris dancing. But this was the first time I had considered playing one.

I decided to buy a two-row Hohner Pokerwork melodeon in the keys of D and G. Of course, I could not play the instrument yet, but I was determined to learn. I picked up the melodeon and tried to hold it properly. Ted—for that was the name of the one-eyed old man who sat on the bentwood chair—instructed me how to hold it and said, "Good. Hand it back to me," so I did. Then he proceeded to play two tunes on it. As is customary in East Anglia, he announced the tune's name after each performance, the second being "Speed the Plough." He handed

Nigel Pennick plays melodeon on a megalith, Wales, 1997.
Photo by Rosemarie Kirschmann.

the melodeon back to me and commanded: "Now you play!" I tried to play "Speed the Plough," which I had heard many times before, but naturally it was not so easy. I thanked Ted, paid for the instrument, and went on my way. That was my only melodeon lesson, but it was the way generations of players learnt in rural East Anglia. I practised hard and before long was able to play tolerably well. Within a year I was out in public playing for Northstow Mummers on a four-stop, one-row melodeon I had bought at Bowes & Co., the Cambridge pawnbroker.

Northstow Mummers

On Boxing Day, 1996 (a traditional day for mumming), I saw a mummers' play in a pub at Halesworth in Norfolk and I was captivated. I had seen many performances of Morris and Molly dancing before, and participated as well, but somehow I had never been in the right place to see mumming in person. Having danced with the Duck Race Morris team at Willingham for a few months, and with the Molly dancers at Fenstanton on Plough Monday, I knew people who would, I hoped, appreciate

Northstow Mummers at the Ship Inn, Thornham, Norfolk, 1997. L to R: Nigel Pennick, Sally Tooley, Ann Pennick, Les Randall, Martin Tooley, and Lin Randall.

mumming if I got a team together. One of my favourite traditional songs was "The Derby Ram," and I knew this had a mummers' play associated with it. I contacted people who might have the play, and looked for it in the University Library. I received advice from Peter Cave of Derby Morris Men and members of the Coventry Mummers. We called ourselves Northstow Mummers, after the term for the local Hundred north of Cambridge.[6]

The first team of Northstow Mummers comprised Martin and Sally Tooley,[7] Les and Lin Randall, Ann and me, and occasionally our son Martin who guised as the Old Tup, the Derby Ram. The play we adapted was written down in the 1890s at Ecclesfield near Sheffield, and it had a song—with the music. We adapted the play and played the music for "The Derby Ram." The tune was not the one played on the carillon bells at Derby Cathedral, but something else. We were grateful

---

6. A "hundred" was a traditional subdivision of a county or shire; the term goes back to Anglo-Saxon times.

7. Tragically, Sally Tooley died in 2022.

The Northstow Mummers at Fen Ditton, dressed in their roles for the play "The Old Tup," 2008. (L–R): Nigel Pennick (Little Devil Doubt, with broom); Jon Ward (musician, with fiddle); Helen Starksfield (Bonny Old Lass); Derek Wood (the Doctor); Meggie Hiley (invisible, guising as the Old Tup); and Paul Smith (Butcher-So-Good). Photo by Linda Kelsey-Jones.

that someone had written it down. Martin Tooley constructed a "hobby animal" of the Old Tup from wood, papier maché, and cloth, with a snapping jaw operated by a wire. We rehearsed until we were proficient, and I investigated where we could perform. I had to arrange the gigs in between my frequent trips to Germany and the tours I was conducting in western England and Wales. Our first performance was at the seaside village of Thornham in Norfolk alongside several Morris teams in the centre of the village and at the Lifeboat pub. I was the musician, in tattered jacket and trousers, playing my one-row melodeon. We were well received and invited to perform in King's Lynn on several occasions.

During the first iteration of Northstow Mummers, we performed at events with the Milton Morris Men on May Day in King's Lynn and in Cambridge, where we performed at the

Plough Sunday, Pampisford, 2011: Northstow Mummers, Milton Morris Men, and Gogmagog Molly Dancers in procession.

Maypole pub. Other gigs included Twelfth Night at Duxford; St George's Day at Snape in Suffolk; midsummer in Northampton; folk festivals at Saffron Walden in Essex, Haverhill in Suffolk, and Whitwell and Gressenhall in Norfolk; and the Strawberry Fair in Cambridge. We also mummed in Whittlesea at benefits for the Straw Bear, but never at the festival itself because the Midwinter Mummers were regulars. For several years we performed at the clock tower in Fenstanton in Huntingdonshire, on Boxing Day along with the Fenstanton Morris, and then went on to the White Swan at Conington to perform again. "The Old Tup" play was augmented by several other traditional plays incuding a Horse Play, for which Martin Tooley made the Old Horse in the same manner as the Old Tup. At Conington we performed the Huntingdonshire piece (a short play with Beelzebub as a character) in some years and "The Old Tup" in others.

Sometimes, I guised as the Old Tup. Performing in an animal costume is transformative: one takes on the persona of the animal. I have found myself in combat with dogs, snapping my jaws and frightening them away. Children have cried when the Tup was "killed" by the butcher with his cleaver and I fell to the ground "dead." In the play, the ram (led by Bonny Old Lass) on his way to market in Derby stumbles and falls. Bonny Old Lass is worried and asks Little Devil Doubt what she should do. He says she needs a Butcher, and calls him up. After a struggle, the Butcher kills the Tup. Little Devil Doubt then calls up the Doctor, who brings the Tup back to life, saying: "If you're not quite dead, rise up and bay!"

The Horse play appeared sporadically at other venues, but "The Old Tup" was our favourite. When we performed at a folk event at the Honest John pub at Chatteris in the Cambridgeshire Fens in 2000, I was playing the Horse in the next performance. Because the event was taking place in a marquee (a tent) on the car park, I had to park my own vehicle some distance away. Guising as the Horse, I walked along the street towards the pub to join the team. Seeing me, a group of small boys shouted "It's the horse of death!" and ran off in mock terror.

The first Northstow Mummers team broke up owing to various members' other commitments. I founded the second iteration with Jon Ward as musician; Derek Wood (later Starkwood); Helen Starksfield; Paul Smith, who played the Butcher (and was a butcher in real life [died 2021]); Meggie Hiley; and myself. Meggie, Jon, Helen, and I were members of the Traditional Music of Cambridgeshire Collective (see below). Others from the Cambridge Pagans occasionally rehearsed or played with us, but the core group performed the majority of gigs. We continued our association with the Milton Morris Men and appeared regularly on Plough Monday at Pampisford until that tradition ended when the Milton Morris Men disbanded.

Other performances were on May Day at the Maypole pub and for various village feasts including the Fen Edge Festival at Cottenham. Finally, the continued deterioration of my health and other factors led to the second team disbanding. Subsequently, Northstowe with an "e" was chosen as the name for a new town to be built on the supposed "brownfield" site of the former Oakington airfield, dating from World War II. A plan was drawn up, and the first houses were actually built on greenfield land just outside the village of Longstanton. Historically, Northstow Mummers had no connexion with the new town of Northstowe.

Pub Sessions

In the mid-1990s I started going to blues jam sessions in Cambridge at the Boat Race pub. This was the former Falcon, which had survived the demolition of most of the Kite area, and hosted established blues and ska performers, as well as "open-mic" blues nights. There was electric blues on Sunday afternoons and acoustic blues on Wednesday evenings. Mostly I did not play, as then I still did not have the full set of harmonicas that I later bought. Occasionally, at an acoustic session, I would get up and sing. The only time I sang "Dust My Broom" there was with Ben Smith, a regular, on guitar. Other people had sung Robert Johnson's popular blues and the Boat Race had recently hosted American bluesman Honeyboy Edwards, who once worked with Johnson. I also saw Kent DuChaine, disciple of Johnny Shines, another of Johnson's associates, play "Dust My Broom" there. Such is continuity across generations and across continents.

One night in 2006 I had a dream that I was playing a musical instrument laid in my lap. It was not the *guqin* I had played at the China Cultural Company back in the sixties. Neither was it my homemade *dicros*, with wires stretched over blockboard. It was something else, with frets. When I woke up, I remembered that I had a photocopy of some pages from a book about Appalachia which had an instrument similar to the one in my dream: it was a mountain dulcimer. I vaguely remembered seeing Brian Jones of the Rolling Stones and—at another time—Joni Mitchell playing the instrument on television. I felt an irresistible urge to

Nigel Pennick on electric dulcimer and Helen Starksfield on accordion, Wysing Arts Centre, Cambridgeshire, 2012.

get one. The only place I could think of was Hobgoblin Music in Fitzrovia. On Monday morning, I travelled to London and Hobgoblin had two different mountain dulcimers for sale. One, made in Pakistan, was so poorly constructed that it was clearly not playable; this was evident even to a novice like me (since I already played the guitar, I could also tell whether the fretting was decent or not). The other, a Stoney End dulcimer made in the United States, was far better made, so I bought it even though it was twice the price.

Now I actually had a dulcimer! The Hogoblin Music shop was within walking distance of St Giles's church, where I had to go when at primary school. I sat in a pew for the first time in fifty years, unwrapped the dulcimer from its bubble wrap, and made a sound with it. I could not play it properly yet, but having it there in a church I was visiting for the first time in half a century was a consecration of sorts.

Later, in 2013, musician and master craftsman Russell Paddon rebuilt my Stoney End instrument with chromatic fretting. He also made me a celestial monochord based upon the accurate one in the Paracelsian physician Robert Fludd's writings.[8] I painted it with the planetary, stellar, and empyrean sigils on the correct frets. I was taught technical drawing at grammar school and can make accurate scale or full-size plans of any object I want to make or have made. My Runestaff Crafts artefacts had all been made in this way.

Sessions at the Carlton

The Carlton Arms on the north side of Cambridge hosted a music session where everyone played together and I went there with my dulcimer and sometimes brought my melodeon. Many of the regular musicians were Irish, so most of the tunes played were Irish, too. But it was not an exclusively Irish session; American "Old Time" tunes and English folk songs were played as well. One musician had a keyboard, and Peter Ward would borrow it to play the bossa-nova standard "The Girl from Ipanema" or Meade Lux Lewis's boogie-woogie number "Honky Tonk Train Blues." He also played Irish music on the concertina. It was good to go every week with my dulcimer, even though when I tried to start a tune the background din of the pub often meant that the other musicians could not hear me. But I learnt the standard Irish repertoire at the Carlton. I was also given an instrument that a Carlton regular, who was not a musician, said had been in his garage for thirty years. It was a *Magyar citera* (Hungarian zither), and he gave it to me because he saw a family likeness with my dulcimer. It was in a bad state, but I restored it to playable condition, and used it on some recordings where its ethereal drone enhances the mood.

Apart from the sheer noisiness of the Carlton, I always felt threatened there. There were belligerent people around who were not interested in what we were playing. Several other musicians were harassed for no discernible reason at the Carlton sessions. There were pool tables close by and the clack of the balls was distracting. Outside, there were often people up to no good.

---

8. This appears on a Fludd engraving from 1623. The inaccurate illustration of a monochord appears in the earlier 1617 work *Utriusque Cosmi Maioris Scilicet et Minoris* (On the Two Worlds, namely, the Major and the Minor). The instrument depicted there would be unplayable if constructed.

As I left one evening near midnight, a group of Travellers were standing around in the car park at the front.[9] As I came down the Carlton steps, one young man grabbed at the handles on my dulcimer case and said: "I'll carry it for you." Replying with the firm response of "No you *don't!*" I managed to get to my car, lock the doors, and drive off.

The threat of violence was sometimes real. On one occasion, a car pulled into the Carlton car park, a door opened, and a man, beaten and bleeding from wounds, was thrown out. People went to attend to him and asked if he needed an ambulance, but after a few minutes he staggered to his feet and hobbled off into the night. He appeared to be an Eastern European. Around that time, less than half a mile away in Arbury, the Snow Cat pub was the scene of a stand-up fight between Travellers and a group of Polish men. Apparently, a Pole had been beaten up by the Travellers and his friends showed up to get revenge. Carrying hammers, iron bars, and knives, the Poles attacked the Travellers. Finally, the police arrived. After that, the pub ceased trading and it was converted into a gurdwara. I finally stopped going to the Carlton after one night when I came out to my car to drive home and saw that someone had torn off a wing-mirror. It cost me over £100 to repair. One of the regulars offered me to park in his driveway a few hundred yards away, but walking to that pub in the dark was not exactly a good idea.

The Traditional Music of Cambridgeshire Collective

In 2009 Jon Ward, doyen of the Carlton Session and veteran of Cambridge rock bands and *céilidh* performances, suggested we form the Traditional Music of Cambridgeshire Collective (TMCC). There were four of us at first: Jon on bouzouki, guitar, or hurdy-gurdy; Meggie Hiley on fiddle; Helen Starksfield on piano-accordeon; and myself on mountain dulcimer and one-row melodeon. We performed in public a number of times, including

---

9. "Travellers" is a generic term for peripatetic families of various ethnicities who may be Roma or Sinti (colloquially known as Gypsies), but these were probably "Irish Travellers," aka Pavees or Mincéirs, some of whom are settled north of Cambridge.

Traditional Music of Cambridgeshire Collective at John Clare's house, Helpston, 2010. L to R: Helen Starksfield (piano accordion), Meggie Hiley (fiddle), and Nigel Pennick (mountain dulcimer).

at the Cottenham Feast, and we recorded a CD titled *Music from the North Side of the River*, which we offered for sale and gave to friends. I carried the May Garland through Cambridge that year for the first time since the police banned May Day garlands in 1906. Our musician on that occasion was Helen Starksfield.

Meggie Hiley and I played as the TMCC at the opening of the museum at the "Peasant Poet" John Clare's cottage at Helpston near Peterborough. She played fiddle and I played melodeon. We performed traditional Cambridgeshire pieces and some of Clare's original tunes. During a break when everyone else went outside, we looked round the house. Meggie saw one of Clare's manuscript music books open in a glass case, took out her fiddle and played the tune, direct from the source. It was an inspiring moment of continuity.

In its time, Sturbridge Fair (also known as Stirbitch or Stourbridge) on Stourbridge Common was a great trading fair.[10] When Daniel Defoe visited it in the early eighteenth century, the fair was reputed to be the largest in the world. Merchants from as far away as Turkey and Persia came to sell their wares there, sailing up the then-navigable river directly on to the common. It was chartered by King John in 1209 and was held, every year, until 1932. In 2010, we of the Traditional Music of Cambridgeshire Collective were asked to play in the ancient Stourbridge Leper Chapel on Newmarket Road. At the appointed time, we turned up and were ushered into some wooden chairs in the east end of the chapel, where we played local traditional tunes with Jon Ward on bouzouki, Zoe Austin on fiddle, and myself on mountain dulcimer.

We were dressed in ordinary modern clothes, as we always were when we performed. I wore a traditional farm labourer's (and factory worker's) cloth cap, and a green sash, which—in Cambridgeshire tradition—signifies a musician playing at a village feast or similar ceremonial event. We played two sets, which seemed to have been well received by the audience, yet there were no thanks from the organisers. Later, it emerged that they had assumed we would turn up in cod-medieval costume and play cod-medieval music. But we were contemporary musicians who had performed over the years in jazz and rock bands, folk clubs, blues jams, classical ensembles, experimental and electronic music groups, Morris dancers' processions, the band of the Whittlesey Straw Bear, mumming performances, and more. Moreover, we had played venerable Cambridgeshire tunes such as "The Cambridge Hornpipe," which were good enough for the East Cambridge musicians—men like Harry Day, Herb Reynolds, and their colleagues—who had played at the Sturbridge Fair before the fair's demise in 1932. Through archival research, I had compiled a list of tunes played at the Oyster House in the early twentieth century, so that what we

---

10. The various forms reflect how spellings and even names were changed by nineteenth-century academic mapmakers; the current official name is Stourbridge.

were playing would be authentic.[11] But we were not invited back. People in pastiche medieval costumes were there the next time, complete with a hurdy-gurdy. Jon could have played his, had they asked.

It is bizarre that the organisers of such events have no understanding of the process of continual change that has occurred over 723 years. Medieval costume in 1209 was not the same as in 1309 or 1409, just as modern costume in 1821 was not the same as modern costume in 1921 or 2021. It is a serious lack of perception that fixates itself upon some imagined period and tries to reproduce it.

Yet it is often the case that when one plays traditional folk music, one is expected to be *re-enacting* something rather than actually playing there and then. Jon Ward and I once performed for a fête at an old people's home where Jon's father, Peter, was living. He came out with his concertina and played with us. A woman approached me and pointed at my mountain dulcimer—"When did they play those things?" she asked me. "Now," I replied. One time at a Carlton pub session we were playing an Irish tune when someone asked us, "What do you play?" Jon Ward immediately replied: "We play what we like." On another occasion, I was playing balalaika in a procession of Morris dancers and Northstow Mummers at Pampisford. A melodeon player said to me in a cross voice: "That's not an English instrument!" "And *that's* a German instrument!" I replied.

A musical instrument is something one uses to play music, just as a surgeon uses surgical implements to perform surgery. If one is not playing "Early Music" on real or reconstructed ancient instruments, specifically for the particular sound of the time, one can play on any instrument available. The only hindrances are the technical proficiency of the musician and the compatibility of the music. One cannot play Turkish scales on a chromatically fretted guitar, but one can play "God Save the King" on a B-flat diatonic blues harp. So I have played blues on my electric shahi

---

11. The Oyster House was a pub, demolished in 1957, which was turned over to dancing for the duration of the Sturbridge Fair each year. The local East Cambridge musicians provided the music.

Mendoza and mandolin: Nigel Pennick as the Lord of Misrule and Eric Haynes wassail Trumpington Community Orchard, 2020.

baaja at the Fulbourn Music Club I used to run, and Morris tunes on the balalaika and harmonica. "Fun supplies the power!" as *Cambridge Voice* once said. *We wunt be druv.*

The TMCC was always intended to be flexible in membership. In 2011, at an event held in the Emmanuel United Reformed Church in Cambridge to celebrate the opening of my one-man art show, the group was composed of Jon Ward (bouzouki), Helen Starksfield (accordion), Mary Humphreys (concertina), and myself (mountain dulcimer). As part of my Wildwood Show, a multimedia event I staged in 2012 at Wysing Arts at Bourn in Cambridgeshire, Jon and I were joined by Frances Collinson (vocals) and Russell Paddon on banjo. We performed traditional songs connected with the woodlands. Anna Franklin also gave a talk as part of my event. Previously, I had played at Wysing Arts on separate occasions in duos with Jon and Helen.

Around that time, I was asked to conduct the wassail of the young apple trees in the new community orchard at Trumpington. Appearing as the Lord of Misrule in my tattered jacket and rattling a mendoza (also known as a lagerphone or zob stick), I made a short opening invocation and then the TMCC and other local musicians started to play the wassail tunes I had provided as sheet music. As there are no remaining Cambridge wassail tunes known, I adopted the "Carhampton Wassail" from Somerset. This is how tradition develops. We were invited back again and again, year on year, and the trees grew well.

Music Clubs: Good Times, Bad Times

In the mid-noughties, I would sometimes pick up Ann after work in the post office at Histon. We often went for a drink in the Red Lion pub there before going home. On one occasion, we were sitting at a table when we were joined by a postwoman, Moyra Borg. We got to talking about music and she told me she played in a folk club at a pub in Cottenham called the Jolly Millers, and would I like to come? I became a regular. The landlord enjoyed our songs and music and provided free sandwiches at "halftime" in the evening. Moyra would play "Portsmouth" on her tin whistle and sometimes she and I would duet folk tunes on our harmonicas. I played the dulcimer, which was always the subject of fascination. In the summer we were invited to play at special events in the pub garden under a marquee. It was all very congenial.

But then the landlord was replaced by a landlady, who, it soon became clear, only barely tolerated us. It all came to a head one evening when I arrived early. Liam Browne, a veteran Irish singer, raconteur, and accordion player, was already there. I had sat down with Liam and was talking to him when the landlady

Graham and Ann Steward of Eel Pie with Nigel Pennick at Arrington, 2012. Photo by Linda Kelsey-Jones.

suddenly shouted at us: "I don't want Travellers, unemployed people, or folk singers in my pub!" We remonstrated with her for this unwarranted outburst and were then told, in a near-shriek: "Get out! You're all banned!"

We were shocked. What had we done to provoke this reaction? Nothing. So we went and stood outside to tell the others, including the organiser Graham Steward, who, with his wife Ann, was a member of the Ely folk band Eel Pie. The landlady came out and continued her abuse. I saw a piece of chalk-stone lying on the ground, and with it, I drew a binding-pattern on the pub doorstep while calling a runic invocation. The others watched, but knowing my connexion with the Nameless Art, did not comment. I told them I had magically bound the pub, and it would now go out of business. It did. Years later, in 2021, the Jolly Millers was empty and boarded up. It was a sad end to a good place.

We moved on to the old Conservative Club in Cottenham, an Arts and Crafts building from the early twentieth century with "battered" walls and beautiful, sinuous brass door-fittings.

It was not as congenial as the Jolly Millers had been. In the winter, the Geordie barman opened up when we got there, and the heating did not get going until it was too late. People sat there in their winter coats and scarves, playing and singing. On one particular day in 2013 the barman asked, "What's today, then?' in his Newcastle accent. Nobody knew but me. I played "The Blaydon Races" on the dulcimer, for that day was the 150th anniversary of the event immortalised in the song. He was impressed, and I got a free can of Diet Coke for my efforts.

Moyra was diagnosed with terminal cancer, and I used to pick her up from her home and take her to the club, where she dozed until it was her turn to play. She had obtained an instrument for me as thanks for my kindness. She did not know what it was, but I did—it was an Anglia Harp, a rare fifteen-stringed local instrument which I had sought for years. Moyra died soon afterwards, aged forty-nine, and suffered the disrespect that relatives often give to the deceased. Born in Malta, she had been brought up a Catholic, but in England she attended Methodist churches. Her brothers came from Malta and gave her a Catholic funeral in Cambridge. At the next music session someone had been asked why nobody came and played at the Methodist memorial service in her memory. We would have, gladly. But nobody asked us. Two Pagans I knew were given Christian funerals by their relatives, against their wishes. When my Grandmother Grace died at the age of 103 in 2003, I gave her a Christian funeral, as she had attended church regularly before she became too old to do so. It is only right to respect the spiritual pathways of the dead.

The Silent Instruments

In the noughties of the twenty-first century, the Folk Museum in Cambridge asked Northstow Mummers to perform. The museum was in the former White Horse Inn, an ancient timber-frame building, the last one remaining in that street. I was taken from room to room, where ancient artefacts of Cambridge Town life were displayed. I was looking for a space suitable for our performance. In one room were some poorly conserved musical instruments. One glass case contained a rare thin brass whistle, once owned and played by the last known master of the Cambridge brass whistle, Harry Day, who died in 1964. It is the only one I have ever seen. On top of the case was a battered hammered dulcimer, with one row of bridges. Some bridges and strings were missing, and the frame was cracked, making it unplayable. There was also a melodeon which had been played for the Cambridge Morris Men before World War II. I asked the curator if I could play it. "No," she replied, "it is for posterity." "I *am* posterity," I retorted, but to no avail. The mummers' play went ahead later and everyone was satisfied, though it would have established a measure of continuity if I could have played that melodeon in the old White Horse Inn. Instruments were made by skilled craftspeople in order to be played, not to be worshipped like holy relics in a museum. That is their function. Only if they are so deteriorated as to be unplayable is it acceptable to preserve them "for posterity" in a glass case or hung on the wall of a Hard Rock Cafe. Otherwise, let the good times roll.

When should that instrument be played? Now!

VIII
MATTERS OF LIFE AND DEATH

Illness, illness, always following me,
I'll never be free 'til I'm in the Mole Country.

—from the song "Illness Blues" by Nigel Pennick, 2014

Skuld from the "Emblemata" series of ink illustrations by Nigel Pennick, 2002.

The Fates' Decree

We owe our lives to a series of random or fortuitous events which some perceive as chance and others, providence. There are few people who have reached old age without many a close call with death. Those who have survived life-threatening accidents or illness sometimes ascribe their survival to supernatural intervention. Everyone likes to feel special, to be the "chosen one" in some way. But what happens to you can happen to anyone and, on the wider level, it is a matter of belief what causal forces are behind these occurrences.

The Stoic Emperor Marcus Aurelius saw events as ordained by the "decree of the Fates"—in other words, he believed that the things that happen to us are destined. This concept encapsulates an ancient belief that at birth we are given a particular time to live. It is a view that is evident in both European and African traditional spirituality, as in the saying "He died before his time," and the blues song by Mississippi Fred McDowell:

> *Lord, if I have to die, baby, fo' you think my time have come,*
> *Lord, if I have to die, baby, now fo' you think*
>   *my time have come,*
> *I want you to bury my body out on Highway 61.*

Then, although the body is buried, the spirit will not return to the gods until the designated time, and it will rove the roads as a ghost until then. In 1937 Robert Johnson modernized the concept with burying his body by the highway side "so my old evil spirit can catch that Greyhound Bus and ride." The ghost will disappear from earth once its time is up. Those who die violently—whether they are murdered, killed in battle, executed, or die in an accident—will also remain earthbound until the appointed hour. Of course, some have no belief in a separate spirit, and to them, "Once you're dead, you're done."[1]

We do not know the time of our demise in advance. As an old sundial motto admonishes us: *Watch and pray: for ye know not when the time is*. It is better that way, as those diagnosed with terminal illness or on death row awaiting execution will attest. Though even terminal illness is not determinate in its duration, and on death row one may receive a reprieve. Philosophically, though, we are all terminal cases under sentence of death, "mortal men, doomed to die" as J. R. R. Tolkien put it.[2]

European traditional spirituality is equivocal about the survival of the spirit after death. It is generally accepted that the Druids taught the transmigration of the spirit from one body to another, which is a widespread belief of polytheistic religions in many lands. It is essential to the Eastern concept of *karma*, where the type of rebirth is dependent upon the type of life one has led. This has the propensity to be interpreted cruelly—for example, in the assumption that someone born disabled is being punished for sins in a previous life. Such a belief can lead to vulnerable people being treated badly for the whole of their lives, which is unjust. Furthermore, it enables those born into powerful privileged families to boast that it is a reward for fine and worthy deeds performed in a previous life.

A follow-on from the ancient belief in karmic rebirth appears in the Islamic and Christian religions, where life is indeed a one-way ticket, and good karma ensures admission to Heaven, while bad karma brings eternal punishment in Hell. At school we were told to write something about Heaven and Hell, and I described Hell as "God's concentration camp." Of course,

---

1. From the song "Life's a One-way Ticket" by Cousin Joe of New Orleans, 1973.

2. *Men* meaning "humankind" according to more recent sensibilities.

Odin's Ordeal. Drawing made by Nigel Pennick during recovery from a near-death experience, 2003.

I was punished for this.

Paganism evinces a range of attitudes about life after death, reincarnation, or extinction. The practice of woodland burials is indicative of a belief that one's spirit passes into a tree at death, becoming a sort of dryad. Ancient Pagan and Heathen "scriptures" within a given tradition will vary too. The Eddic poem *Hávamál* (sts. 76–77) recounts that kinsmen and cattle die, and so must the self; the only thing that survives is one's good reputation. Elsewhere, Norse mythological sources tell us how those slain in combat are gathered up by the Valkyries and taken into the entourage of Odin to await the final battle at Ragnarök, after which a new Earth will emerge. In all cases, the condition of the afterlife is determined by our conduct in this life. Spiritual traditions and beliefs provide a means for us to survive and remain mentally balanced under difficult conditions, including long-term illness.

Family Illness

One of my great-grandmothers, Louisa Robinson, born in London in 1878, contracted smallpox as a four-year-old girl when she fell into some contaminated laundry at the bottom of the stairs of the East End tenement block where her family lived. She survived, but suffered lifelong poor health as a result of the infection. She married, and bore one daughter, Grace, in 1899. But as Louisa had heart trouble and during World War I, her husband Charles Robinson was sent home on compassionate leave because she was not expected to survive. Leaving his unit, Charles returned to London and avoided the fate of most of his comrades who were killed fighting in a failed offensive on the Western Front. Louisa lived until 1960, having spent her last year bedridden in the Homoeopathic Hospital. Her daughter, Grace, was my paternal grandmother. Sometimes she recited an epitaph to me that she remembered from an ancient tombstone she saw as a girl:

> *Traveller, as thou pass by,*
> *As you are now, so once was I.*

NIGEL PENNICK

As I am now, so thou must be.
*Prepare thyself to follow me.*³

At eighteen years of age, Grace had lost her first husband, killed in World War I, and in World War II many members of her church congregation died in the crypt of St John's, Red Lion Square, from a direct hit by a *Luftwaffe* bomb. She lived through the whole war in London, earning her living as an insurance agent. So the imminence of death was always a theme in her life, and in her profession as a nurse. Her husband Charles Pennick had a stroke, aged fifty-two, and she had to look after him because he was no longer able to play the drums, nor to do much else. It saddened me to see him reduced to sitting in an armchair all day. Smoking was his only pleasure—the Black Cat cigarettes that he had smoked from his days playing at the Hotel Cecil and the Hungaria Restaurant. The cigarettes must have accelerated his end, but medical understanding then was tolerant of smoking, even for patients in hospital. He died in 1960 at the age of sixty, so my grandmother lost both her second husband and her mother in the space of a month.

My father, Rupert Pennick (1924–1999), was a numerologist who had fatalistic beliefs. From the age of seventeen he had served in the Royal Air Force in World War II and then trained to become a teacher. His fatalism seems to have come from his mother's trauma at losing her first husband in the war at the age of eighteen. One is doomed when fate brings one into an unavoidably fatal situation; if your "number's up" there would be no escape.⁴ This was compounded by a story he used to tell

---

3. Punctuation added (doubtless a seventeenth-century tombstone had none).

4. This belief may originate with the military practice of giving each recruit a unique identity number. The order given to servicemen taken prisoner-of-war was to provide only their name, rank, and number to the enemy. Every soldier was aware of his name, rank, and number as his identity as a member of the armed forces. When a soldier died on the battlefield, then his comrades, reporting it, would say: "His number's up." So, the idea of an enemy bullet having "one's number on it" and thereby being destined to hit that individual is also part of British military folklore.

me about how he was "spared." He and his comrades were on a break and had been playing cards in a hut on the airfield, but he felt he had to go outside and have a smoke. He had walked some distance when a lone *Luftwaffe* aircraft flew over low and targeted the hut with a direct hit. His comrades died, but he survived. Clearly, his number was not up, and he survived the war and much longer until the end of the century, dying aged 74. In 1944 he had a letter published in *The Daily Mirror* predicting that the war would end on its 1,944th day. It did not. He was always noticing numbers—13 and 23 seemed ominous to him, as they proved to be. He told me how 23 occurred in films; street numbers on doors were often 23; and 23 was the New Orleans streetcar route number in *A Streetcar Named Desire*. However, his numerology was put to good use when he won a substantial amount of money on the Football Pools—enough to buy a house.[5]

"Hoojah Moon, toodleoo, 23 skidoo" were my father's last words, written on a piece of paper by his bed the night he died, December 13, 1999. He had served on North Atlantic air bases in World War II in occupied Iceland and later Scotland, which were operating aircraft from both the Royal Air Force and the United States Army Air Corps. The American airmen said "23 skidoo!" when an airman was killed, the equivalent of "Wizard Prang" in the slang of the RAF. While the origins of the phrase "23 skidoo" are disputed,[6] to my father the number 23 represented

---

5. The Football Pools in the UK were a legal gambling system where the results of soccer matches had to be predicted on a coupon, which was then sent with the appropriate stake before the matches were played by mail to the office in Liverpool. Each game was given a number, and sometimes very large prizes were won.

6. In New York City, the Fuller Building (nicknamed the "Flatiron") was built in 1902 at the intersection of Broadway and 5th Avenue at 23rd Street. It was an early example of a high-rise building at a geomantically inappropriate place, channelling heavy gusts of wind that blew up women's skirts and encouraged young men to loiter there. The 1939 *New York City Guide* produced by the Federal Writers' Project of the WPA tells how "policemen used to shoo loungers away from the Twenty-third Street corner, and the expression 'twenty-three skidoo' is supposed to have originated from this association" (pp. 204–5).

NIGEL PENNICK

Rupert Pennick, 1924–1999.

doom, and he died on the thirteenth.

Family illness and disability surrounded me from childhood at the age of six until I was fifty. In 1973 my mother had a stroke and was paralyzed down one side and lost her speech. She spent the rest of her life in a wheelchair, heroically looked after by my father with occasional respite for a week at a time when he took trips abroad to Germany and the Netherlands. Because she could not communicate, she often became very frustrated and sometimes had epileptic fits as a result. She suffered terribly and there was nothing we could do. It was unmitigated stress for all the family, especially her. She survived for twenty-three years in that terrible state.

Lives during Wartime

War! What is it good for? Absolutely nothing!
—Edwin Starr, "War"

War has been the background to the whole of my life. Although I never fought in a war, during my lifetime many wars have been fought in my name as a British subject, though I never approved of a single one of them. Thirty years before I was born, Sydney Dale, who was the twenty-two-year-old brother of the woman who later became my grandmother, was killed in 1916 in France in the Battle of Delville Wood near Longueval, a small area half a mile in circumference.[7] During the Battle of the Somme, the devastated remains of Delville Wood had been lost and retaken several times by the British Army and the opposing Germans. Over the course of several weeks, thousands had died fighting over these few yards of ground, now dug with trenches amid the splintered standing stumps of the woodland's trees, gas-filled craters, and churned-up ground containing the mangled remains of young British and German men. On Sunday July 23, men of the 1st East Surrey regiment were sent into the remains of Delville Wood to expel German units that had again taken most of the wood back from British Empire troops. At 3:40 a.m., the East Surreys along with units from Northumberland, Yorkshire, and Cornwall were sent forward into the zone, but after taking some territory, German machine-gun fire forced them back to their starting-point. Sydney Dale was one of many English soldiers mown down that morning. His remains were never found.

The names of the slain can still be seen listed on war memorials that were erected in every city, town, and village once the war had ended. The First World War (or "The Great War for Civilisation," as it is inscribed upon the medals), especially the Battle of the Somme, was instrumental in destroying the ancient culture of traditional rural life that had persisted for centuries in essentially the same way. So many young men were taken away to fight for the Empire, never to return. Horses were requisitioned for the army, and American tractors purchased to till the land. The skills of horsemanry and self-sufficient farming were replaced in a short while by industrialized methods reliant upon imported fossil fuels. Those soldiers that did return from the atrocities and tragedies were traumatized, altered men, and

---

7. The Battle of Delville Wood was fought from July 15 to September 3, 1916.

there was no work for many.

War's blight upon families continues through the generations. Naturally, I was affected. My father's mother lost her first husband, killed in the war in 1918. She became a pacifist, and occasionally talked of the "war-monger Winston Churchill." My mother, born eight years after the Somme, always hated Germans whom she vilified from time to time. My father-in-law, Sidney Trevelyan, had been taken prisoner in 1942 by Japanese forces who occupied Singapore. He was marched away with his comrades and forced to work as a slave labourer on a railway Imperial Japan was constructing through Burma.[8] British prisoners-of-war there were as a matter of course starved, beaten, tortured, and killed. Many were worked to death, and some were thrown to the crocodiles. As American and British forces began to advance, Sidney was taken to Japan, where he was forced to work in a mine. Finally, he was liberated and rescued by American forces.

The wars fought by the British military during my lifetime were many. As a boy, I would hear accounts on the BBC radio news of military actions in Malaya, Kenya, Cyprus, Suez, Aden, and so on.[9] In 1956, I was playing outside with some other boys when my father came out of the house and told us that he had heard on the radio that the Royal Air Force had just bombed Cairo. We all cheered, having been brought up on stories of the heroes of the Battle of Britain and Bomber Command in World War II. What we were living through—though we did not realize it at the time—were episodes in the dissolution of the British Empire with all its bloody consequences. When we grew up, and became taxpayers, it was our money that was used to

---

8. Burma is now called Myanmar.

9. Malaya, now Malaysia, was the locus of a fifteen-year-long war (1945–1960) of British forces against communist insurgents, which ended in the defeat of the communists. Kenya was the nationalist uprising of the Mao Mao; the Cyprus uprising was by Greek Cypriot nationalists (northern Cyprus now occupied by Turkey since 1974); Suez was a short war fought in 1956 by British, French, and Israeli forces against Egypt. Britain was forced to withdraw after international condemnation. Aden is now South Yemen.

William Robinson, 1833–1917.

fund the subsequent wars of post-imperial Britain: the Falklands, two wars against Iraq, the bombing of Belgrade and Libya, and ultimately the lost war in Afghanistan. The thirty years' internal struggle in Northern Ireland was never called a civil war. Like the Falklands, it was a "conflict," or "the troubles."

In 1982 I was seconded to the biology department of the University of Guelph, Ontario, Canada. Shortly before this, a British task force had (with considerable losses) reconquered the Falkland Islands in the south Atlantic, which had been occupied by the Argentine military. Being British, I was taken to task by people at the university, who disapproved of Britain's "imperial war." But I had no say in it, and I felt no need to justify or condemn it to people who were seemingly puzzled by such a war in 1982. Like all the other wars, it was nothing to do with me, apart from my taxes being diverted to pay for the military rather than more useful things like hospitals and transport systems at home. In 2021 a Scottish man who came to repair my heating boiler told me of his experiences as a sailor in the Falklands. He had narrowly escaped from his burning, sinking ship after it was hit by an Argentine missile. His anguish was palpable forty years later. War means hideous suffering on all sides of any conflict. It blights lives long after the fact, and the trauma is transmitted down through the generations.

Eventually, though, memory is lost. I have a photograph of an ancestor, William Robinson, a former Royal Marine who died a Chatham Pensioner in 1917.[10] A note on the back tells that he was decorated by Queen Victoria for some heroic act, now forgotten as all records of the Royal Marines were destroyed when Chatham was bombed by the *Luftwaffe* during World War II. New wars destroy the histories and monuments of earlier ones. But so long as anyone lives who is affected by war, the anguish is not extinguished.

At the Holy Mountain of Alsace

I was diagnosed with diabetes in 1980. I followed the medical advice I was given, attending every appointment at Addenbrooke's Hospital in Cambridge. In 1993 I went for my annual routine eye examination. Shockingly, I was told that my retinas were beginning to haemorrhage, and that something would have to be done about it quickly. I was injected with fluorescent die so that my eyes could be photographed (in those days, digital scanning had not been invented). But I passed out from the injection, and was sent home. A week later I went back for the same test, and this time remained conscious. I was informed that I would have to have laser treatment on my eyes. I postponed the appointment because I had an event to do in Germany.

---

10. Chatham Pensioners were superannuated Royal Marines who lived in a special "hospital" at the naval base at Chatham, Kent. I presume his Irish wife predeceased him before he became a pensioner there.

After the event, the organizer took me to Alsace, France, to visit the geomantic holy mountain of Alsace, Mont Sainte-Odile (aka Odilienberg). The holy mountain is covered with dense woodland and contains ancient cyclopean stone walls. My German friend told me that local German speakers call these *Heidenmauer* ("heathen walls"). Roads and paths snake up the side of the mountain, and on top there is an active monastery with a church containing the tomb of Sainte Odile, the patron saint of Alsace.

Legend asserts that Odile was the daughter of a Pagan king who was blinded for her conversion to Christianity, but whose sight was restored miraculously. Consequently, her cultus is one of healing eye problems. I was told that there was a healing holy well some way down on the rock below the monastery. We stumbled down hundreds of rock-cut steps and came across a grotto with a grille displaying the monastic coat-of-arms in wrought iron. A pipe carrying water ran out through the grille; the water poured out into a stone basin and then ran away. This was the healing spring. With cupped hands, I took water from the pipe, drank some of it, and bathed my eyes in it. This is the recommended procedure for all "eye wells" in Celtic countries. We returned to Germany, and, the next day, I returned to England. A few days later, I visited the eye clinic. When the doctor examined my eyes preparatory to the laser treatment, she was surprised. She told me that my eyes were fine, and I did not need the procedure.

A coda to this came in 2003, when I was in Liège in Belgium. I went there to see the famous Perron, the geomantic centre of the city, but unintentionally it led to a resolution of my experience ten years earlier. In a city church I saw a notice (in French) that one of the priests there had holy water from Mont Sainte-Odile for congregation members with eye ailments. I told my companion the story of my miraculous cure, and we resolved to go there. So we drove into France via Strasbourg, southwards and up to the monastery, and there I was able to light an *ex-voto* candle at the tomb of Sainte Odile. Like Nideck, it was another confluence in Alsace—another unplanned foray into the realms of the weird and the wonderful.

Borough Hotel, Southend, 2022.
Photo by Nigel Pennick.

John Barleycorn: My Part in His Triumph

He'll turn a man into a boy
And a boy into an ass;
He'll turn your gold to silver
And your silver into brass.

—from an East Anglian version of the folk song "John Barleycorn"

In 1860, in his *Les Paradis artificiels*, Charles Baudelaire wrote:

> thinking only of his immediate pleasure, [man] has heedlessly violated the laws of his constitution to find in physical sciences, in pharmaceuticals, in the harshest liquors, in the subtlest scents, in all places, and at all times, the means to flee his wretched dwelling, if only for a

moment. He seeks ... "to carry off Paradise in one go."[11]

A century later, it was no different. People of my generation sought paradise in drink or drugs—or both—and, consequently, many fell by the wayside long before their time. When we are young, we feel we are invincible, but, sooner or later, we discover it is an illusion.

From about the age of ten, my parents allowed me to have a small glass of cider with our customary Sunday dinner. Then, from my early teens, I enjoyed drinking alcohol outside this carefully controlled context. By my mid-teens I was able to go into Off Licenses and purchase alcohol,[12] though it was forbidden below the age of eighteen. Licensees were happy to sell alcohol or cigarettes to underage customers. I did not smoke, so my purchase was cider, and later, beer. By about sixteen, I began to go into public houses and drink. I enjoyed alcohol and my consumption increased when I went to college in Cambridge and frequented the local pubs around East Road: the Granville, the Tiger, the Ancient Druids, and the Nelson. When I visited my grandmother in London, I used to go to the Queen's Larder pub about a hundred yards north of her apartment, or Ye Olde Cheshire Cheese in Fleet Street, an inn built in 1667 which still retained the literary ambience of Dr Samuel Johnson and Charles Dickens.

Although I found pleasure in drinking and got drunk, I never fell into the condition of "I woke up this morning and got myself a beer ... ," as described in Jim Morrison's "Roadhouse Blues." Neither did I take Alfred Jarry's view that alcohol was a means of attaining the absolute. In my *Cambridge Voice* days at Peabodys, we frequently enjoyed all kinds of alcohol—wine, beer, tequila, and whisky—once the work was over. And when I visited *The Times* newspaper offices to meet with Tony Roberts, I had a swig of whisky from his hip flask before we repaired

---

11. Baudelaire, *Artificial Paradises*, trans. Stacy Diamond (New York: Citadel, 1996), 32.

12. An off-license is a liquor store in Britain.

for a "liquid lunch" at the Black Friars pub nearby. At CCAP, lunchtime every Friday saw several of us drive a mile north to either the Traveller's Rest on Huntingdon Road or half a mile south to the Isaac Newton. There we bought lunch and had a few pints of beer before going back to work. In the evening and at weekends I was in pubs, meeting friends and discussing geomancy and Paganism. In 1978 Jacky Craig and I founded and ran a Pagan Moot at the Mitre pub in Bridge Street in Cambridge, where alcohol flowed freely. Later the Moot moved next door to the Baron of Beef and thence around to other venues, always to the accompaniment of alcohol. In 1986 at the Baron of Beef I established an annual Scot-Ale to celebrate the Winter Solstice, which continued unbroken annually until 2019.

In my travels in Britain, I frequently talked at meetings in pubs, inns, and hotels, where members of my audience were only too happy to buy me a beer. Outside Great Britain, I was able to partake of exotic alcohol. As a drinker, I sought authenticity and was able to visit breweries where my tipple was made. One used to get free samples after the tour. So I visited both Guinness breweries—the original at St James's Gate in Dublin and the British one at Park Royal in London—as well as the Heineken brewery in Amsterdam. I even gave a talk at Hürlimann brewery in Zürich. On visits to Zürich in the early 1980s, I also drank *la fée verte*, the "Green Fairy," as absinthe is referred to poetically. It was illegal there at the time, but readily available.[13] On my frequent visits to Stuttgart, I drank *vierteles* (quarter-litre glasses) of local wine, as well as the local Stuttgarter Hofbräu beer and Herren-Pils. In other cities and towns in Germany and Austria, I partook of the local brews, including *Weizenbier* in Bavaria. On a tour in Ireland in 1988, Bushmills, Jameson, and Paddy whiskey flowed freely. Shortly before I gave up alcohol in 1991, I was able to drink a Pilsener at the original site of its production in Plzeň, Czechoslovakia (as it then was).

Pub quizzes offered another opportunity to drink. Between 1987 and 1989, I was a member of the quiz team at my local

---

13. Having been banned in the early twentieth century, absinthe was re-legalized in 2006.

Winning quiz team at all-comers' event, Harlow, 1988.
Fox team: (back row, L to R) Nigel Pennick, Alan Choat, and Rupert Pennick.
Center: landlord and landlady.

pub, the Fox. The other members were my father (a former schoolteacher), Alan Choat (an ex-army officer), and Tim Reid (a civil engineer on the Channel Tunnel). We were one of the best teams in the region, participating in the quiz league of Tolly Brewery, based in Ipswich.

Teams visited pubs where the quizzes were held. Some of the teams were welcoming, playing the quiz for fun, while other teams took the contest in deadly seriousness. After the main rounds, in which one or the other team won, there was a "beer round" where each member was paired off with a player from the opposing side, and asked a question. The loser had to buy the winner a drink. The only time this did not happen was at the Prince Albert in Ely, where the Fox team won by many points. This angered the local drinkers so much that we retreated hastily before violence ensued.

In 1989, the Fox team appeared at the grand final in Ipswich, but did not win, being beaten by one point. We had all gone there in a coach with supporters, who were well oiled by the last questions and protested that we had been unfairly cheated of the winning points. It was the typical partisan supporters' behavior I knew so well from my days as a football fanatic. A very drunken trip back was punctuated with Fox-team supporters' cries that we had been robbed, "it wasn't fair," and so on. That was my last quiz.

In November 1991 I had obtained a quart of duty-free whisky, which I brought back on a long flight from San Francisco. I was totally exhausted after gruelling journeys and crashed out asleep for almost twenty-four hours. Having woken up and feeling better, I waited until the evening to have my whisky. Still feeling a combination of fatigue and the effects of alcohol, I was in a good mood and started to sing an old folk song, which went:

I'm a rambler, I'm a gambler,
I'm a long way from home;
And if you don't like me
Please leave me alone.
I eat when I'm hungry,
I drink when I'm dry,
If the whisky don't kill me ...

Then suddenly I stopped and got up, realizing that the song I was singing was a message to me: the whisky *was* killing me. (The last line is: "*I'll live 'till I die.*") I picked up the bottle and walked to the kitchen sink. Ann was shocked as I unscrewed the cap and poured the rest of the whisky down the drain. That was the last time I ever drank alcohol. Looking back on the state I was in then, I would have died if I had kept on drinking. My unconscious (or Guardian Angel) had made me sing that tune at that time, and I took heed. My life was saved by a folk song.

Ymir

The summer of 2003 was extremely hot. I had just returned from Germany, fatigued and exhausted as always, when I suffered a heart attack. At first, I was not aware what it was, and only after sixteen hours did I find myself in Addenbrooke's

WYRD TIMES

Hospital, Cambridge, undergoing emergency treatment to save my life. During this time I underwent a near-death experience of Ymirish dismemberment, where I felt my body torn to pieces and reassembled.[14] I remember hearing internally the saying from *Beowulf*: "Wyrd often spares a man who is not doomed, so long as his courage holds!"[15] It did.

The following is a recall of my near-death experience of dismemberment and meditations under heart attack and emergency treatment, July 25–28, 2003 (written down in hospital July 31–August 8):

> Ymir, the primal giant, is dismembered by the gods as the primal act in the formation of the world. The various parts of Ymir compose the basic structures of the world. Ymir's bones become the rock, Ymir's hair the plants growing upon the earth. Ymir's blood becomes the sea—the ebb and flow of the tides recalls the ebb and flow of blood in the body, the old way of viewing the pulse. The sea's tides are related to the waxing and waning of the Moon, paralleling the heart as the origin of the bodily blood-tides. The penetrated body bleeds, just as springs of water emerge from within the body of the Earth. The spiritual principle of "as above, so below" links the bodily blood to the tides, and also links the bodily breath to the winds. All is a symbolic way that humans can relate to the materials of the world, from which our bodies are formed, through the physical exchange that links our individual being in interbeing, in continuity, and in separation. The symbolic separation of Ymir's body to make the world gives us a sequence of forms that allows us to relate to the world, part to part. These are manifested in different ways, for example, in the thirteen types of the world

---

14. Ymir is a primordial giant in the cosmogonic mythology recounted in the Eddas. He is ultimately slain and dismembered by Odin and his brothers.

15. *Beowulf*, ll. 572b–73: *Wyrd oft nereð / unfægne eorl, þonne his ellen death!*

Ymir by Nigel Pennick, 2003.

that appear in *Alvissmál*, and the twenty-nine runes of the *Old English Rune Poem*. By isolating the perceptible parts of the interconnected continuum, we can gain insights and understanding of them, and better relate our own part in this with the whole.

When I had recovered, I recounted this experience to a witch I knew, and she said: "Now you are a Shaman!" But in my ancestral traditions from working-class Londoners and Old West Surrey farmhands there is no such thing, and I am true to my ancestral tradition. So, I would never call myself that.

Before I was out of hospital and rehabilitation, I endured a long struggle. Despite being on strong painkillers, I still had to practice runic meditation to overcome the discomfort. After several days in intensive care, the medics decided that I should have stents inserted in my heart blood vessels, which had to be done at Papworth Hospital, fifteen miles away. But as the "superbug" MRSA was rife at Addenbrooke's, it was deemed that patients had to have negative tests before being sent there for surgery. I spent three weeks in a very hot ward without air conditioning, during which time the electric fans we had for relief from the heat were taken to another ward. It was scarcely possible to sleep from the incessant noise and the desperate melancholy of my fellow patients, making the environment hardly conducive to recovery.

While I was in Addenbrooke's, Michael Clarke—the East Anglian magician, toadman, and collector of esoteric artifacts—came ninety miles from Great Yarmouth to see me and asked if he could get me anything. I requested a copy of the *Prose Edda*—and two days later, a copy was delivered to me at the hospital. It was a great consolation, which assisted in my survival. Two friends from the Norwich pagan moot, Val Thomas and Chris Wood, came to visit me at Addenbrooke's as well. Also, from Oxford, Celtic spiritual authors John and Caitlin Matthews sent me a set of drawing pencils and a sketch pad. My Ymir drawing was done using them (I later re-drew it in ink).

After a week or so, I was able to walk slowly and found

a space just outside the ward in a corridor where the heat was less oppressive. Sometimes I was joined there by an old Polish Jewish man, Josef, who had survived the horrors of World War II, a stroke, and now a heart attack. His stoic will to survive was admirable. We mused on life and death as a trolley covered with a brown blanket carrying the dead wheeled past. I never knew what happened to him. People disappeared from the ward continuously, either to another hospital or home—or to the mortuary.

Finally, I was signed off to go to Papworth and was wheeled in a wheelchair to an ambulance to take me there. At Papworth, stents were inserted in my heart by "keyhole surgery" while I was conscious in an operating theatre ominously named "The Laboratory." The operation was a success and I was sent home with frequent visits to Addenbrooke's Hospital for rehabilitation. A car would be sent to pick me up and to drop me off afterwards.

On my last visit to rehab, I had just been signed off, so I went to the outpatients' café to have a cup of tea before my driver came for me. There I saw an old friend from the Tech, Mark Seal. Known as the doyen of Cambridge buses—he knew everything about them; he had written a piece in *Cambridge Voice* about their history and published a book on the subject—I had not seen him for years. He had deteriorating eyesight, caused initially by a car crash in the 1960s and worsened by the fact that he had been beaten up in Bedford, the victim of a disability hate crime. I called to him and touched him on the shoulder. He recognized my voice and I saw his white stick. We sat down together and he told me that he had just been signed off by the eye clinic; they could do no more for him, and now he was registered blind. It was a strange confluence meeting there and then, as we were both signed off for different reasons.

Some years later, my deteriorating heart condition caused a second heart attack, which necessitated more stents, and in 2014 after suffering from the air pollution on a trip to Edinburgh,[16]

---

16. Edinburgh's traditional nickname was "Auld Reekie" (Old Smoky), recalling the smoke from coal-burning that polluted the air of the Scottish capital for hundreds of years. My lungs were affected by petrochemical smog.

Nigel Pennick on the occasion of his 72nd birthday.
Photo by Ann Pennick.

I experienced a collapsed lung and, subsequently, heart failure. Ann saved my life by her prompt summoning of the paramedics. I was resuscitated at Addenbrooke's Hospital and then, also suffering from kidney failure, transferred to Papworth where, after hallucinating a phantom bicycle and a sprite resembling one seen and drawn by my friend Helen Field a decade earlier, I had a pacemaker implanted to keep my heart beating. I was told that it was the "Rolls-Royce of pacemakers," made in Boston, Massachusetts.

More recently, I was given a communicator that connected to the hospital via a cellphone network dongle. Carrying the name "Latitude,"[17] it uses wireless technology to interrogate

---

17. Manufactured equipment is often given a grandiose or meaningless name, as exemplified by cars ranging from the *Silver Shadow*, *Terraplane*, and *Mustang* to the (at the time of writing) *Duster* and *Qashqai*. Autonomous delivery boxes on wheels trundling driverless round parts of Cambridgeshire

and monitor the chip that runs the pacemaker. Malfunctions are picked up and transmitted to hospital staff, who can then contact the patient. This useful apparatus picked up two instances where my pacemaker suddenly altered its function to default mode, and both times I was summoned so that the doctors of the devices clinic could rectify it. I traced the timing of the two incidents to two visits I made to the Waitrose supermarket in St Ives, where, apparently, the detectors one must walk through to leave the store had affected my pacemaker. I have never been back there. In September 2022, however, the technology detected a worse malfunction, and I was summoned to hospital immediately.

One of the leads from my pacemaker into my heart had faulty insulation, affecting its efficiency. The devices clinic closed down that lead, and my pacemaker was reset on a default mode using the remaining two. I was told I was now on the waiting list for a replacement. The waiting lists of the National Health Service are politically contentious, as some people have to wait years for what are called "routine" operations. I had no idea how long it would be, but clearly I was a priority. Just over two weeks later, I received a phone call that I would be operated on the next day. So, on September 21, 2022, I prepared myself and was at the hospital on time. I was tested for Covid, and prepared for the procedure. As before, I was conscious during the operation, which lasted an hour and three-quarters. There were problems in inserting the replacement lead, and it was decided to remove the existing pacemaker and replace it with a new one. The old lead was closed off and abandoned inside me, as it was not removable. By the evening, I was back home, recovering from the ordeal—still alive. It was thanks to these interventions that I was enabled to continue my work, and to complete this memoir, *inter alia*.

In my father's words, I had been "spared" yet again, and I still have in my collection of esoterica a Roman coin with the goddess Providentia on it. My connexion with Northern

---

as I write are called by the ludicrous name *Starship*, while actual space vehicles have played fast-and-loose with the names of sacred beings such as *Thor*, *Apollo*, *Artemis* and so on, because they are—according to the delusions of grandeur of their makers—going on "missions."

WYRD TIMES

Tradition philosophy enabled me to survive extremely stressful, painful, and horrifying experiences of illness. Allied in many ways to Stoicism, it has become a means of bearing the unbearable. Often overlooked is the Northern Tradition's compassionate and heroic attitude towards disability. No other religious system overtly accepts disability, and stanza 71 of the *Hávamál* celebrates that a lame man can still ride a horse (or in modern terms, drive a car); a deaf man can still be a fighter who prevails in combat; and if one loses one's sight, it is better to live in that condition than to be dead. Even death must be accepted when it is inevitable. This acceptance is present in Ragnar Loðbrok's death song "I laugh as I die!" or Earl Siward's ritual suicide, when he jumped from the battlements of York with sword in hand rather than dying "on straw like an animal."

But none can escape in the end. As noted blues pianist Cousin Joe of New Orleans sang, "Life's a one-way ticket: there ain't no second time around." My Irish English teacher used to say "time is short," and my grandmother Grace used to say of something speculative "I should live so long." Despite her East End saying of Jewish origin, she *did* live so long, surviving through the whole of the twentieth century, from 1899 until 2003. But she buried two husbands and a son in that time. Life is fragile and limited, and "the end is always near." A motto from a seventeenth-century Emblem Book says it all: *Tempora labuntur, tacitisque sensecimus anni; et fugiunt fræno non remorante dies*— "The times speed onwards and we grow old as the years pass unnoticed; and the days pass with no brake to hold them back."

Ultimately, we have only one option: to *dree our wyrd*, accepting with good grace whatever the "decree of the Fates" brings us.

EPILOGOS

VAST AND STRANGE REALMS: A CONTINUING QUEST FOR KNOWLEDGE

The Enlightenment of Menw the Aged by the Awen.
Ink drawing (original in colour) by Nigel Pennick, 1999.

This memoir is a record of my life as I experienced it. My relationship to the world, my principles and practices, were conditioned by experience and they remain so. As far back as I can remember, I always tried to understand what was happening to me, and why. Since my early days, my life has been a quest for knowledge and understanding of everything I have encountered.

At quite an early age I learnt not to be a passive recipient of information, but to question what I was told. If something did not feel right to me I could not accept it, even when my teachers punished me and forced me to say things I felt were false. I am not sure when I realized that my world was not random or simple in the slightest, but was the current expression of countless events and things that had preceded it. In the Northern Tradition, this is called "Orlog" (ørlǫg). These earlier states of existence were not just a matter of history—which to my elders was so often the history of "The War"—but had much more mysterious and deeper origins.

Of course, I was told that the ultimate origin was God, who made everything, but this mythic simplification did not satisfy my curiosity—for I was living in the present and not at the origin-point of existence, which was what "creation" meant. Clearly, the continually changing, multiform complexity of the world and the cosmos was of a totally different order. I soon found out that there are numerous conflicting and contradictory accounts of how the world was made—if it was "made" at all!—and I had been taught only one of them

Living in a cosmopolitan city, but of indigenous English

descent through an urban father and a rural mother, I experienced what now would be called "the Other" embedded in everyday life. My paternal grandmother, who had been brought up in Clapton, East London, in the early twentieth century, used vernacular Cockney language that included certain terms that clearly were not normal English, but, as I discovered later, were Yiddish in origin. She was not Jewish, being brought up in the Church of England and later converted to Anglo-Catholicism. When proposing a toast with an alcoholic drink she would always say "Muzzletoff!" (Yiddish *mazel tov*), and to a sneeze would respond "Gesundheit!" We used to call anything that we considered authentic or genuine "kosher," an argument was a "schemozzle," and a person who stood round giving unwanted advice was a "kibitzer." From other people I heard the words "meschuggah" (or "meschugginer") for a deranged person and "sheigetz" for someone who was considered a waste of time. The use of these alternative words as part of everyday discourse must have impressed me with an awareness that there were other modes of expression, from different languages, and these had deeper connexions, even if not easily discovered. There were alternative ways of seeing the world.

Everyday life has its own tenor—a familiar reality or *habitus*—that one takes for granted. It covers a large range of experience, but has its particular limits. Outside of that familiar realm are other things and other states of being, which are rarely experienced by the majority except in special circumstances. Vast and strange realms lie outside the circumscribed area. Even when encountered, the stock response is to ignore or deny them. But this does not change the greater reality which persists, regardless of whether all its hidden parts are acknowledged.

The past is one of these strange realms. I was fortunate to live near the British Museum, which was crammed with artifacts from times and cultures whose modes of being were far removed from the beliefs and mores of mid twentieth-century London. What I saw in the British Museum were clearly the archaic antecedents of present existence. I could perceive their numinous qualities, qualitatively different from a mundane bus

The Queen of Time statue (sculpted by Gilbert Bayes, 1930) on the Selfridges building, Oxford Street, London. Photo by Petr Brož.

or schoolbook.

Closer to home culturally than the carvings of Sekhmet or Egyptian talismans to ward off scorpions that I saw in the museum, were sculptures and artworks on the buildings I passed in the city. A golden mosaic of the sun with a sundial and a gilded bronze Father Time with his scythe adorned the Imperial Hotel overlooking Russell Square. On Selfridges in Oxford Street was the magnificent polychrome bronze sculpture of the Queen of Time, while visible from my front doorstep were the Cosmic Eggs on the Passmore Edwards Settlement (now Mary Ward House). These emblems of time and creation were immediate and spoke to any passerby who bothered to take notice of them. Then there were the London Baroque churches I was taken to. These had been designed in the seventeenth and eighteenth century by men who had studied the ruins of ancient pagan temples and tombs. The top architects of their day—Sir Christopher Wren, James Gibbs, James Archer, Nicholas Hawksmoor, and,

The Spire of St George's Church, Bloomsbury, London.
Drawing by Nigel Pennick, 2008.

later, Henry Flitcroft—had taken the geometric and spiritual principles of these ancient buildings and created structures that embodied more than just the mere material that went into their construction. One I walked past every day on the way to school was St George's Church in Bloomsbury, designed by Hawksmoor and built in 1721. It had a stepped-pyramid steeple whose design referred back to the Tomb of Mausolus at Halicarnassus—one of the Seven Wonders of the Ancient World. Even stranger was the presence, two hundred yards away in the British Museum, of the excavated remains of the original Mausoleum. These relics had been taken there a century after Hawksmoor's church was built. This part of Bloomsbury contained a strange confluence of place, which to me was significant, though I could not explain why. Other similar confluences have appeared to me throughout my life.

The religious services I was compelled to attend never meant anything to me. The tired and bored clergy and congregation just went through the motions, mechanically reciting obscure texts and never daring to address the vast expanses of time and the grandeur of the limitless cosmos. To me, it was all so petty and mindless. I was just waiting for the time when it was over, so I could go and do something more interesting. As architectural creations, however, the old churches expressed the cosmic symbolism that was so sadly lacking in the lukewarm ministrations of the clergy. It was as though their spirit had been driven away by literalism, as William Blake had noticed a century and a half before.

My first major illness at the age of ten where I had an out-of-the-body experience was a traumatic event which dragged me from familiar reality into invisible realms. (I had experienced something similar a few years earlier when I was in the church of St Giles-in-the-Fields and had a reverie of the limitless cosmos, so brutally negated later that day by an unsympathetic teacher.) Once I recovered from my illness and returned to my normal surroundings, I understood that what I had experienced—invisible reality—was a state most people could not comprehend, having never experienced it. I told nobody about it because I did not understand what had happened to me and they would not have listened anyway.

So, without any instruction or even knowing that what I was doing was a practice, I began to meditate and developed the faculty to visualize things that were not actually present. When I came across the runes, I began to use my ability to visualize their forms and meanings. I sought out knowledge about these aspects of invisible reality, and from the Atlantis Bookshop, which is a stone's throw from the British Museum, I obtained cheap secondhand copies of occult books. I studied them avidly. They dealt with the inner workings of causality and contained techniques for accessing the invisible realms, which I practiced. These included books on ghosts and spirits, parapsychology, magic, the Qabalah, and texts that dealt with various arcane alphabets, exoteric and esoteric. I worked these techniques in the spirit of Albertus Magnus, who said of the Philosopher's Stone: "If it exists, I want to know what it is like. If it does not exist, I want to understand the meaning of such an illusion."

I came to understand that magic was not a fanciful forerunner of science, but something powerful in its own right, and that analogical causality was a reality. Magical techniques provide a means of access to the unseen mystery that underlies and shapes humanity. I recognized that the unifying principle is that all parts of the cosmos communicate with one another and comprise a single whole, a correspondence between the microcosm and the macrocosm as in the medieval English maxim "IN ON IS AL" ("in one is all").

Autonomously, I learnt to observe the things around me, and later I was trained to observe in both artistic and scientific ways. As Louis Pasteur noted: "Where observation is concerned, chance favours only the prepared mind."[1] In spiritual terms, this means taking note of *ostenta* when they present themselves.

Although steered into a scientific direction at school, I had a great interest in art—not just ancient artifacts, but contemporary art as well. When I could, I visited London art galleries and read books on modern art and artists. Although I was studying chemistry, physics, and biology for my advanced level examinations, I opted to do an ordinary level exam in art as an addition. My art teacher was a fan of Wassily Kandinsky and I came across the latter's text *Concerning the Spiritual in Art*, which gave another viewpoint on the link between the visual world and invisible reality. William Blake asserted that a work of art is not only a manifestation of liberty, but the means by which Nature can be perfected. In my work in various fields, I have always attempted to embody as far as possible the spiritual qualities that informed our ancestors' lives and works.

Place is an important element in all we do. To do something at the right place, and at the right time, is the foundation of all

---

1. The original French appears as an inscription on the former Medical School building at Cambridge: "*Dans les champs de l'observation le hazard ne favorise que le esprits préparés.*" The quote is from Pasteur's inaugural lecture at the University of Lille in 1854, and refers to Hans Christian Oersted's "serendipitous" discovery in 1822 of the deflection of a magnetized needle near a copper wire carrying current, which lead to the invention of the electric motor.

**Nigel Pennick by the ancient Celtic cross at St Neot, Cornwall.
Photo by Ann Pennick.**

success. I came to realize this in the early 1960s. On a school trip to see the new cathedral at Coventry, I felt immediately that something was not right. Much of the city had been destroyed by the German *Luftwaffe* in November 1940. The devastation was so great that the word *coventration* was coined to mean a city destroyed by bombing. The original medieval cathedral had been burnt out, though its tower and spire still stood. Like the sister church almost next to it, Holy Trinity Coventry, it was orientated due east–west. Unfortunately, the new stone-clad concrete cathedral was built at right angles to it, with its altar in the north. This would be correct for a Northern Tradition holy building, but it was not so for a church. So I felt unease immediately upon entering it. The 1960s cathedral is in the wrong place, and the ruins of the earlier one stand to the south of it, seemingly as a reproach. Later I learnt that the technique of finding the right place and the right times involved the ancient sciences of geomancy and electional astrology—traditional techniques sadly

Nigel Pennick with Ian Read and Ingrid Fischer at the artist's "Visionary Steeples" exhibition, Emmanuel United Reform Church, Cambridge, 2011.

ignored by officialdom after World War II.[2]

From my early teens onwards, I wandered through vague terrains in search of the weird and wonderful. In more than sixty years of travelling in Europe and North America, I visited places I came to know well and places I can't remember and shouldn't have been in. I survived three car crashes, one coach crash, a bus fire, and two near-misses in aircraft—it has been a "long strange trip," to quote the Grateful Dead. "By my travelling" I saw many things and learnt a lot from local people who *knew*. I always sought out the authentic.

In 1967 in Amsterdam it was explained to me that the buildings of the Amsterdamse School (1913–1940) embodied Theosophical principles and contained eternal symbols that condensed physical and cosmic energies: *"Eeuwige levende*

---

2. An exception was the rebuilding of the devastated city of Plymouth, where the town planner, Patrick Abercrombie, used feng-shui principles to lay out a new axial boulevard and the (modernist) civic buildings.

teekens." A woman I knew, scion of an Amsterdam patrician family, told me of her grandfather's house, built for him in the 1920s according to a particular geomantic praxis that melded Dutch and Indonesian principles. Shortly afterwards I encountered Chinese feng shui, which was not the Indonesian art, but which I realized was analogous to what my ancestors had practiced in ancient times in Britain. All of these techniques are rooted in the realities of the landscapes: the directions, the stations of the sun, hills and dales, the energies of wind and of water, "flow water and blow wind." In 1985 in Germany I was taught Runic Yoga, and in 1991 I stayed in a Buddhist temple in California. A feng-shui master noted that through Chinese history, there were periods of stagnation. These were caused by legalism and ritual. When litigation became rife, nothing could get done without endless wrangling and vast expense; when ritual reigned, prolonged rites and ceremonies preceded any event, costing money and time for no purpose. Only when legalism and ritual appear in the proper places can society function smoothly. In the twenty-first century, we are plagued by both ritualism *and* legalism.

I have lived in a remarkably rich and pluralistic culture, where numerous spiritual currents underlie so much of everyday life. Overt forms of religion with their external manifestations in symbols, clothing, dietary rules, and rituals often appear only as institutions that guarantee the status and power of particular groups and individuals who benefit from them. But nobody has a monopoly on the truth, and dogma—be it religious, political, or economic—becomes a hindrance in variable situations where the strictures of doctrine cannot deal with the contingent necessity of the moment.

The unregulated powers of nature manifest to humans through *ostenta* and the emanations of the eldritch world. I have always been open to these possibilities. I view all supernatural beings perceived by humans to be manifestations of the same order: sprites, daemons, angels, saints, and gods. They are imperfectly glimpsed images of the invisible world, flashes of the celestial light in the mundane realm. The Spiritual Arts and Crafts enable us to express these unseen powers in physical form, as did the craftspeople of old making their artifacts in the spirit of meditation or for the glory of the gods.

William Blake noted that anything that it is possible to believe is an image of truth, so we can find, in scriptures and writings of all lands, timeless wisdom in texts that otherwise may be unacceptable to current political or religious sensibilities. In an attempt to retain and increase their power, priesthoods—whether religious, political, or of the commentariat—thrust labels upon people whom they wish to condemn. A laughable example of this, which should be noted by anyone tempted to condemn others in grandiose "creative-writing" terms, is the case of the noted poet, writer, mountaineer, and magician, Aleister Crowley. In his lifetime he was labelled the "wickedest man in the world"—at a time when Stalin was conducting his genocide in Ukraine and purging his terrified Russian subjects. One must always keep things in perspective.

In anyone's life, there are changes. A person may believe something, even promote it widely, at one stage of their life; then later abandon or repudiate it and take up another belief or way of life. To label a person as being that one thing immutably for the whole of their life is absurd. I knew a person who was brought up in the Church of England, converted first to Buddhism, then to Wicca, and finally to Judaism. Then she died at the age of forty-nine. Religious and political affiliations change frequently during many people's lives, as leading politicians—prime ministers, even—have jumped from one party to another. Perhaps it is only dyed-in-the-wool football supporters who retain allegiance to their club unto death. As the Biblical book of Matthew (7:1-2) tells us: "Judge not, that ye be not judged. For with what judgment ye judge, ye shall be judged: and with what measure ye mete, it shall be measured to you again."

Other titles featuring Nigel Pennick available from Arcana Europa Media

The Eldritch World

By Nigel Pennick

ISBN 978-0999724538, 190 + iv pages, clothbound, $40.00

For most of us, life is a largely monotonous affair—an endless round of school, work, and social and family commitments, punctuated by idle chatter. But beyond this drab and uninspiring reality, there is another world altogether, a world where the contours are sharper and the colors are brighter. This is the domain described by mystics and Surrealists, esoteric poets and psychedelic voyagers. For Nigel Pennick, who has spent much of his life mapping out this hidden terrain, there is a name for it: the Eldritch World.

The way that we experience the eldritch is invariably tied to the circumstances of our birth, or to what philosophers might call our being-in-the-world. The eldritch has a history and its roots run deep in the land. In Nigel Pennick's case, it manifests through the myths, folklore, and customs of his native Britain. A gentleman scholar in the Victorian style, Pennick has made a career out of documenting these fast-disappearing traditions and of working toward their revival. He is a mummer and a magician, a Pagan, and a practitioner of the traditional arts and crafts.

Yet unlike many of Pennick's other writings, *The Eldritch World* is not about runes, or geomancy, or the ancient customs of pre-Christian Europe. *The Eldritch World* is a meditation on what these things mean and why Pennick has devoted his life to them. It is also a manifesto: against the soulless mediocrity of the modern world, and for a reinvigorated Spirit of Place.

Presented in a fine clothbound edition, *The Eldritch World* is beautifully set in seventeenth-century type and illustrated throughout with eerie archival images and photographs depicting various folk traditions and beliefs.

TYR: Myth, Culture, Tradition 1

Edited by Joshua Buckley
and Michael Moynihan

ISBN 978-0999724568, 286 pages, paperback, $20.00

Stephen Edred Flowers on "Integral Culture," Joscelyn Godwin on the Italian esotericist Julius Evola, French philosopher Alain de Benoist's interview with "new comparative mythologist" Georges Dumezil, Nigel Pennick on the "Spiritual Arts and Crafts," Steve Pollington on the Germanic war god Woden, Michael Moynihan on divine traces in the Nibelungenlied, Collin Cleary on the anti-modern television series *The Prisoner*, Joshua Buckley's interview with Ian Read of the English heathen music group Fire + Ice, and much more.

TYR: Myth, Culture, Tradition 2

Edited by Joshua Buckley
and Michael Moynihan

ISBN 978-0999724576, 430 pages, paperback, $25.00

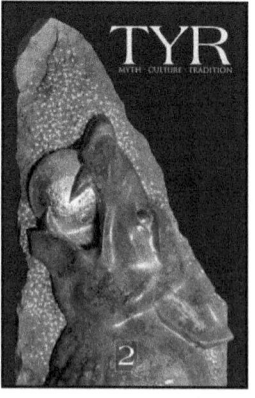

Julius Evola on "The Doctrine of Battle and Victory," Charles Champetier's interview with Alain de Benoist, Alain de Benoist on "Thoughts on God," Collin Cleary on "Summoning the Gods," Stephen McNallen on the "Ásatrú Revival," Nigel Pennick on "Heathen Holy Places," John Matthews on "The Guardians of Albion," Steve Pollington on "The Germanic Warband," Michael Moynihan on "Disparate Myths of Divine Sacrifice," Christian Rätsch on "The Sacred Plants of our Ancestors," Joscelyn Godwin on Herman Wirth, Peter Bahn on "The Friedrich Hielscher Legend," Markus Wolff on Ludwig Fahrenkrog, Stephen Flowers on "The Northern Renaissance," Joshua Buckley's interview with "technosophical" musicians Allerseelen, and an extensive book and music review section, featuring sidebar interviews with Coil and P. D. Brown.

TYR: Myth, Culture, Tradition 3

Edited by Joshua Buckley
and Michael Moynihan

ISBN 978-0999724552, 538 pages, paperback, $25.00

Thomas Naylor on "Cipherspace," Annie Le Brun on "Catastrophe Pending," Pentti Linkola on "Survival Theory," Michael O'Meara on "The Primordial and the Perennial," Alain de Benoist on "Spiritual Authority and Temporal Power," Nigel Pennick on "The Web of Wyrd," Thierry Jolif on "The Abode of the Gods and the Great Beyond," Stephen Flowers on "The Spear of Destiny," Joscelyn Godwin on Philip Pullman's "Dark Materials" trilogy, Ian Read on "Humour in the Icelandic Sagas," Geza von Neményi on the "Hávamál," Gordon Kennedy on the "Children of the Sonne," Michael Moynihan on "Carl Larsson's Greatest Sacrifice," Christopher McIntosh on "Iceland's Pagan Renaissance," Jónína Berg on Sveinbjörn Beinteinsson, "Selected Poems" by Sveinbjörn Beinteinsson, Vilius Rudra Dundzila on "Baltic Lithuanian Religion," James Reagan on "The End Times," interviews with the stalwart folk singer Andrew King and the modern minnesinger Roland Kroell, Collin Cleary on "Paganism Without Gods," Róbert Hórvath on Mark Sedgwick's "Against the Modern World," and extensive book and music review sections.

TYR: Myth, Culture, Tradition 4

Edited by Joshua Buckley
and Michael Moynihan

ISBN 978-0972029247, 430 pages, paperback, $25.00

Alain de Benoist on "What is Religion?", Collin Cleary on "What is Odinism?", Nigel Pennick on "Traditional Time-Telling in Old England," Claude Lecouteux on "Garden Dwarves" and "Geiler von Kaiserberg and the Furious Army," Steve Harris on "Barbarian Suffering," Stephen Pollington on "Germanic Art in the First Millennium," Michael Moynihan on "Rockwell Kent's Northern Compass," and Christian Rätsch on "The Mead of Inspiration," interviews with pioneering psychedelic explorer Ralph Metzner, Sequentia's Benjamin Bagby, and Cult of Youth's Sean Ragon, and much more.

TYR: Myth, Culture, Tradition 5

Edited by Joshua Buckley and Michael Moynihan

ISBN 978-0999724521, 394 pages, paperback, $25.00

Collin Cleary's "On Being and Waking," Jack Donovan on "Starting the Sacred World," Bradley Taylor-Hicks on "Reclaiming Sacred Space," Joscelyn Godwin on "Alain Daniélou in the Age of Conflicts," Steven Posch on "The Last Pagans of the Hindu Kush," Nigel Pennick on "Northern Cosmology: The World Tree and Irminsul," Richard Rudgley on "Pagan Palingenesis," Stephen Edred Flowers on "Germanic and Iranian Culture and Myth," Wolf-Dieter Storl on "Indo-European Healing Lore," Michael Moynihan on the cult film *Koyaanisqatsi*, interviews with traditional bladesmith J. Arthur Loose and avant-garde composer Dylan Sheets; and much more.

www.arcanaeuropamedia.com

www.ingramcontent.com/pod-product-compliance
Lightning Source LLC
Chambersburg PA
CBHW060106170426
43198CB00010B/793